D1714756

GREEK VASE PAINTING
Form, Figure, and Narrative

❀

TREASURES *of* THE NATIONAL
ARCHAEOLOGICAL MUSEUM *in* MADRID

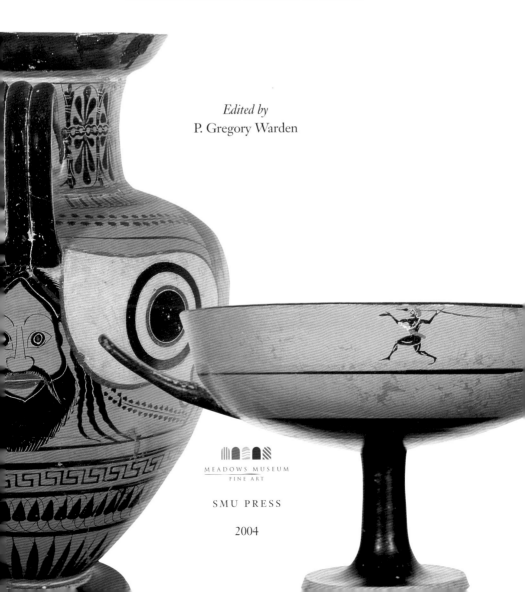

Edited by
P. Gregory Warden

MEADOWS MUSEUM
FINE ART

SMU PRESS

2004

The exhibition and accompanying catalogue have been underwritten, in part, through the generosity of a grant from the Meadows Foundation, Dallas. The Embassy of Spain in Washington, D.C., has also contributed significantly to the success of this project. ESPAÑA ACCIÓN CULTURAL EXTERIOR

Published by:

Meadows Museum
Southern Methodist University
5900 Bishop Boulevard
Dallas, TX 75275-0357

Southern Methodist University Press
P.O. Box 750415
Dallas, TX 75275-0415

Translator: Jennifer Meehan
Coordinating Editors: Jeanne Lil Chvosta, Bridget LaRocque Marx and Courtney E. Kennedy
Design by: Tom Dawson, Dallas, Texas
Printed by: Authentic Press LLC, Fort Worth, Texas
Separations by: K&W Group, Inc., Jackson, Mississippi
Bound by: Universal Book Bindery, San Antonio, Texas

LIBRARY OF CONGRESS CATALOGING-IN-PUBLICATION DATA

Greek vase painting : form, figure, and narrative : treasures of the National Archaeological Museum
  in Madrid / edited by P. Gregory Warden.
    p. cm.
    Published in conjunction with an exhibition at Meadows Museum, Dallas.
    Includes bibliographical references.
    ISBN 0-87074-489-5 (alk. paper)
      1. Vases, Greek—Exhibitions. 2. Vase-painting, Greek—Exhibitions. 3. Vases—Spain—
    Madrid—Exhibitions. 4. Museo Arqueolâgico Nacional (Spain)—Exhibitions. I. Warden,
    P. Gregory. II. Meadows Museum.

NK4623.5.S7M334 2004
738'.0938'0747642812—dc22   2003067324

Frontispiece: *Amphora with Dionysian masks* (detail), inv. no. 10.905; H: 40 cm; maximum width: 26 cm; Attic black figure, Antimenes Painter; 520 B.C. and *Lip cup with hunter and bull* (detail), inv. no. 1999/99/70; H: 8.8 cm; diameter at rim: 13.9 cm; diameter at foot: 5.9 cm; Attic black figure, The Centaur Painter; 540 B.C.

Contents

Form, Figure, and Narrative in Greek Vase Painting

❀

P. GREGORY WARDEN

What is new about Greek vases? Why study and display works of art that, splendid though they may be, are by now familiar to most museum goers? After all, there is good classical art all around us. Fine vases can be found in many museum collections, and excellent ones can certainly be seen in our own region, at the Dallas Museum of Art, in the Kimbell Museum in Fort Worth, and in the San Antonio Museum of Art, to mention just some of the collections closest to the Meadows Museum. These are the objects and galleries that most museum goers walk by quickly, with only a casual nod and at best a brief pause, as they proceed on to the Old Masters, or more likely, to the painters of the late 19th century and their offspring. But if this type of object is familiar, it is no less important. The artists who created these vases are in fact the ancestors of those later artists who populate the blockbuster exhibits. These vases are the first works of art in the western tradition that are actually signed by the artists. They are the first testament to the later commonplace of a workshop dominated by a master artist, and some of these vases are clearly masterpieces of the potter's and painter's art. They are highly creative, extremely sophisticated, and innovative. We can see artists who define the formal conventions of later western drawing and painting, artists who grapple with the expression of naturalism, scale, and spatial definition. In these vases we can see the historical development of such fundamental elements over almost six centuries, as Greek artists pursued their single-minded obsession with the naturalism of the human form and its inherent narrative possibilities. But familiarity can lead, if not to contempt, at least to complacency. It may well be that the fundamental quality of classical art—its closeness to us in spirit, substance, and tradition—makes it hard for us to see it anew.

Exhibitions tell a story; the story may not always be new, but what is important is the telling. Exhibitions instruct us, and here again it is not the content that is paramount, but the way the content is presented, the questions that are asked, the issues that are raised. In the case of this exhibit, these vases are more than a set of splendid objects; they are of interest in the context of current practice in the disciplines of art history and archaeology, in the context of the study of the classical past. This exhibit is not just about the vases and what they seem to tell us about the classical world; the other important part of the story is the way that we have used, or the way that we are using, these vases for the construction of our own understanding of early western European art.

The title chosen for this exhibit, *"Form, Figure, and Narrative in Greek Vase Painting,"* is deliberately conventional. Almost every word raises important questions, some of which are not merely semantic. First, "Greek" is used here very broadly to encompass art created by and for cultures that are in fact linguistically and ethnically not Greek. "Painting" is also used loosely, albeit in this case conventionally, for, while the term vase "painting" is ubiquitous, scholars are well aware that the technique is much more akin to what we would now consider drawing. In the black-figure style found on many of the early fabrics color is used to create silhouette (thus also contour) while incised line is used for the details, a technique in some ways more reminiscent of metal-working than of painting. In the red-figure technique a brush is used, but line is still supreme. The result is still closer to a kind of drawing than to what we would consider painting today.

However, this exhibit is not just about painting, it is about the painted surface, and the vases are no less important than the decoration. Foremost is the question of the relationship of the decoration to the vase itself, the connection between painting and pot, between painter and potter. The decoration is sometimes so fine that we can forget that these vases are exquisite examples of ceramic art. Even more interesting is the question of relationship of the one to the other. Certain painters become adept at using the surface of the vase to enhance the effect of the line; one of the most notable examples is the Berlin Painter with his single figures that flow across and are formed by the three-dimensional surfaces of the vase (22). There is also the relationship between decoration and the function of the vase. Can there be any doubt that the scene painted on the Apulian *rhyton* (37), depicting Actaeon being torn asunder by his hunting dogs, relates to the fact that the vase is shaped like a dog's head? What would it have been like to drink out of a vessel that is so intimately connected to its violent mythological decoration? What would the message have been, for the maker and for the user? Greek vases had very specific functions, and thus very specific social contexts, and painters were well aware of these contexts and often chose their imagery with function in mind. The imagery of vases themselves and the evidence thus provided for social contexts is discussed by Jenifer Neils in this catalogue. Recent research has taken a more anthropological approach by investigating connections of function and decoration, especially in the context of the Greek symposium where many of these vases were used.[1] Thus social rituals, and even political statements, can be enacted and symbolized through the use of the object.[2] It has recently even been argued that certain early Attic red-figure painters created scenes that, in their complexity and through visual paradoxes or pictorial riddles, visually paralleled sympotic literature, the riddles and puns that were part of the discourse at a Greek symposium.[3] In any case, the careful attention to form and decoration (traditional connoisseurship), combined with questions of context and meaning, can lead to very nuanced readings and new insights, as Neils demonstrates in her essay.

But if exhibitions are narratives, then what is this exhibit really about? What is the story told by these forty-four vases? One clear message is that of the historical development of Greek art from the Geometric to the Hellenistic period, the evolution of a figure style that will inform western art to the present day. The vases in this exhibit, selected from the superb collections of the National Archaeological Museum of Spain, were chosen with that theme in mind. Another important criterion is quality. These are all outstanding examples of their type. The word masterpiece is much overused these days, but there is no question that there are masterpieces here, that is, vases that are of the highest artistic quality and also profoundly important for the understanding of the development of the medium. A good example is the bilingual amphora signed by Psiax as painter and Andokides as potter/maker (20). This is a vase that, apart from the quality of its shape and decoration, documents the shift from the black-figure style to the innovative red-figure painting in Athens at the beginning of the fourth quarter of the sixth century B.C. It is a kind of vase that scholars have dubbed "bilingual," since it speaks two visual languages.[4] Although scholars are still debating the reasons for this dramatic change in painting technique, there can be little doubt that an important component for the change is formal; the interest in vase painters in developing a technique that is more painterly and would allow them greater freedom in defining form and space.[5] Because Greek monumental painting, which would have been done on panels, has not been preserved, vases like this provide essential evidence for a broader range of art. The amphora thus documents a profound moment in the history of western painting.

Another vase in the exhibit that surely would be considered a masterpiece by anyone's definition is the *kylix*, painted by Aison, that depicts the labors of Theseus (29). The scale of this drinking cup is much more modest than the bilingual amphora, but the scope of its red figure decoration is vast, and of all the vases in this exhibit it has received the greatest scholarly attention. On its surface is a complex narrative whose sophisticated structure reveals a great deal about Greek modes of visual expression. It also brings up an interesting issue of terminology, for all the objects in this exhibit would, by modern standards, be considered "minor" arts, yet a vase like the Aison *kylix* is in no way minor. The post-Renaissance division of "great art" and the minor arts simply does not apply in the classical world,[6] and while there is still lively scholarly debate about the ancient perceptions of value,[7] there is no doubt in my mind that these are major works of art created by some of the most important artists of their day. Despite the attention that the Aison *kylix* has received, it has only traveled outside Madrid once, to a recent exhibition in Berlin, and we are privileged to have it come to Dallas. As Paloma Cabrera explains in her historiographic essay on the collections of the National Archaeological Museum in Madrid, the bilingual amphora and Aison *kylix* have been part of the museum's collections since the 19th century and have a distinguished pedigree before that, but there are also surprises in this exhibit, vases that are not nearly so well known. About half of the vases were recently acquired by the National Archaeological Museum and were displayed for the first time, and published, in an inaugural exhibition in the fall of 2003. These vases are relatively unknown even to scholars. Their quality is also exceptional.

But if one part of the story told by this exhibit is historical, another part is geographical. The vases have been grouped under the rubric of Greek art, but they encompass a wide geographical and cultural range. When we think of Greek art today, we are usually thinking of Athens, and indeed many of the vases in this show are Attic, that is, from Athens or the area around Athens. Yet there are vases from other parts of mainland Greece, for instance Corinth (4–8), Laconia or Sparta (11), or even possibly from east Greece or Ionia, on the other shore of the Aegean (9). There is also a large group of vases (32–40), generally somewhat later in date (fourth century B.C.) from southern Italy or greater Greece, Magna Graecia as it came to be called. These vases are no less Greek but have a far less "classical" feel. Their decoration is more florid, their form more Baroque, and their narrative expression quite different from the earlier Attic vases. While Attic narrative was linear, usually focused on single defining moments, South Italian vases present more complex, multivalent narratives that require closer attention and even greater knowledge on the part of the viewer. And finally there are the Etruscan/Italic vases (41–44). These are not really Greek at all, even if these central Italian artists were heavily influenced by Greek art. Recent scholarship on Etruscan art has focused on questions of reception, on how Etruscan cultural idioms come to be expressed in a Greek visual language. The four central Italian vases in this exhibit are good examples of this fundamentally non-Greek message expressed in terms that are influenced by Greek art.

If the geographical, chronological, and cultural range of the vases in this exhibit is vast, what is all the more remarkable is that the vases all adhere to a shared aesthetic. The structure of the decoration is invariably connected to form, and the occurrence of this phenomenon (repetition) is investigated in this volume by Ann Steiner who uses new methodological approaches in her essay. And then, there is the decoration itself, the wealth of imagery found on Greek vases that is unparalleled in other media in the ancient Mediterranean. There are thousands of scenes, imagery so vast that it is no wonder that the early study of Greek vases focused on issues of attribution, classification and taxonomy, although as Sarah Peirce points out in her essay, the choice of imagery is in many ways circumscribed.

AN INTRODUCTION TO THE STUDY OF GREEK VASE-PAINTING is provided in this catalogue by Karl Kilinski. The study of Greek vases is a rich and complex one, pioneered by Sir John Beazley whose approach so interestingly parallels the work of that other pioneer, Bernard Berenson, in Italian Renaissance art. Beazley literally created the foundation for the study of Greek vase painting,[8] the structure on which the field is based, but as is the case with most pioneers his work is now decidedly out of fashion,

and it is indeed now the vogue to decry the pervasive influence of Beazley "in keeping the focus on the search for masters and on authorship as the ultimate explanation
for vase painting."[9] It is easy to criticize a pioneer, and if Beazley's influence was
pervasive and thus constrictive, it has also been pointed out that the problem lies
perhaps not with Beazley but with the scholars who followed him.[10] A new generation of scholars, however, has moved from structure and taxonomy to issues of representation and meaning in order to pursue questions that are at the core of prevailing
theory of the art historical discipline, to wit, what is the nature of representation on
these vases? It used to be thought that the visual repertoire could be divided into two
parts, scenes of mythology and scenes of everyday life, and that the latter group
presented us with evidence of the realities of Greek life. Of late the very basis for this
division has been called into question, but there is no doubt about the richness of
imagery and its usefulness. Even if it cannot always be used in a strict documentary
sense, it reveals a great deal about the broader contexts of the Greek world.[11] But
even so, there remains the question of what is represented.

This question, the nature of representation, is of interest not just to the specialist but to anyone interested in visual arts. Part of the problem is that the visual
language is so familiar. It is the way that the images are structured, their seeming
naturalism, the rationally composed and spatially defined "window" that is so familiar to the western viewer. Can these scenes be considered genre? Is the artist observing nature and reproducing it as observed? Is this reality or a construct? What did this
scene mean to the artist who created it, or to the person who viewed it while using
the vase? The issues have been neatly summarized by Neer: "Realist accounts of vase-
painting have been much criticized in recent years…. The central, oft-repeated point
is that pictures do not reproduce reality: they transform it…. The existence of some
relationship between daily life and vase-painting is not really at issue. The problem
rather, is to define those relationships: to separate realism—which is a genre—from
the real as such." The nature of representation and the construction of the image,
topics that are at the core of current scholarship on Greek vase-painting, are investigated in this catalogue by Sarah Peirce. Also at the heart of the debate are issues about
the nature of narrative, and the way that the human figure and its spatial definition
are used to construct narrative.[12] The importance of these vases for understanding
the classical idiom cannot be overestimated.[13]

The point of this exhibit is thus twofold, to display objects of the highest quality
and importance while using them to evoke issues that are of both historical and theoretical importance. The aim is to take something that is familiar and to look at it in a
new way, and thanks to the work of a new generation of scholars who are pushing the
limits of the discipline, this is now possible. Of late it has become fashionable to talk
about the two art histories,[14] the one practiced in museum galleries by curators who
stress the dominance of the object as work of art, and the other practiced in the classroom by teachers and scholars who lean to increasingly theoretical approaches that
subsume the object in a greater socio-cultural matrix. The difference is sometimes

presented as a contest between the practical and the theoretical. It need not be a contest. As a scholar who has lately come to the museum world, but also an archaeologist who is thus rooted in the ritual practices of the discipline, I am happy to have the opportunity to present an exhibit that celebrates the work of art while placing that work of art, as object, in its cultural context. This is a wonderful time to present an exhibit on Greek vase-painting, and I wish to thank the Meadows Museum and its Director, Dr. Edmund Pillsbury for the opportunity to do so. I am also profoundly grateful to the National Archaeological Museum in Madrid and its Director, Dr. Miguel Ángel Elvira, and its Curator of Greek art, Dr. Paloma Cabrera, for their extraordinary generosity in allowing these wonderful vases to leave Spain and come to Texas. I would also like to acknowledge the support of the Meadows Foundation and its CEO, Linda Evans, and of the Meadows School of the Arts and its Dean, Dr. Carole Brandt. I also wish to thank the curatorial staff of the Meadows Museum, Jeanne Chvosta, Kay Johnson, Will Johnson, Courtney Kennedy, Lisa Lombard, and Bridget Marx, as well as my teaching assistant, Katy Blanchard, for all their help, but especially Dr. Mark Roglán, who traveled to Spain with me to plan the show and who lent his excellent curatorial eye to the enterprise. Finally, my thanks go to the contributors to this volume who gave their valuable time willingly and their great expertise most graciously.

NOTES

[1] For instance Lissarague 1990.

[2] "...an object might in itself be a political act—not the hypostasis or signifier of a political act, but the very thing itself." Neer 2002, 25.

[3] Neer 2002, 27–86.

[4] Cohen 1978.

[5] For the development or "invention" of red-figure painting: Robertson 1992, 7–9.

[6] For a sensible discussion of these vases as art, or for the distinction between art and craft, see Robertson 1992, 3.

[7] For instance, the theories of Vickers and Gill regarding the monetary value of vases and the argument that they are merely cheap imitations of metal ware. The bibliography is large and ever-growing, but see Vickers and Gill 1994 for the premise and, for the rebuttal: Neer 2002, 206–215, with previous bibliography.

[8] For Beazley as a scholar and the breadth of his influence as a teacher: Kurtz 1985.

[9] Ferrari 2002, 1.

[10] Robertson 1992, 4, on Beazley: "...that he has made it seem that the most important thing about any vase is who painted it, and so has sadly narrowed the study, has I think some force (though it is perhaps less Beazley's fault than his followers')..."

[11] For the knowledge that can be gained from careful examination of the visual repertoire, see, for instance the intriguing set of essays about liminal areas of Greek society or the Greek world: Cohen 2000.

[12] For broader contexts: Shapiro 1994 and Carpenter, 1991.

[13] For general aspects of ancient narrative: Small 1999, 562–575. These issues are of course important for all two-dimensional media, and not just in the Greek world: Brilliant 1984.

[14] See for instance the proceeding of the 1999 conference held at the Clark Institute: Haxthausen 2002.

Painters, Pots, and Pictures: an Introduction to Greek Vases

❀

KARL KILINSKI II

A Hellenistic poem, *Kiln*, preserved in a *Life of Homer* recounts the myriad hazards that may befall the contents of the potter's kiln during that vulnerable time when all the recent efforts expended in crafting and decorating a batch of vases is at risk.[1] In this hour of truth the potter's skills in preparing the clay, shaping the forms, stacking the kiln, and judging the temperatures in firing the vases are subject to natural forces over which he has limited control. For as the poem states, once the kiln is fired, the personifications of destruction may run amuck within, so that Smasher and Crasher, Shaker and Collapser, Scorcher and Crumbler might frolic in their mischievous demolition of the precious wares inducing a loud, disparaging wail from the helpless potter. The Greek ceramics craft was a business of heat, smoke, and muck producing extraordinary products in elegant, yet durable forms and decorated with captivating scenes of myth, ritual, and daily life that provide us with a portal into the mind and matter of ancient Greece.

Although there were often a number of apprentices and laborers on hand, the primary craftsmen in the ceramics industry were potters (actually shaping vases) and painters (those decorating them), the former sometimes serving in both capacities. Painters generally worked for a potter, often in small groups, or sometimes for more than one potter, and might join efforts with another painter in decorating a single vase.[2] Such close collaboration among artists no doubt led to the diffusion of artistic ideas as well as much collegiality in the trade, yet rivalries surely flourished among these craftsmen as we are reminded by the boast, "as never Euphronios," inscribed by the Attic vase painter Euthymides to his contemporary Euphronios in a scene depicting a magisterial rendering of a twisting reveler.[3] Rivalries, some jocular and others fervent, were natural in a competitive atmosphere (as in all business), but that in the Greek pottery trade appears to have been notorious, so that we hear "potter against potter" used as a metaphor for rivalry from Hesiod (*Op.* 25) to Aristotle (*Rh.* II.4.21). In major centers such as Athens, Corinth, and in southern Italy where Greeks had settled, potters and vase painters probably practiced their trade on a full-time basis; the demand for their products requiring a continual supply. Here their collective numbers and ample paraphernalia were established in a specific district, or potters quarter, sometimes en route out of town to the clay beds. In Greek outlying areas and smaller villages such craftsmen may have worked alone, stoking a kiln as the need arose and alternating this occupation with other demands on their time.[4]

Not all ceramicists working in one location were necessarily of local origin. The names of several Athenian artists (e.g., "Thrax" from? Thrace, "Skythes" from? Scythia [Crimea], "Kolchos" from? the Black Sea region of modern Georgia, "Mys" from? Mysia [northwest Anatolia], "Sikelos" from? Sicily, and "Syriskos" the little Syrian?) may indicate that they were *metics* (immigrant craftsmen or merchants) or even slaves.[5] The Athenian vase painter Lydos ('the Lydian') may have emigrated from Asia Minor (or possibly his parents did), the nickname perhaps referencing a former homeland, but his style is purely Athenian.[6] His contemporary Amasis may have had ties to Egypt (or more likely to Ionian ceramicists having business there), as his name is an adaptation of that for an Egyptian king.[7] Some potters and vase painters took diverse opportunities to migrate. The potter Teisias, upon abandoning Athens for Tanagra in Boeotia (central Greece), began to sign his work with the epithet "the Athenian" appended to his name, which perhaps boasted not only of his training in the 'metropolis' noted for fine wares but of personal pride as well.[8] The lettering applied to a vase made in Attica (the territory of Athens) by the Polyphemus Painter indicates that he was schooled on the neighboring island of Aegina.[9] In the sixth century B.C. certain Athenian black-figure vase-painters immigrated to Boeotia,[10] and another painter whose script derives from the large Aegean island of Euboea settled in a Greek colony in southern Italy,[11] while others still from Corinth had already immigrated to Etruria (Tuscany) where an Etrusco-Corinthian style ultimately flourished,[12] all introducing their art in their new regions and many likely seeking an enhanced market share beyond that possible at home. In Athens the Andokides Painter was possibly from Ionia (Asia Minor) as his style of drawing is reflective of East Greece.[13] At least one artist steeped in a tradition of greater polychrome usage (a muralist?) than his new neighbors, left Ionia for Caere in Italy where he produced some of the most colorful and vividly animated scenes on *hydriae* (water jars).[14] Another potter likely from Ionia settled in Etruria where he produced colorful 'Pontic' vases, and this endeavor inspired local potteries blossoming into genuine Etruscan black-figure styles (42–43).[15] Some Corinthian artists may have immigrated to Athens by governmental invitation in the early sixth century B.C.,[16] while in the fifth century B.C. artists emigrated from Attica to southern Italy to perpetuate a style of vase painting (red-figure) that was slowly dying out at home.[17] From these beginnings several South Italian red-figure vase-painting schools (32–40) would flourish in the fourth century B.C.

As vase painters generally worked for potters, the latter were more often shop owners in the larger vase producing centers. A potter making and decorating his own pots along side other vase painters in his shop may not be obliged to carry on both processes consistently. One shop proprietor, the potter Euphronios, also signs as painter, but not in his later years when vases bearing his potter's signature clearly carry decoration in the styles of others; giving rise to speculation that he ceased painting with failing eyesight as an elder.[18] Successful activity in a pottery, perhaps for decades, probably contributed to a higher economic status for some artists who demonstrated their financial gains and pious gratitude through dedications on the Athenian Acropolis.[19] Several artists dedicated painted plaques and vases there, including Epiktetos (who painted 21), often with images of Athena. Other potters, including Andokides (see 20) and Euphronios, dedicated expensive sculptural monuments to the goddess of the city, while yet another artist commissioned a sculptured marble relief depicting a ceramicist holding his wares.[20] How much this action or the financial basis for it might have contributed to the social status of a potter or painter is difficult to determine, but most artists in the pottery industry were likely considered to be ordinary men performing a skilled trade. While some, like Euphronios, may have become rather wealthy, others were less fortunate. Some, such as another Lydos who declares himself a slave,[21] were subject to harsh treatment and little benefit. Yet the artist's perception of his skills and the trade in general could be wrought with high esteem. A rare scene of an active vase shop on a *hydria* in Milan by the Leningrad Painter shows three men and a woman working intently on vases with Athena, patron of the arts, bestowing honor on the primary craftsman and Nikes, acknowledgers of merit, doing likewise to the other men.[22] Although a woman artist is present, she appears to be ignored, and by the body of information on hand pottery production in ancient Greece lay virtually in the male domain.[23]

As few artists in the pottery craft signed their work, modern scholars have bestowed names upon those painters whose specific styles have been recognized on multiple vases. These names may be devised from various affiliations with the anonymous artist, some more inspired than others. A designation might incorporate the name of a signed potter with whom a painter regularly worked (e.g., Brygos Painter), or may derive from a city (Berlin Painter: 22) or collection (Bareiss Painter) in which a prime example of his œuvre resides, or from a specific subject (Achilles Painter) or stylistic trait (the Affecter) in his work. In situations where an actual artist's signature exists, it sometimes includes the name of his father who was also a ceramicist, indicating what we might suspect that the craft was often family taught and sons succeeded fathers in the trade.[24]

Signatures of potters and vase painters commence with the rise of the individual in Greek society during the Archaic era (as do those of other artists and self-references by Lyric poets) and likely display the craftsman's pride in his work (20).[25] The term 'signature' is perhaps misleading as we are uncertain as to exactly who wrote the artists' names: painters, potters, or an inscriber (a 'letterer') charged with the task. Whereas the word *egrapsen* ('painted') apportioned to a name on a vase may be a frank declaration, the word *epoiesen* ('made') is more problematic in that in one instance it might apply to the individual potter (meaning 'shaper') of a vase while in another it might imply the proprietor (i.e., 'producer') of the pottery in which one or more potters and painters worked. A unique case on an Attic black-figure vase by Oikophe-les employs the word *ekerameusen* (literally 'potted'), appearing in an inscription repeating the artist's name and including *egrapsen* (meaning 'and painted'), so that we are more assured that this artist actually shaped and decorated the vessel.[26] It is little wonder that contrary opinions are abundant on the meaning(s) of vase signatures.[27] Yet most vases, even those by the best artists, go unsigned.

The names of gods, heroes (e.g., 21, 26, 34), monsters, animals, and inanimate objects are applied from time to time which assist in revealing an identification or particular narrative, and all were included to attract the viewer's attention. The lack of identifying names (e.g., 21, 22) often leaves modern minds questioning whether or not the painter meant to represent particular characters in a scene when more specific attributes and/or actions are not apparent, but to the ancient Greeks such distinctions may not have been (or needed to be) so explicit. Actual captions are rare, so that narrative is usually a silent presentation in pictures. Utterances from characters depicted are infrequent in black figure scenes, such as Odysseus tied to the mast of his ship crying out 'lus[o]n' ("loose me") upon hearing the alluring song of the irre-sistible sirens.[28] Such occurrences become more common among the first full gener-ation of Attic red-figure vase painters, of which Epiktetos ranks among the most sublime of draftsmen (21). *Kalos* (handsome) or 'love' names of young men inscribed on Greek vases were most popular during the late Archaic period when referencing a specific individual provides a glimpse into the world of who was renowned in high society of the times.[29] The name need not refer to a character in the actual scene in which it occurs, but likely to a contemporary youth who was considered especially notable for his appearance or perhaps outstanding accomplishment (athletics?) in Athenian social circles. Roughly two hundred names are known from this category and several are identified, later as adults, from various accounts. The role of *kalos* names may have evolved over time in the changing atmosphere brought about in the wake of democratic rule established in Athens near the end of the sixth century so that those names appearing on vases by Exekias and his peers of the third quarter of the sixth century might not have been selected for the same reasons or carry the same meaning as those bandied about by artists at the end of the century. Whereas some might hold that the ceramicists were simply referencing the fashionable elite of the time and need not have any acquaintance with their subjects, others consider the array of explicit courting scenes and the like on vases where these names occur as a possible indicator that the artists had intimate familiarity with certain young members of the nobility.[30] One element of interest here is that all of the ceramicists involved were potters,[31] therefore, possible if not probable, proprietors and possibly with means that might elevate their status in Athenian society. The implication stems largely from a handful of vases where known ceramicists are identified by name in conjunction with noted youths and on occasion in cultivated environments, and espe-cially a vase on which we are led to believe the ceramicist Euphronios is importuning the young dandy Leagros (later to become an Athenian general), as both are named.[32]

Although the Euphronios/Leagros case may be an exception, other scholars consider these juxtapositions of ceramicists and the young aristocrats to be jovial whimsies on the part of mere tawdry practitioners, especially since these scenes appear on vessels meant for the rowdy symposium.[33] Those women named on Athenian vases who were praised for their beauty (*kale*) were likely courtesans, as marriageable girls would have been largely out of sight at home and as Thucydides (2.45) informs us through the words of Pericles that the highest admiration for married women was not to be discussed by men with either praise or criticism. Many other inscriptions are nonsense or even imitation letters (e.g., 13, 19, 30), often simply rows of dots, indicating an illiterate (or lazy) artist, but one with an eye to the market where such enhancements were valued.

Ceramic vase shapes were inspired by containers in metal, stone, wood, basketry (cf. 2), and horn, yet other shapes motivated the potters' designs including animals, eggs, body parts (animal and human heads, hands, crab claws, a woman's breast [the *mastos*], a man's genitalia) as well as animal skins, shells, organs, and bones, so that very little escaped the potter's eye. Form followed function, giving rise to thumb props (5, 42) and spouts (8, 42) for pouring control, narrow necks to curtail evaporation and spillage (4, 6–7, 30–31), lids to contain heat or valuables (40), and handles arranged for lifting as well as pouring from a single vase (16–17), but all usually guided by a sense of aesthetics (28). Although the pottery industry catered largely to the needs of Greek banqueting, vase usage was not solely for dispensing food and drink. Vessels of divergent forms and sizes were employed in ritual (e.g., funerary and marriage), or designed for cosmetics, domestic craft, amusement, storage, shipping, and as votive offerings (to gods and heroes) or prizes. Most shapes served rather designated functions, and though their original names are often problematical for scholars, many have been applied for convenience.[34] The *pyxis* (2), *aryballos* (4, 6) and *alabastron* (7) were used for cosmetic purposes, the first to contain jewelry and makeup, herbs and incense, the last two for scented oils or perfumes. The *hydria* (16) carried water, the amphora (e.g., 9, 14, 20) held oil or wine, kraters (24) were for mixing wine, different pitchers (e.g., *oinochoe* (1), *olpe* (5)) for dispensing it, and various cups (e.g., 11, 18, 26) for consuming it. The *situla* (39), originally derived from an Egyptian shape, was commonly used for ritual in the Greek world, as was the *rhyton* (37).[35] An array of open bowls, platters, mugs (28), plates, and covered dishes made up regular dinner ware. Certain vases had gender affiliations, although this might vary, especially in different regions or eras. The *alabastron, hydria, pyxis, lebes gamikos*, belly- or shoulder-handled amphora, and *lutrophoros-hydria* were affiliated with women, while the neck-handled amphora, krater, *kantharos, aryballos*, and *lutrophoros*-amphora were generally associated with men.

Plastic (modeled or molded) attachments to vases have a very long history in Greece going back to the Bronze Age. In what might seem to modern eyes an ostentatious stage of ornamentation, a number of vessels carried figures in clay relief, gilding, and/or appliqués (32, 38), while some were melded into an amalgamated composition with others (38). The last were often ritual vases and their elaborate designs were partially a consequence of their restricted usage, while other ritual shapes such as the handle-less *phiale* (for pouring libations; note that depicted on 38), inspired by eastern metal models, could be quite simple. Other forms were also designed for specific functions: sprinklers, siphons, baby feeders, fishplates (with central depression for sauce), and *epinetra* (thigh covers for handling raw wool) were all products of the pottery. Rattling cups (with loose beads sealed in a hollow foot) and other trick vases (cups with false bottoms or covered and filled from an internal siphon that prevented emptying it without drinking) were witty creations of the potter's craft meant to amuse and confuse the partygoer.[36] Even infusing vases unavoidably drawn to the nose (i.e., cups) with spices for sensual pleasure was apparently not beyond the potter's imagination or skill.[37] *Rhyta* in various molded forms of animals, human or animal heads (37), body parts, and even full figures are embellished adaptations of drinking-horns, while other, more practical, 'oddities' such as the *psykter* (wine cooler), often designed with a self-contained compartment for the coolant (that is not unlike some glass wine decanters today), challenged the potter's skill. Another clever trick was to attach a thimble-like cup at the base of the neck inside a *lekythos* (oil vase), sealing off the bulk of the container below and thus requiring the potter to cut a vent hole in it (often concealed by the handle) to keep the vase from exploding in the kiln when fired (30). The objective was to present the impression of a vessel completely filled with oil when in reality only the neck carried the precious commodity. These vases were meant for the grave, whose occupant cared not about the quantity of oil presented but whose survivors observed a vessel seemingly quite full! Some specialty vases, namely Panathenaic amphoras awarded as prizes in the contests at Athens, were commissioned by the state,[38] while other large and elaborately decorated vessels consuming several days work (e.g., Kleitias' krater in Florence) most certainly were private commissions.[39] That aforementioned piece signed by Kleitias, with over two hundred and fifty painted figures, was probably intended for a wedding.[40]

It is interesting that the majority of finer Athenian vases have been retrieved from Italy, a phenomenon perhaps due in part to chance finds, in part to forms of burial practice (graves where vases can be crushed in Greece, protective tombs in Italy), and also due to a wealthy market in the West. Specific shapes (e.g., Tyrrhenian and Nikosthenic amphoras and *kyathoi*) were designed by certain Athenian potteries specifically for export to cities in Etruria.[41] The décor of the first combined vivid color on layered animal friezes and lively scenes of myth in typical Corinthian fashion, which was already appreciated locally. Nikosthenic amphoras and *kyathoi* addressed the particulars of shape, which imitated corresponding ones produced by the Etruscans. Later, Athenian red-figure vases imitated shapes peculiar to southern Italy that are never found on the Greek mainland, a solid indication of products intended for export.[42] Other Greek vases were destined for the East. A Thracian cup design imitated in Athens and decorated by the Eretria Painter with Thracian warriors in full regalia found its way to Thrace, and the Athenian potter Sotades made *rhyta* mimicking Persian drinking-horns, some with scenes showing Greeks *defeated* by Amazons or Persians.[43] It would seem that protocol took a back seat to profit here.

Of the tens of thousands of extant Greek vases probably less than one percent has survived from the total produced. This meager survival rate and the lofty aesthetic value placed on them by connoisseurs of the eighteenth and nineteenth centuries, who compared them to renowned Renaissance paintings, have bequeathed Greek vases with a worth vastly inordinate to that placed on them by their makers and original consumers.[44] If we assume the average decorated vase was worth about the equivalent of a day's wage, with larger and/or more elaborate vases costing much more, while others plain, small, or of mediocre quality substantially less, then we arrive at an approximate understanding of their original value. Overseas distribution added the inevitable charges for shipping and handling and foreign ports were not likely to admit competitive wares without some sort of imposed duty, thereby increasing the purchase price. Competition for the market with other vase-painting schools and even with vessels in other materials could be severe. Gilding or a thin silver slip was sometimes applied to black Etruscan bucchero vases to imitate precious metal wares,[45] and a red ground slip was applied on larger Corinthian vases perhaps to rival their corresponding (and ever more marketable) Athenian counterparts, which had naturally reddish clay.[46] Yet the law of supply and demand meant that lesser quality works unacceptable at home might be eagerly sought abroad, perhaps for more easily pleased clientele, and there was certainly greater profit from assembly-line products. Whole dinner collections appear in Etruscan towns and tombs,[47] and there is literary evidence for volume sets available for symposia or banquets as rentals, so that not everyone felt compelled to make large purchases of elegant pottery in order to keep socially active.[48] But there are clear indicators that fine vessels were highly prized in antiquity. The frequent depictions of vases within the contexts of the painted scenes provide a clear indication of the artists' awareness of the importance of the vessels in Greek culture.[49] Furthermore, a number of vases, once broken (sometimes into several pieces), were patched with alien parts and/or repaired with lead staples lacing fragments together (29).[50] Such vessels may not always have been functional thereafter, but they were obviously cherished despite their condition.[51]

The subject matter selected for depiction on Greek vases was under little constraint. Artists took inspiration from a broad array of real life around them, including flora and fauna, and drew on the exhaustive panoply of religion, myth, and fantasy as well. Depending on the vase shape and picture placement, figural scenes were often fringed by floral and/or linear designs. Many painters decorated their wares in free-hand, while the better painters often applied a preliminary sketch (e.g., 21, 24), especially for complex scenes, as testified by visual remnants of a design on vase surfaces, and erasures were often telltale after firing due to a change in color (light to dark) of the glaze.[52] There were natural and imposed limitations in vase painting. Adapting a subject to a curved surface frequently irregular in shape and dodging handle attachments were matter-of-fact challenges for the vase painter. Vases frequently had a 'front' (obverse) and a 'back' (reverse) where a primary or complex subject occupied the former with a generic or lesser theme for the latter (e.g., 24). Yet a vase painter often utilized the double-sided nature of his 'canvas' to assemble equilibrium of forms (15) or more creatively to formulate a narrative leading from one scene to the other as a continuance (12, 22–23, 26), inducing the viewer to turn the vessel in order to conclude the theme. Figural decoration began in simple silhouette (3), then introduced forms in outline, mainly flora and fauna (4), largely of eastern origin, but also for humans until a new technique, "black-figure", perhaps inspired from engraved metalwork, originated in Corinth about 700 B.C. (6) and ultimately engulfed most schools of Greek vase decoration during the Archaic era. The figures were still painted in glaze that would, after firing, turn solid black against the lighter clay surface, but the key to image enhancement involved incising internal details (anatomical features, attire, ornament, structural components, etc.). White and/or dark red were applied for contrast, visual enrichment, and further clarification: the former for women's flesh (15), the latter for men, but such conventions were not firm (7, 18).[53] Although draftsmanship evolved and perspective was enhanced by simple overlapping of forms, the art remained in essence a two-dimensional expression. About 525 B.C., an Athenian artist, probably the Andokides Painter or perhaps Psiax (20), introduced a simple but revolutionizing change.[54] Here the background was filled in with glaze and the figures were left reserved but with different brushes providing lines of divergent thickness for internal details. This process produced a greater fluidity of form with the brush than could be achieved with the incisor and also allowed for enhanced clarity of details and whole figures, especially in congested scenes (29). This new "red-figure" technique (Attic clay, rich in iron, fires reddish) was essentially a photonegative of the older black figure one, yet the same firing process applied to both as none of the materials had changed, only the distribution of glaze on a vase surface. It was then advantageous for an artist to display similar scenes, but in two different techniques, on opposite sides of the same vase (20) to demonstrate the advantages of the one over the other while simultaneously avoiding a complete break with the time-honored technique associated with the art and times of his forefathers. This may help explain why the subsidiary décor of floral designs adorning a red figure vase remained in the traditional black for some time after the introduction of red figure. Some very early red figure vases also have an incised black figure scene on the opposite side. Modern scholars have dubbed these vessels, ornamented in both techniques, "bilingual" vases, since they express themselves to us in a dual fashion. Athenian black-figure vases with backgrounds covered in white (made from an unadulterated clay) commenced in the late Archaic period (19) and white ground was perpetuated on red-figure vases with drawn figures and ultimately with various colors added (some after firing) in the Classical era (30–31); their light backgrounds and polychrome décor were perhaps inspired or encouraged by murals.

Regional schools varied in their primary tastes for subjects. Corinth (4–8) and East Greece (9) adhered to a longstanding preference for animal friezes often in conjunction with clustered floral forms, perhaps inspired by tapestries.[55] In Attica, vase painters gravitated to larger forms (e.g., 3, 16, 20, 25) than those favored in Corinth and were more inclined to adorn them largely with mythological subjects and scenes of heroic action, eventually supplementing these with scenes of more ordinary human activity. Laconia (Spartan territory) took inspiration from both Corinth and Athens, as did Boeotia, while injecting their vase shapes and scenes with a certain amount of local flavor (11).[56] Boeotia in the late fifth and fourth centuries B.C. produced decorated vases in the one comic school of Greek art: Kabiric ware.[57] Euboea drew on the Cycladic islands and Attica for inspiration, while the Greek colonies in southern Italy and Sicily and the Etruscan cities, as noted above, created styles inspired or adapted from Athens, Corinth, and East Greece.[58] A particular fondness for reflecting scenes from the Greek theater (35, 36) was prominent in certain South Italian schools of the late Classical era.[59]

The choice of decoration was often selected with the type and/or purpose of a vase shape in mind. A *hydria* is decorated with a scene of women bearing *hydriae* to a fountain house (16). Women (38) bathing in the presence of winged Eros while another prepares an offering from a *phiale* for good fortune and holds a mirror (an attribute of Aphrodite) are appropriate selections for a *lebes gamikos* (wedding vase), which may have held refreshments for the new couple or perhaps the purification water required for a girl's marriage bath.[60] Many were recovered from the Sanctuary of Hera (goddess of marriage) at Paestum where this vase was made.[61] Men cavort to music or find amusement with a drinking cup on the interiors of them (11, 21), while others revel midst the nocturnal den of fellow symposiasts on a wine krater (24). Heroic subjects were also fitting on wine cups (12–13, 21, 26, 29) as assurances of manliness for the all male symposium (drinking party). Further male dominated spheres, such as the *palaestra* (25), were likewise appropriate subjects for symposium vessels. Yet other vases with seemingly less explicit scenes of assertive activity were also psychologically suited for male affiliation. A wine amphora from East Greece appears to be whimsically decorated with animal friezes (9), yet the hounds chasing hares and a goat caught between pawing sphinxes emit similar connotations of aggressive behavior. Symbolism was much a part of Greek vase painting décor. Special meanings were often infused in seemingly incidental elements. A palm tree set within a scene may constitute a location (the East), a single bird in flight might signify an omen, the presence of a goose, devotion, while hares or cocks were appropriate love gifts. Other symbols appear on vases to reference familial, civic (28), ritualistic (14), or talismanic (10, 14, 18) affiliations. The last served to protect the vessel, its contents, and, especially when debilitating wine was involved, its consumer. While such images were invested with a serious sense of potency, many artists did not hesitate to instill a playful element into the placement or arrangement of these symbols. A frontal-faced gorgon, Medusa or a sister, with grimacing expression faces out from a cup (18) to protect its contents, while the interior is embellished with a disembodied gorgoneion, which repeatedly projects its petrifying stare at the one imbibing from the cup each time he drains the vessel and slowly becomes 'stoned.' Disembodied eyes (14) were meant to ward off evil.[62] Yet such pairs of apotropaic eyes set on either side of a vase could be augmented with the addition of a nose painted between them (10) creating a clownish image, which when the cup was lifted to the lips took on the appearance of a garish face with the handles likened to ears (*ous* is Greek for handle and for ear) and the hollow ring foot serving as a gaping mouth. Many vases were destined for the grave or tomb, some scenes on larger upright vessels, perhaps symbolically representing the deceased, depicting the *prothesis* (mourners at a wake) in the Geometric era (3). During the early Archaic period these vases appear with mythological subjects often violent, among them monsters and demonic forces readily vanquished by gods or heroes to ease our minds. Others later in this epoch and also in the Classical era perpetuate the mourning scenes and later still bear images heroizing the dead (32), many enhanced by mythological narratives associated with the Underworld (33). Other large and small vases, generally *lekythoi*, of the Classical period, are decorated with underworld characters (e.g., Charon the boatman, Hermes who escorts spirits, and the twins Sleep and Death), while others still display the grave monument with attendants (30), projecting the promise of remembrance, or on occasion with a life-like image of the deceased before the tomb (31).[63]

A number of subjects were influenced by other arts. From observing sculptures, vase painters were inspired by various compositions, drapery styles, and poses, and by the fourth century they commanded the draftsmanship to execute subtle nuances of figures unachievable before (the arrangement of gods relaxing together on 39 is loosely reminiscent of their display on the Parthenon frieze), but generally such depictions are liberated impressions, perhaps unconscious in most instances. Standing architecture no doubt guided them in depicting fountain houses (16), shrines (32, 33), and funerary monuments (30–33). Theatrical performances on the Greek stage were reflected in vase scenes (35–36 and ? 34). Mural paintings, known from literary descriptions, eventually affected perspective, color, subjects, poses (22), and compositions on the smaller-scaled vessels. And of course poetry, whence much of the mythical narratives derive from Homer onward, played a vital role in shaping the selection and depiction of such subjects on Greek vases. But painters, like poets and playwrights, readily altered or adapted traditional mythical narrative for a diversity of motives, in many instances substituting what might well be their own conceptions, which demonstrates the metamorphic aptitude of myth.[64]

A variety of subjects selected for depiction appear to be reflections of ordinary Greek life, although many display trappings of glorified versions that are more likely presumed anachronisms on behalf of the painter or even products of a social construct than a portal to the present.[65] Yet, glimpses inside the merchants' establishments appear to reveal a daily activity not far removed from our own. The painters take us inside the shops of the butcher, cobbler, sculptor, baker, vintner, and armorer. And we are shown the various activities of the foundry, olive press, and not least of all the pottery.[66] The array of subjects is nearly as diverse as life itself, and yet such pictures of "ordinary life" are far from the normal fare on Greek vases and perhaps are the products of special commissions involving those engaged in the activities presented.[67] To these may be added other scenes, whether 'real' or contrived, of the swimming hole, the classroom, music and dance lessons, and of weddings (17), children at play, funerals (3), and tombs (30–33) of the dead. We encounter foreigners, both real (e.g., Africans, Etruscans, Thracians, Persians)[68] and mythical (15), hunting scenes (12, 19), warriors taking leave (16), and full-fledged combat (13). Music and dance[69] to accompany ritual and for symposia (6, 11), in which one found entertainment[70] in song, conversation, spectacle (27), erotic engagement, and/or amusing games (21),[71] was endemic of Greek life. The purpose of symposia might differ by region and are much a part of banqueting (42), the latter including tables for food as well as couches for reclining (of eastern derivation) while the paraphernalia of drinking parties (24) focuses more explicitly on the containers and dispensers of the essential ingredient: wine.[72]

Erotic scenes (10), are often, but not always, more explicit for males than for females (38). Many involve ritual, while those seemingly outside this determinate are proportionally few in number, and mostly occur on vases from ca. 570 to 450 B.C.[73] Prominent among the scenes lacking explicit sexual intercourse are representations of homoerotic courtship between aristocratic males of whom a mature lover (erastês) pursues a beloved youth (erômenos).[74] Such relationships were more than sexual, however, for they offered spiritual, intellectual, and educational benefits provided by the more worldly erastês to his chosen erômenos, in addition to a token love gift. The lack of explicit sexual intercourse of any form in these scenes lends credence to the idea that these relationships were considered primarily spiritual in nature. The popularity of such courtship scenes on Athenian vases during the latter half of the sixth century was likely in response to the elevated social status of Athenian male nobility under the governance of the aristocratic, Peisitratid family who promoted patrician values and a worldly extravagance then currently associated with East Greece with which the Peisistratids had political ties. Courting an admired adolescent of a noble family by an older aristocrat who was likely married with children of his own was upheld and lauded in Greek elitist poetry of the time. Once the youth outgrew adolescence he was no longer considered an eligible erômenos and would eventually marry and have children but would also become an erastês himself, commencing a new cycle in male homosexual relationships. While young male aristocrats would have the leisure time and financial means to experience sexual dalliances about town with servant girls and slaves, they were precluded by Athenian society from having such encounters with marriageable girls of their own rank, as these were closely supervised and generally at home.[75] Courtship scenes appear on vases largely used in the all-male symposium, thus reinforcing the notion of such behavior. Their dwindling numbers in the early fifth century was likely caused by a backlash against aristocratic values and activities associated with Peisistratid rule by the burgeoning Athenian democracy.

Gender statements abound on Greek vases. Female servants or slaves[76] but also married and marriageable women (16, 38)[77] are shown busy with domestic activities while men are engaged in more aggressive actions in unrestricted environments, such as hunting (12), sport (25), and combat (13, 22), or affiliated with status symbols (17), imbibing communally (24), in revelry (6, 11), or simply at leisure (34). Other women, not socially (or legally in Athens) acceptable for marriage to citizens, namely *hetairai* (courtesans, like geisha), carry on a more lively vocation for the general enjoyment of men,[78] while depictions of non-Greek females pursuing traditional male roles (15) serve as a warning to society of the potentially calamitous results when gender lines are transgressed.[79] However, men played both sex roles on the stage (36).[80]

Environment was addressed minimally. Interior scenes (24–25, 27, 34, 36) are denoted by windows and doors, wall hangings and/or furniture. Outdoor settings may simply lack those furnishings or are indicated by elements of landscape, such as a tree (29) or rock, a building façade (29), and, by mid-fifth century B.C., contour lines for irregular terrain. Actual architectural elements were represented in diverse orders (16, 23: Doric, and 29, 33: Ionic), as well as for structures already noted above, to which we should add houses, shrines (32–33), altars (11, 21, 40), grandstands, stage façades, and even potters' kilns. Sculptures of gods and heroes are depicted in a variety of scenes ranging from myth to daily life. Here, too, are found representations of traditional furniture (e.g., 27, 29), looms, ships, chariots (17), carts, arms and armor (32), musical instruments (e.g., 11, 20, 27, 32), assorted containers and crafted vessels (e.g., 16, 30).[81] Animals, whether domestic (9, 15), wild (4–5, 8, 11, 41), or fantastic (7, 10, 23, 25, 39, 43) and mixed together (9, 42), as well as demonic creatures (17–18) all make their appearances.

Action dominates much of vase scenes from dramatic encounters (13, 22–23, 29, 37) to caricatures (35). Yet drama may be in the making, and the artist focuses on a preceding or even subsequent moment to an encounter, or he might minimize the number of participants in a familiar subject (37), known from traditional oral or visual guides, in order to infuse his scene with an arresting air by rousing the viewer's imagination. Personifications (e.g., Justice, Fate, Strife, Vengeance, Peace, Hellas, Sleep, Death, and Old Age) manifest in various scenes to clarify actions.[82] Personalized images of contemporaries without being modern portraits, such as of the vase painters Euphronios and Euthymides,[83] are very rare as are historical personages, namely celebrated kings (Arkesilas of Cyrene, Kroisos of Lydia, Darius of Persia) and renowned poets, such as Anacreon, Alcaeus, and Sappho, yet most of these characters at the times of depiction belonged to the distant past. Contemporary events of a historical nature were basically ignored, although Greeks fighting Persians do appear on vases soon after the actual conflict between the two peoples ceased.[84] Theater followed suit with Aeschylus' performance of the *Persians* soon after the war, a rare exception to the norm of mythical subjects for the stage.[85]

Myth in Greek art melds the remote and improbable with the present and real, in part by dressing its mythical characters in current attire and conversely by exalting contemporary themes with heroic paraphernalia. So we see Apollo (19) wears the cloak of an ordinary man, and a departing warrior takes his leave in a chariot (16), a vehicle not utilized in Greek warfare of the time but part of the distant past. While this process may now cause moderns some consternation in clarifying the authenticity of a visual program, for the ancients it validated their traditions as history. Much of Greek myth focuses on the champion, and with good reason since the bridge between gods and mortals is the realm of heroes, the most popular theme for vase decoration.[86] Greek heroes often had divine parentage on one side and royalty on the other, setting them apart from mere mortals by their ancestry as well as by their superhuman accomplishments, but binding them to humans through their mortality. More than themes with gods, who are by definition more removed from the mortal world, heroic subjects can be infused with greater narrative. These portray the hero overcoming insurmountable tasks, dispatching or outmaneuvering monstrous adversaries through brain or brawn, or mustering god-given magical powers to charm or manipulate.[87] The heroes invariably succeed in these endeavors, dispelling human nightmares of the psyche and restoring order where chaos reigned, threatening ordinary life. Thus Theseus is depicted (29) striking down wild beasts, brigands, and other scoundrels in preliminary combats to demonstrate his prowess and worthiness prior to confronting a formidable hybrid monster (the Minotaur) praying on Athenian youth (29). Heracles, among his many deeds, dispatches the aggressive centaurs, surmounting odds of three to one (21); his finely wrought sword over-powering their crude branches and stones demonstrates that Greek civilization is superior to barbarism. Yet despite the hero's courage and prowess, and his ability to successfully intervene for the common good, he is also subject to fallibility, which can be painfully destructive to himself, those around him, and even his descendants, demonstrating his humanness. So the youthful Pelops challenging the oppressive and murderous King Oinomaos to a chariot race (26) to win the despot's daughter runs afoul of a curse that ravages his family line for generations.[88] The sagas of others take on a different twist. The rape of Persephone by Hades (33), the triumph of the priestess Io (34) who endures a prolonged transformation as a cow after her tryst with Zeus, and the death of Actaeon (37) who unwittingly offended Artemis, have much in common despite the diversification of their particular scenarios. All three subjects are hapless victims of divine intervention in their lives, a mishap occurring while they were temporarily alone, and they become heroic through their extraordinary sufferance and by being the focus of divine contact.[89] Other heroes, in some cases alluding to real characters in revered settings, often remain anonymous due to their lack (or our ignorance) of mythical narrative (32), but they could be pertinent to a regional tradition of heroism.[90]

Typical narrative on Greek vases displays figures in profile, but dramatic encounters may on occasion be punctuated with frontal faces, which intentionally confront the viewer with extremes (e.g., anxiety, agony, sleep, and death). When borne by fantastic beasts and monsters (7, 18) they are meant to intimidate, while that of the god Dionysos is more enigmatic. Partaking of the god of wine through his drink, as Euripides says in the *Bacchae* ("Dionysos is himself poured out"), is a direct method of engaging him, as best as mortals might, so that coming face to face with the mask of Dionysos, especially when flanked by apotropaic eyes on a wine amphora (12) or cup, is a disquieting experience perhaps meant to heighten awareness of one's imperfection while offering liberation from the constraints of an artificially lucid world.

Dionysos serves to carry us into the Olympian world of the divine. The Greek gods represented natural forces that tempered and colored the cosmos in which mortals toiled. The Greek perception of them in anthropomorphic form was a means of expressing their super*human* character, while the powers attributed to them set them apart from common culture in an elitist society of their own. The Greek pantheon consisted of twelve (as on the Parthenon frieze) primary divinities but other secondary gods (e.g., Eros, 38) and demigods (e.g., Pan, 39) abounded in Greek myth and religion. While most gods experienced a degree of universal recognition throughout the Greek world, many varied in their particular characteristics or domains of influence from region to region.

In vase painting the divinities are discernable (aside from inscriptions) through pose, attire, stature, juxtapositions, and/or action, but most readily by attributes. Thus the king of the gods, omnipotent Zeus, may hold his thunderbolts, be seated or ride while others stand or walk. His sister/wife Hera may appear stately, holding a scepter and/or wearing a crown, or unveil herself before him as a bride. Poseidon, lord of the sea, carries his trident. Demeter, as goddess of the grain, often holds corn or wheat, or on occasion a torch in search of her daughter Persephone who was kidnapped by Hades, King of the Underworld (33), whose appearance in Greek art is understandably uncommon. Hephaestus, the smithy, is lame, and works his forge or carries his tools. Dionysos, as god of wine, bears a drinking cup, often a horn or a *kantharos*, but he is not the only one to do so (39). However, he regularly appears in the midst of his cohorts, satyrs and maenads, who cavort entranced under his mind-liberating spell, while vines swirl about him like lightning emanating from an irrational and irresistible cosmic force (20). His half brother Apollo conversely represents order, which he enforces with his bow (19), but also plays the lyre or *kithara* (20) as god of music and poetry, or holds the laurel (39), a symbol of his prophetic powers.[91] His twin sister Artemis is mistress of animals and goddess of the hunt, who brandishes a bow and quiver (20, 33). Hermes was the messenger of Zeus, and thus carries his *kerykeion* or herald's staff (39), but also served as a guide for mortals, both living and dead. The war god, Ares, was little liked by a people almost constantly in conflict, but is regularly attired in armor, and here (20) appropriately with a fighting cock for a shield blazon. Another militant was Athena, a virgin goddess whose armored image is seen bolstering heroic escapades (29) or plunging into combat (33). Another irresistible force was Aphrodite, goddess of seduction and fertility, whose companion is often

Eros, god of love (33, 38). The Greek divinities were often depicted in assemblages of their own, on occasion relaxing (39), partaking of ceremony, or fighting common foes. In general they look statelier in the Archaic and early Classical periods, becoming younger in appearance or in some cases more ordinary in the late Classical era (cf. 20 with 39). When not grouped together they are frequently seen escorting or conferring honors on heroes, or receiving such themselves (39), yet often they are officiating, mitigating, misleading, wooing, or chastising, but in one way or another frequently interacting with the world of Greek mortals whence these wonderful vases have survived.

In glancing back over the exhibition of vases assembled here from the National Archaeological Museum collection in Madrid, it is clear how indicative this consortium is in presenting the breadth and scope of ancient Greek pottery. Within this select display of over forty vases we encounter a good diversity of vessel shapes and sizes, while the varied subjects depicted on them range over a broad spectrum of Greek consciousness that includes scenes of gods and goddesses, fabled heroes and their deeds, fantasized encounters, fantastic creatures, rituals, and artfully composed narratives of life and death. We are also privileged to compare differences in vase shapes and approaches to painted subjects representative of several divergent regional schools of vase production as well as distinctions in various techniques of vase painting, all components of a Greek vase exhibition only found in the landmark expositions on the subject in more recent years. It is to the credit of the Antiquities Department in the Madrid National Archaeological Museum that its vision of such a Greek vase anthology has been meticulously fulfilled over the years of collecting, and it is the privilege of the Meadows Museum to receive this bounty as the single-venue destination in the United States.

NOTES

[1] Translated by Marjorie Milne in Noble 1988, 190–191.

[2] For Beazley's classic 1944 lecture on the subject: Kurtz 1989, chapter 3; Arafat and Morgan 1989; Williams 1995. The vase painters Oltos (whose extant vases number over one hundred and fifty) and Epiktetos (21) each worked for at least half a dozen potters, while the potters Euphronios and Kachrylion each provided vases for at least ten different vase painters: Beazley in Kurtz 1989, 55; Webster 1972, 13–14; Cook 1997, 260. The case of Archikles and Glaukytes both signing as potters for a large *Band cup* is well known: Beazley 1986, 51. Multiple painters of a single vessel are not uncommon, such as the Andokides and Lysippides Painters on bilingual vases, while other artists divided the labor between human and animal subjects on a vase, or primary and secondary figures, obverse and reverse sides, interiors and exteriors (e.g., the Penthesileia Painter's workshop: Robertson 1992, 160–167) and even apprentices, perhaps, executed border designs while other artists engaged the figure scenes: Webster 1972, 14–17; Hemelrijk 1991, 252–254.

[33] Simon 1981, pl. 113. For a different interpretation of the phrase that focuses instead on the *komarchos* (revel leader) figure in the scene: Engelmann 1987; Arafat and Morgan 1989, 320.

[4] For the techniques and processes of the Greek ceramic industry: Noble 1988; Scheibler 1995; Schreiber 1999.

[5] Opinions are divided: Keuls 1988; Robertson 1992, 137; Williams 1995, 143 and 151–155; and Boardman 2001, 144, all inclined; Cook 1997, 260, disinclined.

[6] Tiverios 1976.

[7] Von Bothmer 1985, 33–35; Boardman 1987a.

[8] Kilinski 1992. The Boeotian poet Pindar, already renowned at a young age in Teisias' time, praises the cups from Athens: Pindar fr. 124 SM. On the ancient reputation of Athenian pottery: Boardman 1987b, 294.

[9] Morris 1984, 17.

[10] Kilinski 1990, 4–5, 13, 23, and 35.

[11] Rumpf 1927; Iozzo 1993.

[12] For the case of the Corinthian Demaratos who settled Corinthian artists with him in Tarquinia: Boardman 1994, 228. For Etrusco-Corinthian: Szilágyi and Szász Graziani 1992.

[13] Boardman 2001, 82. For the Andokides Painter: Cohen 1978; Robertson 1992, 9–14.

[14] Hemelrijk 1984.

[15] Ducati 1932; Hannested 1974 and 1976; Lund and Rathje 1988 with updates on Hannested.

[16] Plutarch, *Solon* 24.

[17] Trendall 1989, 17; Denoyelle 1997.

[18] Beazley in Kurtz 1989, 55; but see also Robertson 1992, 44–46 and Hemelrijk 1991, 253. For Euphronios in general: Musée du Louvre 1990.

[19] One is reminded of Aristotle's perhaps prejudiced view (*Politics* III.1278a) that the majority of artisans were rich.

[20] Beazley in Kurtz 1989, 48–49; Webster 1972, 4–7 and 12; Wagner 2000.

[21] Canciani 1978.

[22] Noble 1988, 13, fig. 2. Speculation by some scholars proposes that particular accoutrements on the large vessels in this scene, despite being handled by artists with brushes in hand, are metal vases: Vickers and Gill 1994, 171–172.

[23] On women in the Athenian work force: Brock 1994; Lewis 2002, 91–98.

[24] E.g., Eucheiros names the potter Ergotimos as his father. Tleson, the potter, who is likely the Tleson Painter, and Ergoteles sign as sons of Nearchos, who was both a potter and a painter. Another potter, Kleophrades, cites his father Amasis (a potter if not also a vase painter) in his signatures: Webster 1972, 9–11; Robertson 1992, 32. Euthymides, however, was the son of the sculptor Polias. The practice of perpetuating a family occupation extended to other arts in Classical Greece as well, including the theater: Rehm 1994, 23–24.

[25] The earliest known Greek vase signature occurs on a krater fragment from Pithekoussai (Ischia) of around 700 B.C. The inscription is written retrograde in a local variant of Euboean script: "…inos me poies…" (…inos made me), the beginning of the artist's name is lost. Boardman 1980, 167, fig. 204. Some signatures include patronymics, which provide welcome evidence for determining relative chronologies and artist relationships: see supra n. 24.

[26] Beazley 1956, 349, bottom; Beazley 1971, 159–160.

[27] Beazley in Kurtz 1989, 107–115; Cook 1971; Robertson 1972; Eisman 1974; Arafat and Morgan 1989, 319–321; Immerwahr 1990; Cohen 1991. An unorthodox suggestion with negligible following proposes that the 'signatures' on ceramic vases were actually the names of the designers and metal smiths who produced vessels in precious metals (now mostly lost due to their intrinsic value) which were 'emulated' in ceramic forms: Vickers and Gill 1994, chapter 5, with bibliography.

[28] Boardman 1974, 201 and fig. 286.

[29] Robinson and Fluck 1937; Carpenter 1989, 147–148 and 388–399. These range over a century from roughly 550 to 450 B.C. on Attic vases. *Kalos* names appear earlier outside of Attica: Wachter 1989, on a Boeotian black-figure '*kothon*' of the second quarter of the sixth century B.C.

[30] Boardman 1974, 201, listing twelve vases by Euphronios with *Leagros kalos* inscribed on them. Boardman 1992; Boardman 2001, 148–149 and 297.

[31] Robertson 1992, 26–27; Neer 2002, 91, where the data is summarized.

[32] Neer 2002, 133–134 for a list of vases 'depicting' or referencing these ceramicists. Frel 1983 for "Euphronios with Leagros."

[33] Robertson 1992, 26–27, following Keuls 1988; Neer 2002, 91.

[34] For shapes and names of Greek vases in general see: Richter and Milne 1935; Kanowski 1984.

[35] On *rhyta*: Hoffmann 1989.

36 Kilinski 1986; Lissarrague 1987, 48–52.
37 Athenaeus 464c-d: claimed to be Rhodian cups impregnated with assortments of myrrh, saffron, cinnamon, anise, cardamom, and other aromatics that also enhance the flavor of the wine.
38 Bentz 1998.
39 On Commissions: Webster 1972, chapter 2.
40 Studies abound, but see Beazley 1986, chapter 2; Stewart 1983.
41 Carpenter 1983; Carpenter 1984; Rasmussen 1985.
42 Burn 1991; Todisco and Sisto 1998.
43 Hoffmann 1997, chapter 7; Lezzi-Hafter 1997.
44 On ancient prices: Webster 1972, 273–278; Johnston 1979, 33–35.
45 Ramage 1970, 11; Strøm 1981.
46 Cook 1997, 57–59.
47 Rathje 1990, 280; Gran-Aymerisch 1999.
48 Athenaeus 164f–165a and 229b. Webster 1972, xiii, noted long ago his hypothesis that Attic pottery of the highest quality might have been commissioned for a single symposium only to make its way to Etruria through the second-hand market.
49 Oenbrink 1996.
50 Von Bothmer 1972; Noble 1988, 175; Elston 1990; Hemelrijk 1991, 254–255.
51 The fifth-century Samian poet Choerilos wrote, "I hold in my hand my wealth, the chipped sherd of a broken cup...": Choerilos frag. 9, Kinkel 1877, 270. Neer 2002, 214, translation by G.L. Huxley.
52 Corbett 1965; Noble 1988, 103–107; Boss 1997.
53 Sirens, traditionally female since Homer, were occasionally male on some Corinthian vases, but these creatures are generally designated by beards: Amyx 1988, 661. The siren on 7 lacks a beard and would be presumably female, except that its face is colored red.
54 Robertson 1992, 9–14.
55 Payne 1931; Amyx 1988.
56 Laconian: Stibbe 1972 and 1994; Boeotian: Ruckert 1976; Kilinski 1990.
57 Bruns 1940; Braun 1981.
58 Euboean: Boardman 1952 and 1957; von Bothmer 1969; Kilinski 1994, with bibliography. For East Greek wares and other schools of vase production in the Greek world, see Cook 1997 and Boardman 1998 bibliographies.
59 Trendall and Webster 1971; Trendall 1989 index under "Theatre".
60 Oakley and Sinos 1993, 6. For Eros assisting a bride with her bath water: Oakley and Sinos 1993, figs. 20–21.
61 Trendall 1953, 161.
62 Jordan 1988.
63 Oakley 2004.
64 Shapiro 1994.
65 See most recently: Ferrari 2003.
66 For images of the pottery industry: Noble 1988; Scheibler 1995.
67 Webster 1972, especially 42–62; see also Shapiro 1997.
68 Shapiro 1983; Cohen 2000, part III.
69 In general see: West 1992 and Anderson 1994, for music; Lonsdale 1993, for dance.
70 Fehr 1990.
71 Athenaeus 28b, 479d, 665d–667c, and 782b on the game of *kottabos*; Sparkes 1960; Jahn 1967; Lissarrague 1987, 80–86.
72 Dentzer 1982; Lissarrague 1990c and 1990d; Boardman 1990; Rathje 1990; Smith 2000.
73 "Males" includes satyrs: Lissarrague 1990a. On scenes of human eroticism: Dover 1978; Sutton 1992; Stewart 1997, especially chapters 2 and 8. On discerning erotica in Greek art: Kilmer 1993; Lewis 2002, 116–129. On Athenian governance of sexual relations: Winkler 1990; Halperin 1990, 88–112; Cohen 1993. Ancient Greek male sexual promiscuity was mirrored in and 'justified' by the amorous pursuits of the great Olympians: Kaempf-Dimitriadou 1979; Sergent 1984; Shapiro 1992, 58–72; Kilinski 1998; Calimach 2002.

74 Dover 1978, especially 91–99; Shapiro 1981; Halperin 1990; Shapiro 1992, 53–58; Canterella 1992, chapter 2; DeVries 1997; Brisson 2002, 64–65; Halperin 2002, 138–154.

75 For the life of Athenian women: Reeder 1995, 20–26 and 30; Lissarrague 1995; Brock 1994; Blundell 1995; Lewis 2002. Female homosexuality exists in ancient Greek literature but apparently not in Greek art: Shapiro 1992, 72, n. 2. The scene on a cup in Tarquinia by Apollodoros of one nude woman crouching before another and touching the latter's pubic hair is likely to be one of *hetairai* grooming, and depicted on the interior of a wine cup for the titillation of male symposiasts: Beazley 1971, 333, *9bis*; Dover 1978, fig. R207. The hydria in Athens belonging to the Polygnotos Group and depicting Sappho reading in the midst of other women does not appear especially erotic: Beazley 1963, 1060, 145; Matheson 1995, 174, pl. 149. See, Halperin 1996, 722. Whereas male homosexuality among the nobility contributed to aristocratic bonding and apparently did not detract from fatherhood, such activity among women was likely perceived by men as threatening to their own sexuality: Dover 1978, 171–184; Cantarella 1992, chapter 4. In Plato's *Symposium*, Aristophanes' well-known dialogue on the origin of sexual preferences concludes (191D–192B) that of the three (i.e., heterosexuality, female homosexuality, and male homosexuality) male homosexuality is superior because men are seen to cherish their like and are those who become prominent citizens, while a woman homosexual was considered a *tribas* (uncouth, alien, and unpredictable). Cf. Brisson 2002, 75–81.

76 Williams 1983; Oakley 2000.

77 Hannestad 1984, notes a distinction in the social character of women depicted in the fountain scenes on *hydriae* before and after the onset of democracy in late sixth-century Athens. In referencing women in black-figure scenes at the fountain house, Ferrari 2003, 43–51, also perceives them to be members of the Athenian citizenry, but nostalgic emblems of a traditional past as opposed to reflections of contemporary life. The association of scenes depicting a departing warrior by chariot (an anachronism by the painters) on some of these *hydriae* (as on the Madrid vase) may lend support to this notion. But see Neils' essay (*Vases on Vases*) in this catalogue. See also: Manakidou 1992; Manfrini-Aragno 1992. As for the issue of what type of women were at the fountain, note that Aristophanes (*Lysistrata* 327–333) informs us that, presumably at least by the later fifth century, both wives and slaves ventured to the springs of Athens.

78 Williams 1983; Keuls 1985, especially chapters 6–7; Peschel 1987; Kurke 1997; Davidson 1997, chapter 3; Neils 2000; Lewis 2002, especially 98–129, 146–149, 185–201.

79 Militant, avid equestrians, roving adventurers, totting traditional male weapons (spears) and accompanied by hunting hounds, shunning marriage, promiscuous, and preferring female over male children, the Amazons display characteristics antithetical to Greek male perspectives about their women. As Hoffmann notes 1997, 92, "A greater contrast to the traditional image of the docile Athenian wife can not be imagined." Tyrrell 1984; Cantarella 1987, 16–18; Davison 1991, 57; Castriota 1992, 43–46 and 143–151; Cohen 2000, 101–106.

80 Rehm 1994, 20–30; still valuable: Gebhard 1969.

81 See Neils' essay (*Vases on Vases*) in this catalogue.

82 Shapiro 1993.

83 Most recently: Neer 2002, chapter 3, with a catalogue of the images.

84 Williams 1986, with a list of vases. Some of these vases may have been executed during the time of conflict.

85 Though Phrynicus produced the play *Capture of Miletus* (now lost), perhaps in 492 B.C. (technically before the Persian Wars but after the sack of Miletus in 494 B.C. by the Persians), he was fined by the Athenians for doing so as it bitterly reminded them of the destruction of their fellow countrymen (Herodotus 6.21), and, perhaps, because they had done too little to assist them.

86 Carpenter 1991; Shapiro 1994; Woodford 2003.

87 See Steiner's essay in this catalogue regarding the winged horses of Pelops' chariot (26).

88 Gantz 1993, chapter 15.

89 Persephone, of course, is a goddess, but was taken by force at the instigation of Zeus and Hades; male, superior gods to herself. *Homeric Hymn to Demeter* 1–4.

90 Andronikos 1968; Burkert 1985, chapter IV, 4 "The Heroes." See also: Lohmann 1979; Morris 1992, chapter 5, "Monuments to the dead: display and wealth in classical Greece."

91 *Homeric Hymn to Pythian Apollo*, 395–396.

Vases on Vases

❧

JENIFER NEILS

"Oh father Zeus, would that I might get rich!"
Prayer spoken by a shop proprietor as inscribed on an Attic *pelike* (Vatican 413).

Self-advertisement is hardly a new idea. In the realm of Greek vase-painting artists first represented their wares on vases dating to the Geometric period (eighth century B.C.), although the practice did not become commonplace before the early sixth century.[1] By the fifth century B.C. depictions of vases on vases abound, and these representations are useful in demonstrating how various ceramic shapes were actually used in antiquity before they were interred in Etruscan tombs or displayed as isolated *objets d'art* in our museums. Vases on vases can serve as props in the narrative, elements of setting, attributes for identification of the figures who hold them, memorials to the deceased, and even as three-dimensional knobs for larger vases, as we shall see.

In art historical parlance this practice is sometimes referred to as *mis en abîme*, a French term which describes an identical image within an image. In this discussion it refers to a vase on a vase of the same or similar shape. This artistic device not only is visual mimicking, but it also makes a statement about the vase painter's craft. Obvious instances of self-promotion on the part of ceramic workshops appear on a number of vases that represent the workings of the establishment complete with potter's wheels, kilns, and painters hard at work.[2] A unique red-figure cup in Baltimore (Fig. A) shows what looks like a customer with his money pouch admiring and presumably about to purchase a set of pots.[3] These include a pointed wine amphora resting in a cylindrical stand, a *kylix* or wine cup set into the mouth of the amphora, and a large basin with handles known as a *lekane*. This be-wreathed young man may well be acquiring vessels for the evening's symposium: an amphora for transporting the wine, a *kylix* for drinking it, and a *lekane* for regurgitating it into. (A line from the fifth-century Attic comedian Kratinos mentions vomiting into a *lekane*, and the practice is depicted on an Athenian *kylix* in Copenhagen by the Brygos Painter.[4]) Perhaps the vase painter considered it good luck to depict a well-to-do and handsome customer buying his wares, but in any case the scene is definitely self-referential as well as self-serving.

Women's Work

In our examination of Greek vases on vases let us begin with one of the most famous specimens in the archaeological museum of Madrid (16). This black-figure *hydria* or water-jar is the name-vase of the so-called Painter of the Madrid Fountain, and the only vase by

Fig A: *Attic red-figure kylix* (detail), signed by Phintias, earthenware, c. 520–510 B.C., Baltimore Society of the Archaeological Institute of America B4. (Photo: Johns Hopkins University)

this artist with a fountain scene, although his colleague the Priam Painter decorated over a half dozen similar *hydriae* with fountains.[5] This particular fountain is a small structure consisting of three Doric columns, a triglyph-and-metope frieze, and a low triangular pediment. Inside on the back wall are two feline water spouts and two white blocks. Although the block is normally used as a place to set the *hydria* in order to fill it with water, in this instance it serves as a shower stall for a young boy who is crouching beneath the spigot.[6] The fountain house is flanked by five draped women, each of whom has her own *hydria*. The two closest are holding their vases both by the high vertical handle at the back and the distinct foot. The others carry their water jars on their heads either upright or in one case on its side. (It is presumably empty.) Three of the five painted *hydriae* echo the shape of the vase on which they are painted—with its vertical handle, horizontal lip, flat shoulder, and pronounced disk foot. The other two are different; they have a rounded shoulder and lower handle, and so resemble another form of water pitcher known as the *kalpis*. The *kalpis* was a newer shape in the Attic potter's repertoire, and so we could conjecture that the painter is deliberately showing off his latest wares as a form of self-advertisement.

At first glance this vase-painting looks like a genre scene, i.e. Athenian women fetching water at the local fountain, but there are problems with reading this and some eighty similar pictures as snapshots of Greek daily life.[7] Because black-figure *hydriae* with fountain scenes date to circa 520–500 B.C. they have been interpreted as political propaganda on the part of the Peisistratids, the sixth-century Athenian tyrants who provided the city with an elaborate nine-spouted fountain house called the Enneakrounos.[8] Other scholars have interpreted these scenes as religious rituals, either the Hydrophoria procession held on the third day of the Anthesteria, a festival of Dionysos, or the transporting of water for the bride's ritual bath.[9] On the basis of the names inscribed on some of the vases and the fact that in one painting the girls have tattoos, it has been suggested that the women are slaves.[10] According to the historian Herodotos (6.137.3) in the early days of the city the Athenian women had to fetch their own water because they lacked slaves. Presumably at the time these vases were painted, the duty of water collection was relegated to household servants, and so the vases probably represent either slaves or other non-citizen women like *hetairai* (prostitutes). The latest interpretation has identified these scenes as set in the remote past when Athens was a primitive city and when women moved freely outside the household.[11] This last suggestion is perhaps belied by the presence in these scenes of two types of *hydria* which indicate a given point in time when both types were in use, namely circa 520–500 B.C. Since many of these vases were found in Etruscan tombs at Vulci, it has been hypothesized that they were made specifically for the Etruscan market—a female scene to balance the martial imagery of other black-figure *hydriae* which feature chariot scenes.[12] Whatever the impetus for their production these *hydriae* with fountain houses certainly do serve the potter in advertising his wares.

The Symposium

Approximately thirty years later than the Madrid *hydria* is an early red-figure *kylix* or wine cup attributed to the prolific cup-painter Epiktetos (21). The tondo on the interior provides a glimpse of an adult male symposiast, half-draped and wearing a garland around his head. Propped up by a striped pillow on his banquet couch, he is in the act of flinging the wine dregs from his *kylix* toward an invisible target at the left in a common drinking game known as *kottabos*.[13] Our symposiast is equipped with not one but three *kylixes*. In addition to the one in his raised right hand, he holds a second in his lowered left hand, while a third rests on the floor below. Each of these *kylixes* is a stemmed cup with offset lip. Thus, in shape they are more like some of the earlier black-figure cups than the cup on which they are depicted. This cup has a continuous curve from stem to lip.

As if his three cups were not enough, this symposiast also has a large wine amphora propped up near his feet. Since this type of pointed coarse-ware amphora was used for the transport of the wine, it is usually depicted in the *komos* or procession to the banquet, and it is rare to find it in scenes of the symposium proper. On other cups by Epiktetos the pointed amphora is in the hands of satyrs who cavort with or drink from it.[14] It is also depicted in the hand of a *hetaira* reclining on a symposium cushion.[15] These associations suggest that the presence of a transport amphora is inappropriate at the civilized symposium, and is an attribute of the barbaric Other. Possibly the artist is subtly alluding to one of the scenes on the exterior, namely Heracles' fight with the centaurs that ensued after the centaur Pholos opened a jar of wine causing the inebriated beasts to start a row. The moral of this vase may be that excessive drinking leads to the loss of self-control in both life and myth.

While scenes of the symposium are naturally common on wine cups, they also appear regularly on the centerpiece of the Greek symposium, the krater.[16] Used for the mixing of wine and water this bowl was the largest piece of symposium equipment. There are many varieties of this shape, but the sturdiest was the column krater with its thick vertical handles attached to the rim with handle plates. This example by an unidentified later mannerist (24) dates to around 460 B.C. and is remarkable in including images of no less than seven vases in addition to a ladle.[17] All but one are ranged along the ground line below the three banqueters; beginning at the left they include an *oinochoe* or wine jug, a *skyphos* on a stand, a *pelike* or Type C amphora, a ladle presumably hanging from the couch, a column krater, and two *skyphoi* of different sizes on a second block. Hanging on the wall beyond the first symposiast is a *kylix* viewed from the underside. While the second symposiast is busy playing his *aulos* or double pipe, and the third is listening intently as evidenced by his right arm slung over his head, the first seems to be looking down in amazement at the array of vases on the floor.

Such a large variety of vase shapes is highly unusual. A series of red-figure vases by the earlier painter Douris and his followers employs a decorative band known as a 'vessel frieze' beneath the banqueters in which a number of different wine vessels are depicted in black silhouette.[18] On the Madrid krater, however, the ensemble suggests the range of shapes available from some Athenian potter's workshop more than a logical arrangement of wine vessels at the symposium where one would expect to find the wine cups in the hands of the symposiasts. Thus, rather than a realistic portrayal of the symposium, it appears that the painter is deliberately displaying the products of his trade as a sort of self-advertisement to the viewer.

A more credible depiction of the symposium appears on a red-figure *situla* (bucket) produced in Apulia in southern Italy in the mid-fourth century B.C. (39).[19] Here one sees a calyx krater with fluted bowl (and so possibly meant to be metal) on the ground next to a table laden with food for the banquet. A small servant moves to the left holding an *oinochoe* and a *phiale* (offering dish), also probably of metal because they are painted white. However, the three symposiasts are not the usual human banqueters as can be seen by the attributes they hold: a laurel branch, a *kerykeion* (messenger's wand), and a *thyrsos*. They are the youthful male divinities Apollo, Hermes, and Dionysos. In addition to his *kerykeion*, Hermes is holding a drinking cup with two high handles known as a *kantharos*. This special cup is the usual attribute of the god of wine, Dionysos (see 20 and 25), but here he seems to have lent it to his guest, while he holds aloft a pomegranate. These gods are resting under a verdant grape vine and are being entertained by a female *aulos*-player, perhaps a maenad, at the right. Strangest of all at this fantastic banquet is the satyr at left who appears to be riding a magic carpet!

The scene on the reverse, as often, is much simpler. It shows a seated Dionysos surrounded by his retinue of satyr and two maenads. Interestingly the god holds, not his traditional *kantharos* or the more usual *phiale*, but a perfume vase known as an *alabastron*. Such a vase is usually associated with women at their toilette or funerary ritual. The pomegranate held by Dionysos on the other side of the vase also has funerary connotations, it being the fruit that Persephone was given to eat in the Underworld, and so the wine-god seems to be depicted in his chthonic aspect. In the vases represented, the *alabastron* and the *kantharos*, one might see subtle references to funerary practices and banquets for the dead. Since many South Italian vases were specifically commissioned for the tomb, the iconography is not inappropriate.

Funerary Contexts

Vases played an important role in funerary rituals in all periods in ancient Greece. *Lekythoi* (oil flasks), especially the white-ground variety which suggest expensive marble, were a common offering in Athenian fifth-century graves.[20] X-rays reveal that these vases often have a false interior oil compartment, allowing the donor to economize on the perfumed oil. This example attributed to the Inscription Painter (30), so-called after the nonsense inscriptions on his gravestones, has just such a false interior. The decoration is typical of mid-fifth century B.C. white-ground *lekythoi* in depicting a visit to the grave, an inscribed stone stele on a tall three-step base, by two women. One holds what looks like an egg, the other a long ribbon or fillet with which to bedeck the stele between them. Real eggs, as well as marble and ceramic ones (known as *oa*), have been found in graves, so the egg on this vase could be yet another vase, although the ceramic *oon* is exceedingly rare. Two additional offerings hang in the background: at the left a black-glaze *lekythos* and at the right a knuckle-bone sack or *phormiskos*. Often these funerary *lekythoi* reference themselves by the inclusion of one or more *lekythoi* in the scene, usually on the steps of the gravestone. It represents the most common usage of *mise en abîme* in Attic vase-painting, with the exception of the *choes*, or ritual wine jugs, which regularly depict a wreathed chous.[21]

The most prominent offering of all at this grave is the *kantharos*, a high-handled wine cup, which sits atop the stele. Its handle struts indicate that it is a metal vase, and so an expensive offering. The shape is one used, as we have seen, by Dionysos, but it also appears in the hands of heroes like Heracles. Therefore it almost certainly is a sign to the viewer that the grave is that of a heroized male. On other white-ground *lekythoi* of the Classical period one finds personal possessions such as a wool basket, *diphros* (stool), or wedding vase denoting the graves of women. Like the banquet garlands dedicated at the tombs of men, so too the *kantharos* surely references the all-male symposium as well as the deceased male occupant of the tomb.

The wine cup makes a similar appearance, albeit in a slightly different form, on fourth-century B.C. funerary vases from South Italy. A case in point is the large Apulian *volute* krater attributed to the Baltimore Painter (32). Both sides show grave monuments: a *naiskos* or small temple on the obverse, and a stele tied with ribbons on the reverse. The two warriors in the *naiskos* indicate that this vase commemorates a dead male, as does the broad low *kylix* atop the stele. The color and detailing suggest that this too is meant to be a precious metal vessel.

Women's Toilette

We began this investigation with a woman's vase, the hydria, and we end with another, the *lebes gamikos*, or nuptial bowl with high handles. These are believed to have held water for the bride's ritual bath before her wedding. If so, the image on this fourth-century B.C. example from Paestum attributed to the Asteas Group (38) is appropriate. Two nearly nude women are flanking a large marble *laver* or pedestalled water basin, on which stands the winged god of love, Eros. He holds two vases: an *oinochoe* in his right hand and a *phiale* in his left. He is about to make a ritual libation in honor of the bride who leans towards him, holding forth an egg, here a symbol of fertility. At the base of the *laver* is a white *alabastron*, probably meant to represent the alabaster original, rather than a ceramic perfume flask.

What makes this vase especially striking is its lid, which is almost as tall as the vase itself. The knob takes the form of a miniature *lekanis* (whose lid is missing). This type of shallow lidded dish is also connected with weddings, and was used by the bride to store personal items needed for grooming or dressing. Thus, the potter produced two for the price of one. Both the bathing imagery and the ritual shape make this vase particularly appropriate for women, and it is no surprise that most of these vases have been found in female graves at Paestum.[22]

To conclude, these seven vases, ranging in date from the late sixth to late fourth centuries B.C., demonstrate the wide variety of imaginative ways in which vase-painters and potters reference their craft. On the Attic vases (*hydria, kylix,* column krater and *lekythos*) the painters utilize the *mise en abîme* device whereby they portray the actual shape of the vases they are decorating. On the two Apulian vases the artists depict funerary vessels that relate to the function of the vases they decorate. The extravagant Paestan vase is two vases in one, and both shape and imagery reference the Greek wedding. These representations of vases on vases add a layer of meaning that reinforces the message conveyed to the viewer, ancient and modern.

If the cup in Baltimore (Fig. A) is a blatantly commercial scene of the selling and buying of ceramic vases, these other vase paintings we have considered are more subtle in their self promotion. By depicting vases in a specific social context, like the symposium or the cemetery, vase-painters achieve exactly what modern advertisers strive for, namely the viewer's identification with the image. If the Greek man or woman identifies with the context depicted, he or she may be more likely to buy the object which is portrayed as an essential element of that setting, whether it be a krater for the symposium or a *lekythos* for the tomb. The power of suggestion is a powerful tool, and one clearly understood and utilized by the Greek vase painter.

NOTES

[1] A thorough study of vase representations on vases can be found in Gericke 1970. For figured vases represented on vases, see Oenbrink 1996, 81–134. See also Sparkes 1996, 64–89, for discussion of pottery in context.

[2] For representations of pottery workshops see Beazley 1946; Ziomecki 1975; Noble 1988; Philipp 1990, 79–110 and 512–18; Himmelmann 1994, 1–48.

[3] Baltimore Society of the Archaeological Institute of America B4 (on loan to Johns Hopkins University), Attic red-figure kylix signed by Phintias, ca. 520–510 B.C. See *ARV²* 24, 14; Reeder 1984, 139–41, no. 102.

[4] For actual examples of the pots depicted see Sparkes and Talcott 1958, fig. 13. A man vomiting into a *lekane* on an Attic red-figure *kylix* in Copenhagen (National Museum 3880) is shown in fig. 21.

[5] For the Painter of the Madrid Fountain see *ABV* 335, 1–2. For the Priam and A.D. Painters see *ABV* 330–35.

[6] On a well-known black-figure hydria by the Antimenes Painter in Leiden (Rijksmuseum PC 63) two youths are showering under the spigots of a fountain house. See *ABV* 266, 1.

[7] See Manakidou 1992, 51–91. See also Hannestad 1984, 252–55; and Manfrini-Aragno 1992, 127–48; Iozzo 2003, 17–23.

[8] Kolb 1977, 99–138.

[9] Hydrophoria: E. Diehl, *Die Hydria* (Mainz 1964) 130–34. Wedding ritual: E. Götte, *Frauengemachbilder in der Vasenmalerei des fünften Jhs.* (Munich 1957) 7–9.

[10] Williams 1983, 102–105; Neils 2000, 209–10; Shapiro 2003, 96–98.

[11] Ferrari 2003, 44–50.

[12] See Lewis 2002, 1–4 and 71–75.

[13] On *kottabos*, see Sparkes 1960, 202– 207; Jahn 1967, 201–40.

[14] See, for example, the cups by Epiktetos in Baltimore (Boardman, *ARFV* I, fig. 69) and in the British Museum (Boardman, *ARFV* I, fig. 73)

[15] The *hetaira* with transport amphora appears on a palmette-eye cup in New York (56.171.61); see *ARV²* 50, 199.

[16] For the krater as the centerpiece of the symposium see Lissarrague 1990c, 19–46, and 1990d, 196–209. For wine vessels in general see Vierneisel and Kaeser 1990, and Valavanis and Lourkoumelis 1996.

[17] For a description of this vase and symposium scenes by the later Mannerists see Mannack 2001, 100–101 and 148 no. UI.22.

[18] E.g. the cup by Douris in the Vatican (*ARV²* 427, 2; see Boardman *ARFV* I, fig. 284) or the cup by the Triptolemos Painter in Berlin (*ARV²* 364, 52; see Boardman *ARFV* I, fig. 305). For a complete list see Buitron-Oliver 1995, 51, n. 356. To these should be added another *psykter* by the Kleophrades Painter in the Princeton University Art Museum.

[19] This vase belongs to the Group of the Dublin Situlae; see Trendall and Cambitoglou 1991, 105 no. 35b, pl. 22,1.

[20] See Kurtz 1984, 314–28; and Oakley 2003.

[21] The *pelike* also tends to bear depictions of the *pelike*; see Shapiro 1997, 63–70.

[22] Trendall 1987, 128–28. The Madrid vase is no. 186 on p. 128.

New Approaches to Greek Vases: Repetition, Aesthetics, and Meaning

ANN STEINER

Two vases in this exhibit portray the same subject. Both the eighth century B.C. Geometric amphora (3) and the fourth century B.C. Apulian krater (32) portray funerary scenes. Although the subject matter is the same, there are also obvious differences between the two. On the amphora the thin matte produces a dark-on-light effect; the krater uses lustrous glaze to produce a light-on-dark effect. The amphora has figures in simple silhouette; on the krater they are in elaborate red figure. On the amphora the figures are sketchy and angular; the krater has organic figures complete with realistic detail. On the amphora the figural images are outnumbered by the zones of pattern and design; on the krater the figural scenes predominate.

Yet, despite these differences there is still an undeniable shared aesthetic. These fundamental similarities have nothing to do with shared subject-matter, rather they are at a deeper level, expressing a common attitude toward the shape and the way it is decorated. There are similarities in the organization of the shape of the vase: the division of the tall neck, articulated shoulder, and belly tapering to a narrower foot. There is also the way that the decoration is organized according to the division of the shape, the way that the shape itself provides the fields for decoration. On both vases, the neck, shoulder, belly, and foot each have different decoration, whether figural or ornamental, and each of these fields is set off carefully from those adjoining, in many cases by the use of careful horizontal lines. In sum, despite the obvious differences, there are observable aesthetic principles that determine both shape and decoration, and these principles are repeated over the broad chronological and geographical range of Greek vase-painting.

Scholars have for a long time noted this phenomenon of repetition in classical art. They have described how repetition connects to a predilection for consistency, analysis, and categorization that is apparent in the cultural expression of not just Greece, but virtually all of the ancient Mediterranean. Richter more than thirty years ago commented, ". . .For just as Greek poets 'avoided the appearance of originality' and 'treated a traditional theme in a conventional style and form,' so Greek artists used certain accepted types for the expression of their thought."[1]

Pollitt, going further in an attempt to describe this same repetitive phenomenon, identified what he calls two "most essential" aesthetic principles of Greek art that are apparent both in the art produced on the Greek mainland and in the wider presence of Greek culture in eastern Ionia and Magna Graecia; both principles are clearly at work in the many widely disparate examples we are considering. The first, "the analysis of forms into their component parts," is clearly apparent in the way the decorative program emphasizes the parts of the whole vase; the second of these two principles is the "representation of the specific in light of the generic."[2] This principle offers an explanation for why each of these two specific vases (3 and 32) conforms to generic conventions of both plastic form and representation. In general, the second principle "helps to explain why the range of building types in Greek architecture and the range of subjects in Greek sculpture is so deliberately limited."[3] It also explains why there is such a limited repertory of vase shapes over more than four hundred years and wide geographical spans: each specific wine cup is created within the conventions of *kylix* or *skyphos*, just as every water-carrying vessel expresses the standard formal conventions for "*hydria*."

If we look more widely at the examples collected in this exhibition, we see that virtually every example displays the kinds of similarities observed in our comparison of 3 and 32. Careful analysis of the vases in this exhibit shows that repetition of motifs and shapes creates a general style that can have several iterations in divergent local idioms. Further analysis will reveal the role that repetition serves to convey meaning, and the role of repetition as a communicative strategy.[4]

THE AESTHETICS OF REPETITION

Repeated Motives and Shapes

"Subsidiary ornament" is that repertory of decorations not obviously narrative and sometimes not figural, usually extremely stylized, occupying a minor field or serving to separate one field from another. The meander, or Greek key, is prominent in this repertory as are extremely stylized vegetal patterns: rays, palmettes, and lotus. Rays, for instance, are stylized leaves that enter the repertory at the beginning of the Orientalizing period, around 700 B.C. An Etruscan vase (41) is strikingly different in overall effect from the contemporaneous Greek pitcher (5) yet each has the characteristic rays extending up from the base, in the Etruscan case incised and painted in the Greek. Rays also appear in Etruscan and Corinthian productions of the sixth century, the "Pontic" (42) and Corinthian (5, 8) pitchers. There are numerous sixth-century Athenian examples, such as the amphora (14). The motif remains prominent into the fifth century, as on the Attic krater (24). In each case, despite differences in effect, the rays occupy the same place, extending upward from the foot of the vessel; both the rays themselves and their placement on the vases repeat over time and across several different ancient societies.[5]

The same is true for lotus and palmette motifs. Each design is even more long-lived and widespread than the rays: palmettes appear on our examples from sixth-century Etruria (43) to Archaic and Classical Athens (15, 17, 20, 29, 30). Several South Italian examples testify to continued use of the motif throughout the fourth century (32, 34, 37).[6] The lotus has a long life span, represented here on an East Greek amphora (9) to an Athenian example of the second half of the fifth century (27).[7]

The most widespread and long-lived repeated ornament is the Greek key or meander. Fifteen of the vases in this exhibit preserve it; they range from the Orien-talizing to the late Classical periods in date, from Etruria to East Greece geographi-cally. In each case, the meander plays a very similar role, despite the varieties of its form: it is usually arranged in a horizontal band, serving to set off one section of a shape from those that are adjacent.[8]

Subsidiary ornaments are not the only repetitive elements. The shapes them-selves are quite conservative, repeating basic elements of their forms over substantial periods of time. The neck-amphoras, represented here in examples that are Attic Geometric (3), East Greek (9), and early classical Athenian red figure (23) make good examples: all share the articulated, set-off neck, the attachment of the horizontal handles to neck and shoulder, and the body tapering from a broad shoulder to a narrow base and slightly broader foot.

There is a common aesthetic net, uniting the often disparate people who produced and used the vases in the exhibit, cultures that are otherwise distinguished from one another by language, religion, government, burial customs, and architecture.

Repeated Figures

Repetition is also found in the figural compositions. For example, the amphora (15) displays two mounted Amazons, each accompanied by a dog, on each side of the vessel. The so-called *glaux* (28), a small cup, preserves an image of an owl on each side. In one of our latest examples, the red-figure Paestan vase (40), two complete compositions each appear twice in its four interior inserts: a nude youth with altar and a seated female figure.

Apart from these examples of exact or nearly-exact repetition, there are partial repetitions. The cup (18) has two eyes on each side, identical except for the figure between the eyes; in one case this figure is a running winged Gorgon, in the other it is a winged male who appears to flee from her, looking back over his shoulder. Each figure is identically placed between the eyes and is in identical pose. Each figure wears an animal-skin wrap. But the crucial difference, that the male figure looks back at the "female" figure, informs us that he flees from her. This observation conforms to what we know from other sources about the identity of the female figure: she is a Gorgon, and it is her *raison d'être* to pursue. But aside from "making sense," is there any justification for considering repetition as a construct of meaning?

REPETITION AS AN AGENT OF COMMUNICATION

Ancient Vases as Vehicles of Communication

Ancient pottery transmits cultural information. Pottery embodies and communicates aesthetic standards; cultural values and ideals are also expressed, and the images on some vessels communicate myth and legend. Because pottery communicates, it is possible to understand this process through theoretical approaches that explain how messages are sent and received and demonstrate that repetition can and does advance meaning. In general terms, a system with as much repetition and consistency as we observe in the vases in this exhibition is likely to be one that is extremely efficient in delivering its message.

Repetition and Information Theory

Information theory was first articulated in a post World War II publication by an engineer for other engineers; however, its principles can be applied to understand "any system in which a 'message' can be sent from one place to another."[9] Such systems are diverse, including ordinary language, genes, and visual images. A few key concepts of information theory make clear its applicability to repetition on ancient vases.

Information theorists are interested in identifying mechanisms that earmark *messages* as distinct from *noise* and *order* from *disorder* in a communications system. They have identified repetition, or, in the language of information theory, "redundancy," as an essential ordering feature:

> "In nearly all forms of communication, more messages are sent than are strictly necessary to convey the information intended by the sender. Such additional messages diminish the unexpectedness, the surprise effect, of the information itself, making it more predictable. This extra ration of predictability is called redundancy, and it is one of the most important concepts in information theory...."[10]

So, redundancy provides clarity and focus.

Information theory holds that written and visual messages are expressed through codes—languages—and the expression of such messages must conform to the rules of a code shared between sender and receiver. An example in English illustrates the way the rules of grammar enforce repetition and redundancy to reduce "noise" and thereby to get a message across:

In the statement, "I saw four planets," the word "four" tells us that we are in the plural, and the addition of "s" at the end of "planet" confirms it. The redundant aspect, the addition of "s" makes it less likely, although not impossible, that "four" will not be misconstrued as "poor," for example. To illustrate an analogy from the vases collected here, we can look at the interior of the cup by Epiktetos (21). A male figure reclines at a symposium, together with pillows and drinking implements appropriate to that context. The pose and couch and pillows tell the onlooker who is familiar with the code that the context of the scene is a male drinking party. But here Epiktetos repeats one detail to make sure we understand: the *kylix* is pictured not once, but three times. An amphora is also included. Since Greek couches could serve as both beds and dining room furniture, the redundancy assures us that the context is sympotic and not, for example, an image of a man in bed. Our artist makes sure, many times over, that we know the intent of the picture.

Information theory tells us that redundancy is of crucial importance in conveying messages in whatever code is being employed. This alerts us to the fact that we need to see repetition as more than a formal aesthetic principle and to investigate further how it enables communication.

Repetition and Social Anthropology

Social anthropologists have analyzed the function of repetition in cultural systems, and their understanding is derived ultimately from the principles of structural linguistics. As explained by E. Leach, in his work *Claude Levi-Strauss*, "anthropological" redundancy has a great deal in common with that of information theorists. The anecdote he uses to explain the purpose of redundancy treats the code of language at the level of content rather than at the level of form or "grammar," as in the "four planets" example:

> "Now let us imagine the situation of an individual A who is trying to get a message to a friend B who is almost out of earshot, and let us suppose that communication is further hampered by various kinds of interference—noise from wind, passing cars, and so on. What will A do? If he is sensible he will not be satisfied with shouting his message just once; he will shout it several times, and give different wording to the message each time, supplementing his words with visual signals. At the receiving end B may very likely get the meaning of each of the individual messages slightly wrong, but when he puts them together, the redundancies and the mutual consistencies and inconsistencies will make it quite clear what is 'really' being said."[11]

Levi-Strauss, whose ideas Leach is trying to elucidate, uses the phenomenon of redundancy to explain how elders in a society convey a single cultural message to junior members through myths that may vary at the level of language but are uniform in terms of the underlying message. Both the story of Oedipus marrying his mother and the story of Phaedra lusting after Hippolytus, different on the exterior, send a similar message about the bad consequences of allowing expression of sexual feelings between parent (or step-parent) and child. It is extremely important that the message of this particular taboo be absorbed, so the message is sent many times in many different guises. A very large proportion of ancient vases represent myths; since similar renderings of the same myth often appear on the same vase, these observations of social anthropologists are very useful in assessing the purpose of repetition.

Repetition and Semiotics

Semiotics, the "science of signs," is itself integrated with structural linguistics both in origin and application, and it gives us an explanation for why theoretical models developed for verbal language can also be applied to a visual language: the visual imagery on ancient vases is, in effect, an expression of a unified language with its own rules of grammar and syntax, where "reality" is encoded through visual symbols, much as experience and objects are encoded through words in ordinary language.[12]

Semiotics teaches us that the images on an ancient vase are not, then, representations of reality in the same way that a photograph is, no matter how much they may look "real."[13] Ideals and cultural values are expressed through the code of the imagery, so the "meaning" is not at the superficial level of denotation (the "syntagmatic" level), but a deeper level, revealed through "cracking the code," to uncover the connotations, the "paradigmatic" level of what is represented. So, an image of hoplites engaging in battle (13) is not like a photograph of life on the battlefield translated into painting; it is, among other things, a comment on what activities and behaviors the Athenian elite, the users of the vessel, values.[14] A very influential museum exhibition catalog that has become a general handbook, *City of Images*, provides examples of the application of semiotics to imagery on Athenian vases, and those findings can be applied to vase images from other Classical cultures as well.[15]

Repetition, Linguistics, and Narratology

Extending the model provided by semiotics, we can apply the insights of linguists, and in particular narratologists, to the meaning of repetition or redundancy.[16] In attempting to identify a coherent text, narratologists look for, among other things, repetition of "lexical items" and repeated "syntax."[17] The visual equivalent of a "lexical item" is the "minimal formal unit" or the "smallest definable iconographic unit ...[,] the one which cannot have anything removed without disintegration of the recognizable form."[18] So, a "lexical item" can be as large as a garment or as small as an eye, but it cannot be an unrecognizable fragment of one of these. Most often "lexical item" is synonymous with "figure." "Syntax" refers to the way the lexical items are arranged, such as in a sentence at the most fundamental level in written texts. For this discussion, "syntax" includes both the compositional structure of individual fields of the vase and the decorative program of the vase as a whole.[19]

For a linguist and for a narratologist, the fundamental purpose of repetition is to create one text out of many parts. Above all, repetition creates cohesion, and cohesion has many functions.[20] As Bowditch puts it, with my modifications, "In order to understand the point of a story [vase-image], listeners [observers] must understand that the linguistic utterance to which they are attending [at which they are looking] is indeed one text, and neither a series of unrelated sentences [images] nor a sequence of different texts [images]."[21] Such cohesion can be created either through repetition of forms and/or through repetition of content.

The well-known cup depicting seven deeds of Theseus (29) shows how this narratological approach helps us to understand the function of repetition in expressing continuous narrative.[22] Indeed, the cup, by repeating the lexical item, "Theseus," on both sides of the exterior and again in the tondo, reveals its unity, its coherence as a single text. [23] In each instance the artist has carefully repeated the hero's iconography: three times on each side and once in the tondo the hero appears with short hair, no facial hair, and nude except for a baldric scabbard. In two cases, once on each side, he has a short cloak over his arm. This consistency contrasts with his adversaries, all of whom have beards (if they are human) and some idiosyncratic setting element, either landscape or a prop. Indeed, we know that the artist made a deliberate choice in this particular depiction of Theseus, since on other vases the hero wears sandals and/or a hat. There is syntactical consistency as well: in each instance, Theseus is placed to the left of his adversary, and a tree appears at about the middle of each side of the cup. The effect of these repetitions in both iconography and composition, in lexical items and in syntax, is to tell us that we have a unified text, a narrative of at least part of the life of Theseus.

This cup is very unusual, however, in the way it includes, on both sides of the vase, three phases of the narrative in a single field. W. Steiner has remarked, "pictorial art is especially resistant to narrativity: in no other art is the requirement for the subject's repetition so essential, and in no other art is it so non-normative."[24] Indeed, ancient vase-painting, like much Western art, does not often show *continuous* or phased narration in a single field, although it does commonly *refer to* continuous narrations through a variety of mechanisms.[25] A more typical example is the Apulian vase (33) whose side B depicts two crucial, identifying scenes of the Rape of Persephone. These scenes serve to recall the entire narrative to the observer, but do not depict each moment in the story.

Many ancient vases repeat an image in two fields, often so closely that we describe the result as an "exact" repetition; there are numerous examples in this exhibit, cited above. Such repetition surely unites the two images, but it has also been argued that there is no such thing as *exact* repetition: "Two events are never exactly the same. The first event of a series differs from the one that follows it, if only because it is the first and the other is not."[26] Is this true of texts—not only narratives—in general, and those expressed in images in particular? Bal maintains that verbal repetitions, even if they are precise, differ because one must be first: the others follow. The second, third, fourth, and so on differ from the first because they resonate with the previous accounts. Similarly, a viewer cannot see both sides of a vase simultaneously. If an amphora has two images, the viewer must see one first, and that seen second will be interpreted in light of the first. Not surprisingly, scholars will disagree as to whether or not on a vase like the "*glaux*" (28), we see one image repeated, or identical images of two different owls.[27]

CASE STUDIES

A number of vases in this exhibit present compelling instances of repetition that advances meaning. An amphora attributed to the Berlin Painter (22) employs syntax very typical of the painter: a figure stands on each side of the vessel. The figures have a great deal in common: both are adult males, bearded, with short hair, and nude under a voluminous cloak. Each figure holds a sword in his right hand above his head, one with bent elbow lifted high, the other letting it drop below shoulder level. Both hold scabbards high on the hilt, directly out in front of them with their left hands. There are differences too: the two right hands are differently positioned, the figure on side A faces the viewer and wears his *himation* draped over his left shoulder, falling straight down in front and back; the figure on B has his back to the viewer and his *himation* is wrapped around his waist and over his right shoulder. He appears to be retreating, because he looks back over his shoulder at his opponent; his back is turned. A quick glance at the two sides of the amphora might result in a viewer concluding that she saw one figure from two points of view, as if the amphora were transparent. The subtle differences, however, reveal that there are two individuals, one on each side of the vessel. One dominates and attacks, while the other appears to retreat, looking back over his shoulder.

Beazley identified the two figures as Odysseus and Ajax, although there are no inscriptions or identifying attributes.[28] By making an analogy to other vases where inscriptions do identify similar characters, he made a very reasonable assertion. Literary sources report a fight between the two heroes over the arms and armor of the slain hero Achilles, a fight that resulted in the eventual suicide of the loser, Ajax.[29] If the figures do represent this myth, the painter has used a very common technique to represent narrative, the selection of one crucial scene from which the viewer recognizes the narrative. The similarities, the repetitions, between the two figures encourage the viewer to view both sides of the vase as a single coherent text and to engage in a process of close examination. The differences, though subtle, will then separate the two by nuance: two heroes, off the battlefield, both competing on nearly equal ground for the designation as "best" of the surviving Greeks, the man most deserving of Achilles' armor. Odysseus will be victorious, and this result is apparent through the Berlin Painter's presentation of the slightly unmatched pair.

Another vase uses repetition to focus the viewer's attention on crucial aspects of narrative. On the *kylix* (26) each side preserves a scene of a man in a chariot, riding with a woman on side B and with a youth on side A. Each chariot is pulled by two horses. These scenes overall are very similar; a major distinction is that the horses on side B are winged. Winged horses are divine, endowed with special powers of speed that only the gods can impart. In addition, the charioteer-youth on A is replaced by a woman. Because of the inscriptions on the cup, we know that we see on each side one contestant in a deadly race that is described fully in the catalogue entry for this piece: Oinomaos and Pelops; if Pelops wins, he will marry Hippodamía, Oinomaos' daughter; if Pelops loses, he will die and Oinomaos will keep his daughter for himself. The differences, the wings and the chariot-companion, are crucial elements of plot: the woman motivates the action, for she provides the purpose for the race. The wings and the charioteer explain the result, why Pelops defeated Oinomaos: the divine advantage provided by a god endowing Pelops' horses with wings together with the treachery of Oinomaos' groom.

Mentioned above is a *kylix* attributed to Epiktetos (21) where repeated images of the *kylix* itself created a redundancy meant to make sure the "message" of the vessel was received by the viewer. The three images reiterate the intended context of the image and the use-context of the vessel: one is empty, held in position by a symposiast to fling the dregs in the bottom toward the *kottabos* stand; a second is still in the hands of the drinker, held carefully balanced; a third stands ready for use by the lone symposiast, resting on the ground line beneath his couch. As discussed here by Jenifer Neils, there are other examples in this exhibition where an image of the shape appears on the shape itself: 16, *hydria* on *hydria*; 24, column krater on column krater. In each of these cases, the repetition of shape in imagery drives home and clarifies the message, fleshing out information about the ideal context for use. The repetition narrows and makes more precise one aspect of the meaning of the vessel. The imagery is redundant and directive.

Repeated syntax can help to link images that are related in meaning, and sometimes the link informs the viewer of "sameness" or synonymy. A good example is the Apulian krater (32). Each side depicts a central funerary monument centered within a frame of four figures, two above and two below. The repeated frame gives the two monuments a kind of equivalence; although each has its own particular characteristics, each is a grave marker. The similar syntactical arrangement draws attention to this fundamental aspect of "sameness."

Earlier examples create a similar construct for comparison and unity. Both the Attic black-figure amphora (14) and the "Chalkidian" cup (10) provide a frame of repeated syntax in the form of eyes symmetrically disposed on each side. In the case of the amphora, the repeated eyes link masks of Dionysos with satyr-masks. The differences between the two are subtle: the satyrs have noses that broaden significantly at the nostrils and have the ears of horses rather than the god's human ears. The contents of the amphora, undiluted wine, invest the consumer with the divinity's *enthusiasmos*, trading his own persona for the divinity's mask. An aspect of that altered status is the satyr, the god's companion, who represents unlicensed aggressive sexuality. The repeated syntax links the divinity with the aspect of his existence that is satyr-consciousness.

A more overt example of the same phenomenon exists on the "Chalkidian" cup (10). Here the eyes separate two very similar figural compositions, at left a satyr attempting to penetrate his companion, and at right an identically posed human figure engaged in an identical act. The suggestion made by the repetition is that the drinker is equivalent to the satyr; when he ingests wine, the mortal metaphorically becomes the god's rowdy and undisciplined companion. The repetitions in syntax and in composition are essentially creating a visual simile: the man is like the satyr when the god in the form of wine allows him to put on a different mask, to become a different character. Again, the images in combination are almost didactic, with the repetitions acting to drive home the point.

This kind of visual simile appears to be a humorous inversion of the kind of comparisons we observe frequently in Pindaric poetry, where a member of the elite, usually a victor, is compared to heroic prototypes. In Pindar's Sixth Pythian, the poet overtly sets up the epic hero Antilochus and his filial piety as a paradigm for the boy Thrasyboulos, son of the victor Xenocrates named in the poem. Antilochus is cited as an exemplum of ideal behavior when he died to allow his father Priam to live. Mortal Thrasyboulos is then cited as most like the hero Antilochus in his filial piety.[30]

This survey of some of the vases in this exhibition has provided examples of the way that repetition can serve both an aesthetic function and communicate several messages. In each case, repetition links and reiterates. Creating a narrative, identifying the ideal use-setting for the implements of drinking vessels in symposium, establishing the emotional and behavioral status of the drinker, and defining the close proximity of elite symposiasts to heroes and divinities are four of the lessons imparted by repetitions. These vases are exponents of culture that convey and reiterate important messages, and repetition is one of their primary agents of communication.

NOTES

[1] Richter 1969, 57, quoting Thompson 1915, 22.
[2] Pollitt 1972, 5–6.
[3] Pollitt 1972, 9.
[4] Earlier discussions of how repetition advances meaning are Steiner 1993 and 1997. Steiner, *Reading Greek Vases* (Cambridge University Press, in press) is a complete study of this phenomenon.

5 A total of ten vases preserve rays: nos. 5, 6, 12, 14, 16, 17, 20, 29, 41, 43.

6 Palmettes appear on nos. 13, 16, 17, 20, 28, 30, 32, 34, 37, 40.

7 Lotus appears on nos. 9, 14, 16, 25, 29, 43.

8 Examples in this exhibition displaying meander patterns are nos. 9, 14, 19, 22, 23, 29, 28, 32, 33, 37, 38, 39, 40, 43, 44.

9 Campbell 1982, 17.

10 Campbell 1982, 58.

11 Leach 1974, 63–64.

12 The works of E.H. Gombrich 1960 and 1984, Roland Barthes 1982, 251–295 and Seymour Chatman are familiar and well-respected examples of art historical scholarship informed by semiotics. See also Sebeok.

13 Lissarrague and Schnapp 1981, 275–297.

14 See Bérard 1991.

15 Bérard, et al. 1989. Well-known vase-painting studies implementing a semiotic approach are Sourvinou-Inwood 1985, 1987 and 1991 and Lissarague. Marinatos 1993 uses this approach on Bronze Age Aegean art.

16 See Hardee and Henry 1990; Prince 1982, 1987, 1990; Chatman 1978. For understanding the audience for narrative, see Malinowski 1953 and Labov 1972.

17 Ferrari 2002 provides discussion and background. For an explanation of "visual" narratology, see W. Steiner 1982.

18 Bérard 1983, esp. 7f, "unités (iconiques) formelles minimales;" Morgan 1985, 10 and Morgan 1988.

19 Stansbury-O'Donnell 1999, chapter 3, discusses different types of compositions of narratives, or "narrative configuration" and the degree to which each encourages the viewer to associate a particular field with those which are adjacent. Repetition of figures is one other way to encourage association of separate fields. Mackay 1999a also discusses links among different fields of a single vase.

20 Halliday and Hasan 1975; 1989 is a concise presentation of the various ways in which different kinds of repetition create cohesion. Bowditch 1976, 19–37, is a narratological application of some of these principles. Bowditch, relying on Halliday and Hasan's categories, discusses the goals which writers want to achieve through various kinds of repetition.

21 Bowditch 1976, 19.

22 There are many important discussions of the representation of narrative in Athenian vase-painting. Particularly useful are Snodgrass 1982; Froning 1988; Hedreen 1996 and 2001; Csapo and Miller 1998; Stansbury-O'Donnell 1999; Hedreen 2001.

23 W. Steiner 1988, 17, in discussing how one-way repetition creates cohesion in continuous narration, points out that the repetition of a subject, a character, is the primary means for us to know that we are looking at a narrative at all. Since in reality a person cannot be in two places at one time, when we see a figure twice, we conclude that we are seeing two distinct moments in time involving one figure; such a conjunction is likely to represent a narrative. For another discussion of interconnected scenes of the deeds of Theseus on an Attic cup, see Neils 1981.

24 W. Steiner 1988, 20–21.

25 An important summary discussion of typologies for visual narration is Csapo and Miller 1998. In addition, Stansbury-O'Donnell 1999 provides an excellent overview of previous scholarly discussion of the issue.

26 Bal 1985, 77. See also Bal 1991b.

27 Type B *skyphoi*, *ARV* ^{2} 982–84.

28 *ARV* ^{2} 200, 50.

29 Gantz 1993, 629 and *passim*.

30 For a discussion of this poem and its paradigmatic themes, see Kurke 1990.

Myth and Reality on Greek Vases

❀

SARAH PEIRCE

Many Greek vases, like the *kylix* that shows the deeds of Theseus (29), illustrate events of the Greek heroic past. Others, up to half of the total of Greek vases produced in some periods, bear scenes not obviously connected to mythical accounts, because there are no fantastic elements, like the Minotaur, or because the actors in the scenes are anonymous or, more rarely, seem to be identified as real people. These scenes are repeated compositions, the types well-represented in this exhibit. A rough grouping of the most common scenes would include arming scenes, the departure of a warrior (16), hoplites (13) and cavalry (15) assembly and combat, the hunt (12), musical and athletic contests, pursuit, courting, marriage (17), domestic scenes (27), religious ritual (21), symposium (21, 24), *komos* (a revel following drinking) (6, 11), the funeral (3), and tendance of the tomb (30, 31). How is this second category of scenes to be understood?

A survey of current literature on vase-painting shows that there is no agreement on this question. The traditional view, established in the 19th century, is that the scenes on vases can be classified as pertaining to "myth" and to "reality."[1] "Scenes of reality," corresponding to our second category, in this view are to be further subdivided into typical scenes of daily life, "genre," and scenes of specific events, such as a ritual enacted at a particular festival.[2] Adherents to this view agree that scenes on vases represent the artists' visual experience of contemporary life, and that what the painter saw is recoverable by the viewer in the visual experience of the painting.[3] These interpreters do not maintain that the paintings are in all respects accurate renderings of the painters' experiences; a painter may introduce elements that are unrealistic or unfaithful under the influence of ideology or his imagination. These unfaithful elements are the major difficulty in interpreting the scenes.

This view can be designated the perceptualist view, founded as it is on a view of art in which "the painter's task is to transcribe perceptions as accurately as he can, just as it is the viewer's task to receive those relayed perceptions as sensitively as possible . . ." in the words of Bryson.[4] Though for a long time it was a more or less *communis opinio* in classics, it has never been supported unanimously; since the 19th century other interpretations, have been advanced. However, it is only in the last twenty-five years that there has developed a rival consensus.[5] This is represented by the work of a range of scholars whose work has in common that it is informed by linguistic models of the creation of meaning.[6] Scholars viewing vase-painting images in this light "read" them as a language of sorts, as a system of signs. This language of imagery gives access not to the visual experience of the painter but to the collective intellectual system of Greek culture, "*l'imaginaire sociale.*"

The perceptualist view is fading, while linguistic interpretation is gaining ascendancy. Still, perceptualist viewpoints have a firm hold in scholarship.[7] This may owe in part to the fact that practitioners of this method focus on establishing the facts of contemporary Athenian existence—institutions and material objects—as they are documented by the scenes on vases. The findings of this school of thought blend into the landscape of classical scholarship; scholars not following this methodology may accept the results without realizing their source. For example, perceptualist readings of scenes of ritual have played so large a role in the construction of the agendas of Athenian religious festivals that without the "evidence" from the vases little of these agendas would remain.[8] Perceptualist readings of the scene of symposium (21, 24) have long been used as evidence for the history and character of the Athenian symposium, for the dress and behavior of the participants, the furnishings, the entertainment, the availability of female entertainers for sex, even the social evolution of the institution, the admittance of persons of low status.[9] Another group of scenes, represented in this exhibit by 27, has been taken to show the inner workings of Athenian brothels, the professional and social lives and pastimes of madams and prostitutes.[10] A thoroughgoing reform of the methodology of reading vases would result in the disappearance of many scenarios of the everyday life of Athenians, a development to inspire, perhaps, regret.

Quite apart from the merits of competing views, there is remarkably little support in the vases themselves for the notion that the repertory of scenes on Athenian vases documents Athenian life as perceived by the painters. Certainly, some realia, attested in other media, are represented; pots and vases, for example, or clothing and furniture; too, the human figure evolves through time in the direction of greater realism. How realistic, though, is the subject matter as a whole? Though the repertory, as outlined above, is rich, it is also curiously limited, as scholars have noted.[11] There is a very high degree of overlap between the compositions of "scenes of myth" and "scenes of reality," while many aspects of contemporary reality are unrepresented. Athens itself is absent; we do not see the city streets or houses, the Agora, the Pnyx, the law courts, sanctuaries, and the theatre. Landscape is virtually absent. We do not see magistrates, the Assembly, or juries, or public figures, the tyrants, Themistokles, Kimon, Perikles or Sokrates; there is no portraiture. Instead, the cast of characters is both limited and stereotyped: we see primarily, conventionally portrayed, the male citizen, old and young; the youth, the warrior, the well-bred woman, the immodest woman, the man of low status, an occasional child, the male infant. The classes of scenes most often shown are painted over and over in great numbers with minor variations, not a feature of art rendered from observation. Moreover, specific details of rendering—of kinds of drapery, setting, implements, of the composition of groups—can be shown to be specific to particular workshop traditions.

In light of this highly conventional and limited repertory, the conviction that these scenes are windows on daily life in Athens seems quixotic and calls for an explanation. Key to this perception is that it is intuitive, and that it represents to its adherents the "common sense" way of viewing vases. This approach is so naturalized in our culture that it can be invisible. The theory involved is a popular sort of empiricism. The fact that the scenes on vases appear on the face of it to have little to do with real life is trumped by a stronger principle, the tacit conviction that the painters could not or would not paint something they had not seen.[12] This explains why "scenes of myth" and "scenes of reality" are in this view so similar: scenes of myth are based on the painters' perceptions of reality as these are represented in scenes of reality. Interestingly, about the time that these realist interpretations of vase-painting were gaining ascendancy, related views of historiography emerged in historical scholarship. In the 19th century empiricist view of history, the aim of historical writing was objective replication of the past.[13] In these theories of historical writing, objective facts were compared to the exact observations of the scientist. The assembly of these facts was the foundation for the faithful re-creation of the past.[14]

A group of vases represented in the exhibit by catalogue no. 16 can serve as a case-study of the application of the perceptualist and semiotic methods in interpretation. This group of some 79 vases dating circa 520–480 B.C. has recently been brilliantly interpreted on semiotic lines by G. Ferrari; I follow her analysis here.[15] The vases, mostly *hydriae*, like our vase, depict females, and sometimes also youths, filling *hydriae* at a fountain, rendered in various ways. Sometimes males of low status are shown. The women are represented by their dress as well-bred and of citizen class. The fact that gently-reared females are shown drawing water is a central problem for the understanding of the vases, since this seems most unlikely as a feature of Athenian life. Well-off women were sequestered in Athens and menial tasks were performed by their slaves. Several scholars use these scenes as evidence that slave labor was not employed in Athens in the period of the vases;[16] another interprets the activity as a special event, a ritual of the festival of the Anthesteria, when well-born women would carry water.[17] These interpretations obviously are based on the idea that what is seen mirrors an actual occurrence reproduced visually by the painter, and they lead to no verifiable or even coherent results. Indeed, realist methods are foiled decisively by the great variability of the renderings of the fountain. Ferrari resolves the difficulties by relating the representations to Athenian accounts of their early history.[18] As she explains, the vases parallel an account in Herodotos of an idyllic

Athens of the distant past, when the sons and daughters of citizens fetched water from the fountain Enneakrounos. The reading of the vases by Manfrini-Aregno dovetails here with Ferrari's reading; she shows that the females are characterized as girls on the threshold of marriage.[19] The Pelasgian inhabitants of Athens assaulted the youths and maidens at the fountain; the Pelasgians were expelled and social customs changed. Maidens now are sequestered, and slaves draw the water. The key elements of the scenes are read by Ferrari as signs, not as observed realia: the marriageable girls are alluring and in harm's way at the fountain; the low-status men are Pelasgians; a herm on one vase signifies the Pelasgian invention of the herm; there are clues in the scenes that the fountain, inscribed Kallirhoe, is the Kallirhoe identified with Enneakrounos of the primeval city of Athens.

The most productive new work in vase-painting iconography, like the work on the fountain scenes, explores the scenes on vases not as reproductions of actual events but as collocations in visual form of concepts about culture. It is notable that various erstwhile scenes of reality, have, like the fountain scenes, been reassigned, by Ferrari and others, to the realm of imagination. One category is domestic scenes previously accepted as vignettes of the brothel, but revealed by Ferrari to concern the characteristics of marriageable maidens.[20] Another is the scene of nude females celebrating a male symposium, interpreted on realist principles as evidence for the historical recreations of *hetairai*, but reinterpreted semiologically as fantasy or as commentary on the characteristics of Spartan women.[21] It seems quite possible that the entire range of scenes once grouped under the rubric of reality will eventually be reassigned to this category of the imaginary expressed in a conventional system of signs. The location of subject-matter of the scenes on vases in the sphere of the imagination renders moot the distinction between scenes of myth and scenes of reality, by eliminating the relevance of the ideas of myth and reality: the world of social concepts is neither real or mythical.

NOTES

[1] On the origin of the distinction, Bažant 1980, 193–196; Ferrari 2003; for problems, Dummer 1977; for refutation, Bažant 1980, 1981; Ferrari 2003.

[2] On the concept of genre and its relation to contemporary reality, Ferrari 2003.

[3] For examples, Bažant 1981; I give specific examples below in the discussion of fountain scenes.

[4] Bryson 1991, 63.

[5] The new methodology is generally accepted to have been launched with the structuralist analysis of Hoffmann 1977.

[6] The approach, now widespread, can be seen e.g. in Bérard 1983, 5–37; Bérard et al. 1989; and Ferrari 2002, 2003. For a critique of traditional scholarship and useful programmatic statements of method, Lissarrague and Schnapp 1981, 275–82.

[7] See, e.g., the standard handbooks of Boardman 1974, 1975, 1989 and Cook 1997, and the discussion below.

[8] See, for example, the reconstructions of Simon 1983.

[9] E.g. Dentzer 1982, 95–125; a critique of the method, Harvey 1988.

[10] For this scholarship Ferrari 2002, 12–17 and passim for refutation.

[11] Bérard, in Bérard 1989, 110; Lissarrague and Schnapp 1981, 280.

[12] Adhering to the empiricist tag, *nihil in intellectu si non prius in sensu.*

[13] Novick 1988.

[14] On the relation of physical science and 19th century historiographical method, Novick 1988, 31–35. On a similar relation to scientific process of the perceptualist view of art, Bryson 1991, 62.

[15] Ferrari 2003; the vases are collected by Manakidou 1992.

[16] Hannestad 1984; Paradiso 1993.

[17] Diehl 1964.

[18] Herodotos 6.137.3, 2.51.1; Thucydides 2.15.3–6.

[19] Manfrini-Aregno 1992.

[20] Ferrari 2002, passim.

[21] As an actual symposium of *hetairai*, Peschel 1987, 73–74; as fantasies about *hetairai*, Kurke 1999, 205–206; as a commentary on Spartan women, Ferrari 2002, 19–20.

Men, Beasts, and Monsters: Pattern and Narrative in Etruscan Art

P. GREGORY WARDEN

One of the ironies of any major exhibit on Greek vase-painting is that most of the vases will not have come from Greece but from Italy, and not from that thin coastal strip of southern Italy (Magna Graecia) that was Greek in antiquity, but from Etruria, an area populated by a non-Greek population that had a vibrant culture of its own. The Etruscans were avid collectors of Greek vases and deposited huge quantities of them in their tombs. In fact, the likelihood is that most well-preserved Greek vases in a museum or private collection outside Greece were found in Italy, very likely central Italy, ancient Etruria. This irony of provenance resulted in the misconception, until the early 19th century, that Greek vases were Etruscan.[1] Subsequent scholarship revealed the true origin of Greek pottery and the symbiosis of the market mechanisms, that Greek producers and Etruscan consumers were quite aware of each other, and that in the sixth and fifth centuries B.C. potters deliberately created shapes and types of vases that would appeal to the voracious Etrusco-Italic market.[2] There is heated scholarly debate about the ancient value, aesthetic and monetary, of Greek painted pottery, but there can be little doubt that it was much prized and highly valued by the Etruscans.[3]

There is also no doubt about the depth of Greek influence on Etruscan art, and this influence resulted in no small part from the importation of Greek objects into Etruria. In the seventh century B.C. it was Near Eastern art (and possibly Near Eastern artists) that influenced Etruscan "Orientalizing" art.[4] (41) By the sixth century B.C. the influx of Greek art, and Greek artists as well, especially to the rich coastal cities of southern Etruria, profoundly changed Etruscan artistic production at every level. It is safe to say that every part of Etruria, every Etruscan, would have come into contact with Greek art. Even at remote smaller sites on the Etruscan interior good Greek pottery was often in evidence.[5] Even cities in the interior of Tuscany (for instance Chiusi where traditional norms of visualization seem quite resistant to Greek influence) came into contact with Greek art of high quality and considerable scale.[6] A case in point is the magnificent François krater, which somehow found its way into an Etruscan tomb at Chiusi. Despite its size and fragility, this vase was carried overland into the Etruscan interior.[7] Its impressive scale (both size and the scale of its narrative sequences) would have made it the showy centerpiece of any Etruscan banquet.

But if the influence of Greek art is predominant, at times even overwhelming, Etruscan cultural norms are never completely subsumed into the Hellenic mainstream. Etruscans will have banquets that resemble Greek symposia, for instance, and they will use Greek vases and local vases influenced by those Greek imports, but an Etruscan banquet is a far different thing from a Greek symposium, and the two should not be confused, even though the Greek iconography will influence Etruscan depictions.[8] In the same way, much recent scholarship has focused on the way that Etruscan art expresses essentially Etruscan ideas and social constructs.[9] To use a linguistic metaphor, Etruscan art uses a Greek visual language to express a singularly Etruscan message. This phenomenon is best documented in mythological scenes, depicted on engraved bronze mirrors, relief urns, and Etruscan vases. The mythological instances are becoming better known,[10] but in terms of the vases in this exhibit, we might pose the same question of a different type of decoration, the friezes of humans, animals, and fantastic animals (men, beasts, and monsters) that are a virtual cliché of the Etruscan repertoire. My argument is that these friezes are not solely decorative, that they would have embodied a kind of "reality" that had narrative connotations. It may be an oxymoron, but these images are both decorative (more so to the modern viewer) and narrative (to the Etruscan viewer), decorated narratives, so to speak.

The Etruscan vases in this exhibit document this phenomenon in the seventh and sixth centuries B.C. All three vases (Nos. 42–44) represent fantastic creatures. Most unusual is the black-figure amphora (43) that shows a youth running away from a siren, a siren that holds a club, no less. On the belly of this vase is a frieze that combines running youths and horses. Running figures of any sort are a favorite motif for Etruscan artists in the sixth century. The running figure plays to the strength of Etruscan artists who excelled at contour and movement, often creating strong compositions that emphasize movement and gesture, scenes that in tomb painting use a color scheme that seems almost Fauvist and compositions that evoke Matisse. The painter of 43 is no master, but painters of contemporary Etruscan tombs such as the Tomb of the Lionesses at Tarquinia, with its exquisite dancing figures and banqueters, surely qualify as such.[11] The interesting thing about our amphora (43), however, is the combination of human, animal, and vegetal elements, all of which seem to be depicted as equally important (in terms of scale and placement on the vase). These runners (or are they dancers?) are nude youths, but more often than not on Etruscan vases of the Archaic period, they can also be demons, creatures of the Etruscan underworld, hence not real, at least by modern definition. Such creatures are quite common on Etruscan painted vases, although they will not become common in Etruscan tomb painting until two centuries later. And it is not just demons. Silens and satyrs—creatures of the Dionysian realm—are also common.

They too reflect another world. But does the modern distinction, between what is mythological (and hence of another world, not real) and human (observable visually, and hence real), actually apply in an ancient Etruscan context? It has been argued that the Etruscans might have considered the afterlife physically and temporally closer than, say, a place that was physically distant, for instance the South Pole, a place that to us today seems much more real than the Hereafter.[12] The South Pole is real, and even if we have never seen it for ourselves, we know that it exists; we can pinpoint it on a chart. But belief systems are tricky things, and just as there are persons alive today who are absolutely certain that Americans never landed on the moon, there were undoubtedly Etruscans to whom a siren, a demon, a griffin, or a sphinx, would have been just as real as a lion. The issue is one of observation. What we can see, we deem real. The crux of the issue is not what we have observed, but that which is thought to be observable. The possibilities of seeing would, of course, have been very different in the Etruscan world, for those "most religious of all peoples," for that Etruscan elite that felt assured of its continued status in the afterlife. To us the distinction between a lion and chimaera seems obvious. One can be seen, on television if not in a zoo, while the other is fantasy. To an Etruscan, who of course would not have been able to see a lion other than on a work of art, that animal would have been no different from a chimaera or a griffin. This issue is neatly summarized by Small who pointed out that "if the Etruscan artist was personally acquainted with a particular thing, his portrayal was accurate and not fanciful. Since he had not seen monsters (which were as real to him as unicorns were to medieval artists) and certain other animals like lions and panthers, his depictions would not reflect reality."[13]

This modern distinction between observed reality and perceived reality does manifest itself in a visual discontinuity in Etruscan art. A case in point is the life-size hollow-cast bronze statue of a chimaera, the famous Chimaera of Arezzo, that would have been part of a monumental group exhibited in a sanctuary in northern Etruria.[14] Certain parts of this statue, for instance the goat-head and serpent-tail, are extraordinarily naturalistic. Other parts are highly stylized, for instance the mane and snout of the lion. Other parts, the lion's body, fall somewhere in between, looking natural but more like a canine or smaller feline than an actual lion. The incongruities result from the fact that the fourth century artist observed goats and serpents, and recreated them convincingly for the relevant parts of the composite monster, but was unable to observe an actual lion or an animal that had a lion-like mane. The result is a mane that looks more like a series of artichoke leaves than the hair of a lion. The incongruities would not have bothered an Etruscan viewer who would not have seen a lion. A similar thing happens on the Pontic *oinochoe* (42) in this exhibit. The felines, probably panthers, are shown with facing heads that are highly unconvincing to the modern viewer. The ears are huge, closer to a cartoon mouse than to a panther or lion. On the other hand, the sphinxes are realistically painted, with beautiful Archaic female profiles. The latter detail could be observed; the former was more problematic. A sphinx is thus rendered more realistically than a cat.

Etruscan art of the seventh and sixth centuries B.C. abounds with what we call fantastic animals. The very term fantastic stresses the fact that to us they are objects of imagination rather than reality. On a seventh century vase, like the impasto *olla* in this exhibition (41), they form friezes whose main effect today is of decorative pattern. On Greek vases, for instance Corinthian pottery (4–8) and Italo-Corinthian and East Greek Vases (9) influenced by Corinthian models, they are surely decorative. But when they enter other parts of the Etruscan repertoire, they seem to take on a different meaning. They are found incised, painted, and in relief on Etruscan pottery. They are a commonplace on bucchero, that characteristic early Etruscan black pottery. They are found on painted vases of the Archaic period, for instance the Pontic *oinochoe* (42) where they are combined with a "real" banquet scene. Fantastic animals are found in monumental wall painting, on decorated bronzes, on carved ivories. The list is endless and the complexity of combinations is mesmerizing.[15]

It may be the very ubiquity of this kind of decoration that has led us to dismiss much of it as pattern rather than narrative, but there is in fact evidence that it was imbued with significant meaning. Instances where animal decoration is found on a more monumental scale, or in three-dimensional media, hence in a context that is not "decorative" by modern definition, may shed light on the meaning of animal friezes on vases. The sixth-century monumental structure excavated at Murlo (Siena), for instance, had the ridge of its roof decorated with a series of nearly life-size terracotta statues that included human figures as well as a menagerie of animals, fantastic or otherwise: lions, sphinxes, boars, horses, and griffins, to name just a few. Silhouetted against the sky they would have recreated on a grand scale the animal friezes of Etruscan decorative arts. In this context, as part of a building that is approximately sixty meters on a side, they can hardly be considered decorative, even if the interpretation of their meaning is fraught with difficulties.[16]

Another instance of fantastic animals on a more monumental scale are the well-known stone sculptures from Vulci. These statues were probably placed outside tombs, and the repertory here is similar to that found on vases: centaurs, lions, sphinxes, even a human figure riding a hippocamp.[17] The normal explanation for these sculptures is that they served as guardians for the tomb, but the idea of "guardians" has a rather modern tone to it. If in fact these figures were placed outside the tomb, as the evidence suggests, then a better explanation (one that would also help explain the meaning of such figures in other media) is that they serve to mediate between the world of the living and the realm of the dead. They serve to connect two different worlds, two different states of existence, just as Dionysian figures also mediate between two existential environments. If this seems a little too pat an explanation, then we might consider the new discoveries at Cortona, where a large stepped structure was recently excavated at the perimeter of a monumental tumulus tomb that has been known for over a century.[18] The discovery of this altar is dramatic enough, evidence for the cult of the dead in late seventh-century Etruria, and it can certainly be argued that the altar itself mediates, in terms of ritual at least, between living and dead. But most fascinating is the decoration of the antae, for here stood stone sculptures depicting a bloody combat between a human male and a sphinx. These are among the earliest monumental sculptures from the classical world, and man and beast are almost intertwined. The sphinx devours the man (his head is engulfed in the maw of the sphinx) while at the same time the man drives his sword deep into the side of the animal. Clearly, if animals such as sphinxes mediate between two states, at least visually, they belong as much to the Hereafter as to the human world. Their voracity mirrors the ferocity of death; they devour the living. Death in the Etruscan world is often connected to sacrifice,[19] to the shedding of blood, and in fact combats between humans and fantastic animals are not uncommonly represented on Etruscan vases.

Another clue about the meaning of friezes of fantastic animals comes from a particular motif that occurs again and again in Etruscan art but is never, to my knowledge, found in Greek representations. This motif is the animal (often a lion but sometimes a sphinx or fantastic creature) who has another animal or part of a human dangling from its mouth.[20] This grisly detail is quite common in the Etruscan repertoire, and thanks to Etruscan influence it works its way into the visual culture of other Italic and European peoples.[21] The meaning, I think, is clearly connected to the Cortona sphinx combat and other scenes of this kind. Again, the animals symbolize another world, another state, one that has to be negotiated visually and symbolically, just as the Etruscan elites will have to negotiate the dangers of their own journey to the afterlife. In the case of the Etruscans, the Hereafter is a real place, just as the fantastic creatures encountered on our vases are real animals. They exist. This of course brings up the question of what a frieze of fantastic animals is doing on our Pontic *oinochoe* (42) where it is combined with a banquet scene. Does this mean that the banquet has a funerary connotation? I am not sure that we can answer this question, yet,[22] but it does bring up the intriguing notion that certain vases might have been intended for funerary use.[23]

One of the questions posed in this exhibit is about the meaning of representation. What manner of representation do we find on Greek, Italic, and Etruscan vases? Research on Greek vase-painting suggests that what was once considered real, the so-called genre scenes that purportedly reflected the realities of daily life, are actually much more sophisticated constructs than previously thought. Ironically, the Etruscan scenes that are often regarded as pattern or ornament may in fact have been imbued with a meaning that was quite palpable and real to the Etruscan viewer. The nature of reality is mutable, both in life and art.

NOTES

[1] For the historiography of Etruscan art in the eighteenth century: Cristofani 1983. For Greek ceramics in Etruria: Martelli 1979; Small 1994a. For other types of influences and cross-fertilization: Shapiro 2000.

[2] Rasmussen 1985 with previous bibliography.

[3] Vickers and Gill 1994. For an excellent summary of the Etruscan context, and a rebuttal of Vickers and Gill's theories in this context: Small 1994a, 34–58.

[4] Although the phenomenon is actually more complicated than this, since Orientalizing motifs could be transmitted through Greek art, which in turn was influenced by Near Eastern art: Rasmussen 1995.

[5] For instance the recently excavated site, at the north-eastern edge of Etruria, where Attic red-figure has been found. Warden, Thomas, and Galloway 1999, 240, fig. 12.

[6] As evidenced, for instance, by Chiusine "Canopic" urns that continue Villanovan traditions of cremation in anthropomorphisized ossuaries. Gempeler 1973; Warden 2003.

[7] Interestingly, the handles were reinforced, possibly for shipping. Small 1994a, 45, note 60.

[8] For the topic: Small 1994b.

[9] We have come a long way from the singular interest in Etruscan art as a reflection of "superior" Greek culture: "Every phase in the assimilation of Greek civilization by the peoples of Italy is of interest: and Etruscan vase painting throws light on one stage…" Beazley 1947, 10.

[10] For instance: Small 1991, and more recently: Kennedy-Quigley 2001 and Small 2001.

[11] Steingräber 1984, pls. 97, 100.

[12] Warden 2000, which was presented originally as "Where do we go from here? Death and ritual in Etruscan Art," symposium held at the Dallas Museum of Art, 2000.

[13] Small 1994a, 36, n. 11.

[14] Sprenger & Bartolini 1977, 207. Haynes 1988, 76, pl. 156.

[15] An early seventh century bronze repoussé vase, for instance, has a lion, bull, deer, leopard, sphinx, griffin, centaur, chimaera, ostriches, and even a nude female on horseback. Haynes 1988, 251, pl. 16.

[16] The bibliography of the controversies of interpretation is quite extensive: Ingrid Edlund-Berry in Phillips 1993, 107–140, summarizes the bibliography to 1987. It has grown since then.

[17] For a winged lion: Sprenger & Bartoloni 1977, pl. 61 and pl. 60 for the boy riding a hippocamp.

[18] Zamarchi Grassi 1992, pls. 22–29. Bruschetti & Zamarchi Grassi 1999, 39–42, 58.

[19] Of particular importance in this regard is the new evidence, still unpublished, from Pisa, where a tumulus was recently excavated with an altar placed on top of the earthen mound; traces of the sacrificial knife are said to have been found on the altar.

[20] Most often the animal is shown with a human leg in its mouth. Incised bucchero: Bonamici 1974, no. 25, pl. 12b; no. 77, pl. 39b. Sprenger and Bartoloni 1977, pl. 39. Painted vases: Martelli 1987, pl. 48. Sometimes the whole lower torso of a human figure might be shown: Bonamici 1974, no. 73, pl. 34b, for incised bucchero. Bianchi-Bandinelli and Giuliano 1973, pl. 157 for a three-dimensional lion (?) with human torso, bronze decoration for a couch or bed. More unusual is an animal eating another animal: Bonamici 1974, no. 77, pl. 39a.

[21] As, for instance, on a Venetic *situla*: Bianchi Bandinelli and Giuliano 1973, pl. 157.

[22] The answer can only come from continued excavation of habitation settlements. To date the preponderance of Etruscan pottery comes from funerary or sanctuary contexts, but then so does most of Etruscan material culture.

[23] Small 1994a suggests that Greek vases might have been accumulated by the Etruscans primarily for funerary use.

History of the Collection of Greek and Etruscan Antiquities in the National Archaeological Museum of Spain

PALOMA CABRERA

The history of the National Archaeological Museum's Greek and Etruscan Antiquities collection is closely intertwined with the history of royal and private collecting in Spain from the 18th through the 20th centuries. These objects, coveted by collectors in past centuries, as well as pieces showcased in royal cabinets, were the cornerstone of our museum's first collections.

The National Archaeological Museum was created on March 20, 1867, by royal decree of Queen Isabela II. The decree specified that the National Archaeological Museum be established in Madrid, though it did not stipulate its placement or setting. However, the Minister of Public Works had already envisioned the construction of a huge building, a great palace that would house the national library and museums, before the museum legally existed. In 1865 the construction work had begun on a solarium in the Paseo de Recoletos, for which the contract had been awarded to the arquitect Francisco Jareño. In 1866 the cornerstone of the building that would house the National Library and the National Archaeological Museum was laid. Twenty years would pass until the museum occupied the building and the spaces originally set aside for it. It remains there to this day.

In the meantime, from 1867 to 1895, when the museum was housed in the Palacio de Recoletos, it was assigned a "temporary" location in the small palace called the Casino de la Reina.¹ The complex was comprised of buildings, a park and gardens that dated to the beginning of the 19th century and was situated in the Embajadores section of the city. It belonged to the City Government of Madrid, which had given it to Queen Maria Isabel de Braganza, wife of Ferdinand VII. In 1865 Isabela II, the daughter of Ferdinand VII, decided to detach this royal possession from the Crown and give it to the state government. The Ministry of Public Works decided in 1867 to cede this building to the museum until the construction at its permanent location was finished.

The royal decree creating the museum established that the National Archaeological Museum would house all the archaeological and numismatic objects currently housed in the National Library, the Natural History Museum, and the

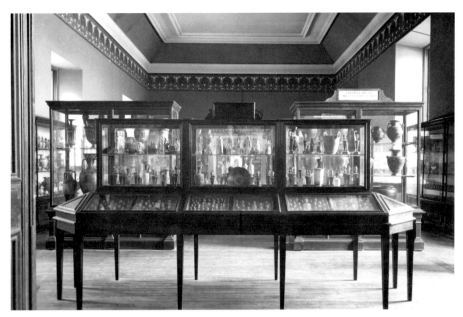

Greek Vase Galleries in 1917

Special Diplomatic School. The first two institutions were created in the 18th century. The Royal Library was constructed during the reign of Philip V (1711); adjacent to it, numismatic pieces and archaeological objects belonging to the royal collections were exhibited. Charles III created the Royal Cabinet of Natural History in 1771, an institution housed in a building designed by the architect Juan de Villanueva that is now the Prado Museum. In addition to the geological, botanical, and zoological collections, manufactured goods and art objects that illustrated "the use that man has made of the natural elements," were displayed in the Royal Cabinet.

The Special Diplomatic School, founded in 1856, was the training ground for a new corps of archivists, librarians and archaeologists and was supplied with a small collection of antiquities for teaching purposes.

Thus came into the Archaeological National Museum from the National Library "a total of 700 objects, among which were a few Egyptian pieces, quite a few Greek, several Roman, some from the Middle Ages, others from the Modern Age, and a few of ethnographic character."[2] The collection included a grouping of fourteen Greek vases, seven Etruscan mirrors, and an Etruscan cinerary urn, which had been described by Basilio Sebastián Castellanos (1847) and Emil Hübner (1862).

The collection of Greek vases included three Attic red-figure vases of exceptional quality. They were extremely rare because of their iconography: the *stamnos* with the procession of old *komasts*; the *pelike* of the Pan Painter showing the motif of the vendor and boy, and the large *pelike* showing Perseus killing Medusa. There was also an Attic black-figure *lekythos* with two goats confronting each other; this was the oldest of the vases. The rest of the vases were of South Italian origin: a column krater and a red-figure Apulian *skyphos*; two Campanian *lekythoi*, also in the red-figure technique; an *oinochoe* of the Gnathian style; several black-glaze vases; and a red-figure "milker," an exceptional piece because of its rarity in the formal Greek repertoire.

Among the Etruscan objects[3] were five mirrors, four decorated with various motifs: a psychostasia scene; one with Herakles and Athena; another showing the battle between Achilles and Penthesilea; a mirror featuring Goloces, Amuces and Losna; a plain one; and another with "figures engraved on the reverse," which are impossible to identify. Among the "objects in the Etruscan style" are many Roman bronzes and an Etruscan urn, the lid of which is decorated with the figure of the deceased woman on a bier with a pillow, and with a combat scene on the front.[4] Hübner describes only eight Greek vases, naturally the *stamnos* and the two Attic red-figure *pelikes*, the black-figure *lekythos*, the Apulian column krater, the two bell-shaped *lekythoi*, and the "milker."[5] He does not mention the black-glaze vases, surely because, according to the aesthetic criteria of the time, such vases did not deserve the same consideration as those decorated with figures.

Where did the Greek vases and Etruscan objects from the National Library come from? Most were in the collections of antiquities that King Charles III had brought with him from his reign in Naples in 1787. However, even though most of the royal collection's objects came from Italy, we are not sure of its particular origin within the country, nor how the objects reached his collection. According to the first

Greek Vase Gallery in 1917

Museum Catalogue, many of the objects in the National Library's collection, especially the classical and Roman ones, "had come to Spain along with the most prized possessions of King Charles III's chambers, having been acquired during the first excavations, ordered and financed by the king, of the unearthed cities of Pompeii and Herculaneum."[6] Years before, Pedro de Madrazo had been far more acute. In his study of two Attic vases from the library collection, he proposed that Charles III had acquired the pieces from Italian collectors or antiquarians.[vii]

Along with the antiquities from the National Library, other antiquities and ethnographic objects from the Royal Cabinet of Natural History (later, the Museum of Natural History) comprised the first of the Archaeological Museum's collections. The Royal Cabinet consisted of the collection that Don Pedro Franco Dávila had acquired throughout his life, in visits to South America and Europe.[8] After trying and failing to get Charles III to purchase his collection, Franco Dávila donated it to the monarch in 1771, on condition that he be named director of the cabinet.

The Royal Cabinet of Natural History's collection included 52 Greek vases, mostly South Italian: Apulian *hydriae*, *pelikes*, kraters, *lebetoi* and *skyphoi*; a Lucanian bell krater; Campanian *skyphoi* and *lekythoi*, all in the red-figure style; two Attic *lekythoi* in the black-figure technique; and several South Italian black glaze vessels. The principal pieces are the Apulian bell kraters described by Hübner along with the other red-figure vases. [9] Missing from Hübner's study, as with the National Library's collection, were the black-glaze vases and those that did not contain any relevant decoration. Describing the Royal Cabinet's collection, Hübner states that a few smaller finds were later added to the Franco Dávila collection, gifts from Charles III and the Infantes Don Gabriel and Don Luis: small Neopolitan bronzes, huge clay amphorae and many of the smaller ceramics. Hübner also recounts that these vases, most featuring Dionysian scenes, must have come from Naples. In any case, the vases in the Franco Dávila collection were most probably of Italian origin, because we know he had close contact with European collectors and antiquarians.[10]

The Escuela Superior de Diplomática, founded October 7, 1856, on the initiative of the Royal Academy of History, contributed only one Greek vase: a red-figure Attic *lekythos*, decorated with the head of Hermes. It is likely this small vase was from Spain, not Greece or Italy, because such vases are very plentiful along the eastern Peninsula, especially from Ampurias and Ibiza.

Building on its impressive base collection, from 1868 to 1895 the museum (which still occupied the Casino de la Reina) continued to seek additional holdings. This was an enormously dynamic period for the museum, despite the volatile historical and political context of the time, including the crisis of Isabelle II's reign, the revolution of 1868, the provisional government of Generals Serrano and Prim, the reign of Amadeus of Savoy, the First Republic, and the beginnings of the Bourbon Restoration under Alfonso XII.

During this period the museum acquired the three great collections of Greek and Etruscan antiquities that would form the nucleus of the Greek archaeology section. Only recently has the museum acquired equally important and large collections. Those early three, in chronological order, were the collection of Greek and Cypriot vases and antiquities gathered during the expedition to the Orient of the frigate *Arapiles*, the collection of the Marquis of Salamanca, and the collection of the consul Asensi.

In 1871, a commission was formed to accompany the war frigate *Arapiles* to the East Mediterranean. The commission was made up of an archaeologist and museum curator, Rada y Delgado; a diplomat, Jorge Zammit y Romero; and an illustrator, Ricardo Velázquez Bosco. Their mission, besides studying the monuments of Greece, Turkey, Syria, Cyprus, and Egypt (wherever the frigate set anchor) was to acquire objects for the museum. This Scientific Expedition, which was recounted in wonderful detail in a three-volume tome,[11] was intended to emulate previous European expeditions of this type as well as add to the knowledge about the monuments and historical geography of the Mediterranean and Orient.

According to Rada y Delgado, "after having toured through practically all of Greece, Turkey, Palestine, part of Egypt and Malta, the commission returned with a great cache of news, drawings, photographs, and 319 objects, stone sculptures, terracottas, glasses, and other such, many of which were the first of their type to reach the Museums of Europe, and some of such great importance that they can be considered unique."[12]

Among the objects acquired by the expedition were eighty-eight Greek vases, several Cypriot sculptures and vases, and nineteen terracottas. The Greek vases came, for the most part, from Athens, a few of them donated by the banker D. Juan Bautista Serpieri, who lived there.[13] Among the donated pieces was a gigantic *lekythos*, possibly from Alopeke, Attica, where similar *lekythoi* have been found, as well as a white-ground *lekythos* (31); a black-figure amphora; and two red-figure nuptial vessels. The principal part of this collection consists of nineteen white-ground *lekythoi* that comprise the most important group of such vases in the museum's collection. He also brought a few late black-figure *lekythoi*, eleven red-figure *lekythoi*, a Corinthian *oinochoe* (7), several black-glaze pieces, among them an intriguing baby bottle, three *pyxides*, and a Geometric cup. The cup, along with a gold band also dating to the Geometric period—a unique piece in the museum's collection—possibly came from a tomb in the Dipylon or Kerameikos in Athens.

The commissioners acquired nine terracottas in Athens, of generally poor quality, except for one Archaic kore figure and a Hellenistic set showing two dancers. Rada y Delgado also brought back from Athens a fragment of an Ionic capital, of Pentelic marble, found in the ruins of the Acropolis. But the commission's principal work in Athens was studying the main classical monuments, drawing sketches of the most notable, and making reproductions of several sculptural reliefs found in the Teseion museum.[14] On its voyage throughout the eastern Mediterranean the expedition visited the ruins of the ancient *Ilium Novum*, where they acquired a Hellenistic relief[15] and several architectural fragments; Smyrna, where the consul of Sweden and

Director Álvarez-Ossorio and personnel of the Museum in 1936

Norway, one Mister Spiegethal, donated five terracottas and a stone head;[16] and Ephesus, where they found a funerary stele showing an infant in the arms of a woman and a servant. From the island of Samos, where the travelers were measuring and sketching the visible ruins at the Heraion, they brought back a fragment of a capital.

The details Rada y Delgado provides on the pieces brought back from Cyprus are the most precise: "on arriving on the island of Cyprus in September of 1871, we had the good fortune to examine the Cesnola collection; and as we also viewed the much smaller, but no less important, collection of sculptural objects and mostly vases gathered by the illustrious General Consul of Italy, Ricardo Colucci, we were very fortunate in that he generously donated a few pieces, even being so generous as to facilitate their transport and shipping."[17] The grouping of twenty-eight sculptures, which Rada defines as Phoenician and Egyptian, and Cypriot vases—also considered "Phoenician"—were found "close to one of the funerary chambers of Larnaca, which was being studied and investigated when the expedition arrived there."[18] Rada y Delgado also found a few Greek vases in Cyprus: two black-figure Attic cups, a black-figure *lekythos*, and an Etruscan bucchero *aryballos*, objects that tie in well with the typology of the furnishings of the necropolis, such as those in Amatunte or Salamis.

The true driving force behind the museum's collection of Greek and Etruscan antiquities was the acquisition in 1874 of the collection belonging to the Marquis of Salamanca. This man, an exceptional impresario and investor, lent his inexhaustible energy to public works: loan houses, banks, the stock market, newspapers, railroads, politics—he became minister of the treasury—theaters, real estate, urbanization projects, and agricultural complexes both in Spain and abroad. He was ruined financially at the end of the 1840s and remade his fortune, considered to be the largest in Spain, only to die again in ruin in 1883.[19] As a good investor and surely also as a lover of the fine arts, he acquired a fine collection of antiquities and *objets d'art*, with which Hübner was familiar, although he did not describe the collection.[20]

The Greek and Etruscan antiquities collection was acquired for the most part in Italy, where the Marquis of Salamanca had lived for many years, overseeing the construction of the two railroads in the Pontifical States.[21] That is where he became a collector and where he sponsored the excavations at the Italian sanctuary at Calvi, in the Campania region. He received permission from the government of Naples to embark on archaeological excavations, with an agreement as to the ownership of the finds discovered there. The objects uncovered during the excavations joined his already impressive collection of Greek vases and terracottas.

After 1865 a series of disastrous business deals almost ruined him. That was when he started trying to sell his antiquities collection, although negotiations with the museum were not finalized to everyone's satisfaction until 1874.

The Marquis's collection comprised 1,500 objects, most from the Classical period: 900 Greek vases, 287 terracottas and a number of Etruscan bronzes. It would be a daunting and tiresome task to ennumerate here all the Greek, Corinthian, Attic, South Italian, and Etruscan vases that form the nucleus of the museum's Greek collection. However, we must cite those objects of exceptional quality, among the best examples of South Italian and Etruscan manufacture, that are the showpieces of our museum. They are: the amphora by the Madrid Painter, showing the battle between Herakles and Apollo for the Delphic tripod, the *hydria* by the Priam Painter, the *hydria* by the Painter of the Fountain of Madrid (16), the *dinos* and the amphora by the Antimenes Painter (14), the Panathenaic amphora by the Kleophrades Painter, the bilingual amphora by Andokides and Psiax (20), the Pamphaios cup, the Oltos cup with the *hetaira* scene, the *pelike* showing Peleus abducting Thetis, the Berlin Painter's *hydria* with the young women at the fountain, the Dwarf Painter's *hydria* with the *hetairae* Archedike and Hapalina, the Aison cup with the feats of Theseus (29), the *calyx* krater by the Meleager Painter with a Dionysian scene, the *calyx* krater attributed to the Pronomus Painter, several monumental Apulian amphorae in the decorated style, among them the one at the tomb of the tragic poet, the *calyx* krater by the Dirce Painter with *phlyax* scene (35), and finally, the Paestum *calyx* krater by the Asteas Painter with the motif of the madness of Herakles. We know the origins of very few of these pieces; for example, the Asteas krater, which was found in a tomb at Paestum, or the black-figure amphora showing Herakles killing Eurytios, which was found at Vulci and became the property of the Marquis of Campana, who gives it as a gift to her friend the Marquis of Salamanca,[22] or the *calyx* krater in the style of the Pronomos Painter, found at Calvi.

As for the collection of terracottas acquired by the Marquis of Salamanca, its principal components were objects "found in the same setting while constructing the Italian railroads at Calvi."[23] This grouping of 157 terracottas, mostly votives representing parts of the human body, of various styles and influences (Greek, Italian and Etruscan), and from different periods (fourth century B.C. to the first century A.D.), points to the existence of a sanctuary dedicated to Italic divinities. The rest of the terracottas in the collection, a total of 322, lacked any clear indication of their origin, but most seem to be of Italian origin and manufacture. Some are in the Archaic style, but most date to the Hellenistic period.[24]

The Salamanca collection also contained an important grouping of ceramics and bronze objects, Villanovan and Etruscan, including bucchero, red- and black-figure vases, as well as three bronze mirrors, one decorated with the images of Lasa and Athena, and two without ornamentation, although the second has an Etruscan inscription.

In 1876 the museum bought the antiquities collection of Don Tomás Asensi, who would become Consul of Spain in Tunis. This collection, described by Hübner,[25] comprised "Egyptian, Phoenician, Etruscan, Greek and Roman objects as well as Greek vases in the Archaic and Oriental styles, and other Italic-Greek pieces of later date, terracottas from Athens, Cyrenaica and various settlements in Asia Minor, and a great quantity of Roman ceramics found in Egypt and Italy, forming a total of 1,000 objects."[26]

Tomás Asensi's collection of Greek vases had 232 pieces. It is said that most came from Cyrenaica and some from Etruria and Campania, but most must have been acquired on the Italian art market. Among them are Etruscan bucchero vases, Etruscan black and red-figure vases, Corinthian vases, Attic black- and red-figure vases (13, 22), and South Italian vessels. The collection also included 137 terracottas and two Etruscan mirrors.

The Asensi collection, especially its Corinthian and Etruscan vases, completed the museum's important Greek and Etruscan holdings. The museum's collection had already been noticeably enriched by the Salamanca acquisition, and this one follows close behind due to its richness, variety and the quality of some of its pieces.

In 1880 Basilio Sebastián Castellanos, who would be the treasurer of the National Library and later director of the National Archaeological Museum, donated a small collection to the museum, made up of 152 objects. Among them were an Etruscan red-figure vase and an Etruscan bronze mirror with an interesting scene of the Theogamia of the Dioscuri, which completed the museum's collection of Etruscan mirrors.

In 1886, the museum bought from Bartolomé Ferrá y Perelló two Greek vases—a large Middle Corinthian *olpe* and an Attic red-figure *hydria*—which have a most interesting story. According to a letter preserved in the museum's archives, "both vases, along with another four, which unfortunately were destroyed, were found by a

The So Called Roman Gallery in 1954

Maiorcan pilot, floating in the Mediterranean crated in a wooden box, some 50 years ago. And these are the only facts I can present with respect to their origin." The origin of these vases found floating on the coast of Maiorca around the 1830s could well be Italian. It wouldn't be strange at all that some antiquities merchant or collector would have shipped these objects from Italy to another part of Europe (England, perhaps?), and that by some happenstance they never arrived at their destination.

In 1900, when Juan Catalina García was director, the museum was given the collection of Theodor Stützel, a Munich merchant residing in Spain. It consisted of "a great number of prehistoric and Bronze Age artifacts, found in Swiss lakes: 21 vases painted in the Corinthian style, Greek, Archaic, and of beautiful style; 14 terracottas; multiple little clay heads; some bronzes; a Roman glass; and a carton with 36 small gold pieces of Greek art..."[27] Some of these objects had been found on the island of Samos and in other locations.[28]

The Greek vase collection was made up of a Boeotian *pyxis* and an Attic lid, both from the Geometric period; an *alabastron*, two *aryballoi* and a lid from Corinth; five black-figure *lekythoi*; a black-figure *alabastron*, and a group of five white-ground *lekythoi*, among which are some of the best of their kind in the museum, such as the ones by the Inscription Painter (30) or the Cane Painter.

Equally interesting was his collection of Greek terracottas, among which are the oldest in the museum's collection:[29] two Boeotian—a goddess and a driver in a cart— both from the seventh century B.C., a seated goddess and a *kore* in the Archaic style, and five Rhodian figures in the Severe style, among them the group showing the abduction of Europa. Hellenistic terracottas were also included: Aphrodite leaning on a rock, several Tanagra, and several animal figures. The collection also had thirty heads mounted on pedestals and 362 heads, torsos and fragments.

The period between 1916 and 1930, with the museum now fully established in its current location, was marked by the direction of José Ramón Mélida, eminent specialist and researcher in the field of classical archaeology, who was responsible for the publication of the first catalogues of Greek antiquities. In 1910, Álvarez-Ossorio published the first catalogue of Greek vases, which would be completed by Leroux in 1912, and in 1921 Laumonier's catalogue on Greek terracottas was released. The acquisition of artworks and private donations continued during this period, although sporadically and on a smaller scale than previously. One highlight, however, was the incorporation in 1920 of the Greek vase collection from the Prado Museum, through an exchange.

The idea of an exchange of objects between the two museums had first been suggested in 1871.[30] Fifty years would go by before the project was finally completed. The National Archaeological Museum donated to the Prado Museum two 18th-century rubbings, a tablet showing Saint Vincent, and the tablet of Saint Domingo of Daroca de Bartolomé Bermejo, in exchange for the "collections of Italian-Greek vases, and porcelains, marbles and other small stone objects from the Buen Retiro collection, plus a Roman funerary stele with an inscription."[31]

The collection contained 53 vases, most of which had been described by Hübner as belonging to the royal collections in the Prado.[32] The vases were mostly South Italian: thirteen Apulian, twelve from Campania, and two from Lucania. The Apulian pieces were the most exceptional: two *loutrophoroi* and two *volute* kraters with funerary scenes, a *calyx* krater with a sacrificial scene, three column kraters, and five bell kraters with Dionysian scenes. The Campanian vases, also high-quality pieces of iconographic interest, included an amphora with a battle scene of Samnite warriors and two *calyx* kraters with Dionysian scenes, along with a bell krater featuring the image of a seated Athena. The Attic pieces were six bell kraters with Dionysian scenes, from the fourth century, a Nolan amphora by the Achilles Painter and another by the Alkimakos Painter; a *pelike*; a column krater and a red-figure *hydria*; and two black-glaze cups. There were also two Middle Corinthian *alabastra*.

Of all these vases, one in particular is worth commenting on, the Nolan amphora by the Achilles Painter. In the catalogue compiled by Álvarez-Ossorio in 1910, it was listed as a South Italian black glaze. A systematic examination of the Greek ceramics undertaken in 1971 brought to light that what had been considered a black glaze vase was actually an Attic red-figure vase, attributable to the Achilles Painter, cracked and grooved, and totally repainted to hide its deterioration and facilitate its sale in the 19th century.[33] This can be explained by the significant hierarchy present in the antiquities markets of the 19th century and the aesthetic criteria of collectors and antiquarians, who preferred apparently intact objects to those in a fragmented state, even if they were originally painted with figures.

Two exceptional pieces also became part of the museum's collection in 1920: two clay sarcophagi from Clazomenae, donated by D. Ignacio Bauer y Landauer, "acquired at a very high price in Paris expressly as a gift to the National Archeological Museum."[34]

During the years of the Second Republic, the acquisition of Greek antiquities dwindled to a few, unimportant pieces. Following that period, the Civil War disrupted all acquisition activity and was truly a dramatic event in the history of the museum, as the pieces exhibited had to be crated to protect them from bombing raids. In the postwar years, economic difficulties and political uncertainty were the dominant themes. Thus in 1944 the Caputi collection of 454 Greek vases was offered for sale to the Spanish government, an acquisition that unfortunately never took place, despite the eagerness of the museum's specialists. This was a great loss, because that collection would have been one of the most notable acquisitions of Greek vases since the Salamanca collection was acquired.

The postwar phase ended in 1951. In the ensuing years, under the direction of Joaquín María de Navascués, the museum experienced a resurgence of scientific study, and exhibitions resumed. Thus began the great museological reforms that would culminate in the 1960s under the direction of Martín Almagro Basch. The building was remodeled, exhibition halls were modernized and expanded in accordance with new museographic criteria, and the storerooms were organized. Collecting began again, both in the form of donations and acquisition of pieces from excavations.

In 1952 a Campanian vase in the shape of a rooster was donated by Joaquín Gumá Herrera, Count of Lagunillas. This Cuban collector had amassed his collection during the 1940s, on the New York and London antiquities markets, and was one of the backers of the Fine Arts Museum in Havana, where his collection was to be one of its essential holdings.[35]

In 1972 the museum acquired a grouping of Greek and Roman pieces from the collection of Fernando Ember Téllez-Girón, which enriched the museum's already important collection of South Italian and Etruscan vases and terracottas. This collection had belonged to the Prince of Anglona, one of the seller's ancestors, and had been described by Hübner, who tells us that it was formed in the 1830s through acquisitions on the art markets in Rome and Naples.[36] Hübner describes only fifty-one objects, although we know from the prince's documents that the collection contained more than a hundred pieces. Perhaps part of the collection had already been sold, or perhaps Hübner described only the outstanding pieces.

The Fernando Ember collection contained an Attic Nolan amphora and a San Valentín *skyphos*; an Apulian *kantharos*, *askos*, *lekythos*, and *volute* krater; an Etruscan *situla* and amphora; various black glaze vases; and several terracottas, among which was a magnificent female bust of the Hellenistic period, a figure of a dancing hermaphrodite, and an *acroterion* in the form of a sphinx.

The same year that the prince's collection was acquired, a donation from Martín Almagro Basch, then director of the museum, added to the collection of Cypriot antiquities. It is made up of twelve pieces, fragments of bowls, an *olpe*—ladle-like bowls in the white-painted style—and two loom weights, which were acquired by the donor when he visited Cyprus in 1966 from antiquarians there.

In 1981, following the extensive remodeling work, the new Greek and Etruscan archeology hall was inaugurated, and the best pieces from the collections already described were put on display. In the past twenty years, the collections have grown through acquisitions, especially from antiquarians' galleries and auction halls. These acquisitions were always made with selective criteria in mind, to find significant pieces that would fill in the scientific and expository gaps in the museum's holdings. But not until 1999 would this policy produce major results, thanks to the acquisition of the collection of José Luis Várez Fisa.

The Várez Fisa collection, compiled during the 1970s and 1980s on the antiquities market, consisted of 188 Egyptian, Iberian, Greek, Etruscan and Roman pieces. This collection, which is enormously important from a scientific, artistic and museographic point of view, contains Egyptian vases and sculptures; Iberian sculptures and Celtic-Iberian weapons; metalwork of Mediterranean silver; Roman sculptures; and more than a hundred Greek vases. It comprises, therefore, a great variety of Mediterranean cultures over a significant chronological spectrum, from the fifth millennium B.C. to the fifth century of the present era.

Among the collection of Greek and Etruscan antiquities the ceramic vases are particularly outstanding, not just in terms of quantity—more than a hundred—but because of their artistic quality and scientific importance. They are from diverse geographic areas in the Greek world: Attica (3, 12, 17–19, 21, 24, 25, 27); Corinth (4–6 and 8), Boeotia; Euboea, Laconia (11), eastern Greece (9), Apulia (32, 34, 37, 38); Campania; Paestum (40); Sicily; and Etruria (41 and 44), and different eras, from the eighth century B.C. to the third century A.D. The Greek vases, in their totality, are of extraordinary interest, because they are first-rate pieces, in some cases created by the best Attic and Southern Italian artists, such as Lydos, Nikosthenes, the Affected Painter, Antimenes, Andokides, Epiktetos (21), the Berlin Painter, the Pan Painter, the Achilles Painter; the Meidias Painter, the Darius Painter, and other great artists from the sixth to the fourth centuries B.C. They are decorated with mythological, religious and quotidian motifs, that in some cases are unique in Greek iconography.

So concludes, to date, the history of the Greek and Etruscan antiquities collection of the National Archaeological Museum. It is a history rich in stories and in the excellent choices made by the staff of this institution, who always intended to make our museum one of the best in Europe in terms of conservation, study and diffusion of the material heritage of the ancient Greek world. Today, the museum is proud to have accomplished that objective and to be one of the principal European museums in the field of Greek archaeology.

NOTES

1 Marcos Pous 1993, 29–33.
2 Catálogo 1883, xi.
3 Castellanos 1847, 29–30, nos. 48–56.
4 Castellanos 1847, 29, no 47; Catalina 1872, 511–539.
5 Hübner 1862, 193–195, nos. 391–398.
6 Catálogo 1883, xi.
7 Madrazo 1872, 78.
8 Calatayud 1988, 83.
9 Hübner 1862, 225f.
10 Calatayud 1988, 76.
11 Rada y Delgado 1876–1882.
12 Catálogo 1883, xxii.
13 Rada y Delgado 1876, 722.
14 Rada y Delgado 1876, 721.
15 Mora 1980.
16 Rada y Delgado 1878, 579.
17 Rada y Delgado 1882, 697–727.
18 Catálogo 1883, 147.
19 Torrente Fortuño 1969.
20 Hübner 1862, vii.
21 Torrente Fortuño 1969, 154.
22 Bienkowski 1899, 604f.
23 Catálogo 1883, 263, nos. 3276–3433.
24 Laumonier 1921, 125–197, nos. 599–921.
25 Hübner 1862, 263f.
26 Catálogo 1883, xxviii.
27 Guía Histórica 1917, 48.
28 Mélida 1901, 559f.
29 Laumonier 1921, 9–76, nos. 20–438.
30 *Revista de Archivos* 1871, 26.
31 Archivo Museo, expediente 1920/13.
32 Hübner 1862, 168–182.
33 Olmos 1976, 9–38
34 Mélida 1922, 5.
35 Olmos 1993.
36 Hübner 1862, 251–260.

The following initials represent contibutors to the catalogue entries:

P.C. - Paloma Cabrera, Chief Curator of the Greek and Roman Antiquities Department, National Archaeological Museum in Madrid, Spain.

M.M. - Margarita Moreno, Doctor in Classical Archaeology, Assistant Curator, Ministry of Culture, Madrid, Spain.

R.O. - Ricardo Olmos, Professor, Consejo Superior de Investigaciones Científicas (CSIC), Madrid, Spain.

C.S. - Cármen Sánchez, Professor, Departamento de Historia del Arte, Universidad Autónoma de Madrid (UAM), Spain.

G.W. - P. Gregory Warden, Professor of Art History, Southern Methodist University, Dallas, Texas.

1. *Oinochoe*

Inv. no. 11.513

H: 21 cm; maximum width: 14 cm; diameter
   at base: 9 cm

Attic. Middle Geometric II

850–770 B.C.

An *oinochoe* of elegant proportions, with a high neck, trilobate mouth and round-sectioned handle that is flatter at the juncture of the lip; globular in shape, with a plain base and with a slight rounded strip at the junction with the body of the vessel. The neck shows a separate clay-colored panel decorated with a central band that has a series of intertwined diamond shapes, with central points, outlined at the top and the bottom by three painted lines. The panel with slightly tapered lateral borders is cut off by the area in which the handle is located. The body of the vessel is totally painted up to the upper quarter, while the middle is decorated with lines that follow the contours of the vase. The lower quarter is also delineated by a painted band that goes all the way to the base.

In the Middle Geometric period the potters more clearly dominate the shapes of the vases, that appear ever slimmer, as well as the distribution of the decoration, obtaining, as in our example, a perfect visual play on colors thanks to the device of alternating clear and dark areas of color. The Attic style can be seen in some of the new motifs, for instance the chained diamonds attached by a central point on the neck of the vase.

Micaceous, clear orange clay.

Perceptible tempers, that in some areas have burst to the surface, appear on the vase.

PROVENANCE:
Marquis of Salamanca Collection.

PUBLICATIONS:
Álvarez-Ossorio 1910, 130

NOTES:
1. For the geometric style, see Coldstream 1968; Coldstream 1977; for the workshops in the Argolid and Corinth respectively: Courbin 1966 and Benson 1989; a good synthesis of the decorative geometric motifs can be found in Kunisch 1998.

M.M.

2. *Geometric goblet with fenestrated foot*

Inv. no. 10.782

H: 9 cm; maximum width: 40 cm

Attic. Late Geometric IIb

730–700 B.C.

This type of vase, characteristic of the Late Geometric period, has a high vertical lip; a low, wide body with two horizontal handles; and a cone-shaped stand with eight apertures or rectangular windows. The lip of the mouth is decorated with a succession of metopes with hatched swastikas outlined by narrow bands akin to triglyphs. The diagonals, and the oblique and horizontal zig-zag lines that follow, are evenly spaced. The lip is separated from the body by thick bands of paint. The space between the handles is filled by two superimposed rows of zig-zags outlined by vertical strokes. The handles are decorated on the outside with this same motif. A wide band of glaze separates the bowl from the stand, which is decorated in the space between the rectangular windows with superimposed zig-zags. A row of points and another row of zig-zags outline the stand at top and bottom.

Goblets with fenestrated stands are characteristic of the Late Geometric IIb and were developed after bowls with a high lip substituted and replaced in their function the flat pyxis. These goblets or bowls with fenestrated stands begin to appear in the transitional period from LGIIa to LGIIb, at first with low stands and twelve or more windows, and finally with small stands and six windows and lip sloping outward. Our bowl, with its border slightly inclined and a reduced number of windows in the stand, can be dated to a later stage of the series.

It has been suggested that these vessels were used for rituals: the windows would allow ventilation so that a fire could be used to warm liquid in the bowl. In any case, these are vessels of prestigious character that accompany the deceased in death. The restricted use of the Geometric style indicates the

selective and aristocratic uses of these bowls. The production of ceramics was placed at the disposal of the competitive and legitimizing strategies of the powerful elite. Although far from the opulent and magnificent exhibits and the use of figured images that configure the great monuments, or *sema*, and the large contemporary funerary urns, these small bowls also contribute to define the formal ritual of death, though perhaps not of the most powerful. The evolution of these bowls toward others with higher stands reinforces this idea, since by using them, their visibility is increased at the most important socially significant moment of the ritual: the presentation and deposit of the funeral dowry.

PROVENANCE:
Oriental Expedition Collection.

PUBLICATIONS:
Álvarez-Ossorio 1910; Leroux 1912; CVA Madrid 1, III H, pl. 1 No. 5; Olmos 1973, 19.

NOTES:
1. Regarding the development of the shape: Coldstream 1968, 86; a similar shape in Kübler 1954, pl. 122, 3371; Coldstream 1968, pl. 15m. On development of later goblets with fenestrated stands, see Kübler 1970, pls. 30 and 72.

P.C.

3. *Geometric amphora with prothesis scene*

Inv. no. 1999/99/26
H: 50.7 cm; diameter at rim: 19.6 cm;
    diameter at foot: 11.9 cm
Attic. Late Geometric period IIa
Circa 730–720 B.C.

Narrow-necked amphora with two flat, vertical handles from neck to shoulder. The body is oval, tapering down to a narrow ringed foot. The neck is slightly concave, and the lip is molded. The figures appear on the neck and shoulder. The rest of the vase is decorated with simple bands alternating with

Side A

Detail Side A

The shoulder panel on side B has been decorated only with three bands of geometric motifs, separated by triple lines of dots, lozenges with centered dots and reticulate triangles.

The image on the two panels on the neck of the vase, both practically identical, is an extension of the principal scene. A succession of six female figures in long skirts, interspersed with geometric motifs (vertical rows of chevrons) appear to comprise a *komos*, or ritual chorus, repeating the gesture of mourning we have seen depicted by the figures surrounding the exposed corpse. This is the ritualized chant of lamentation, the *goos* or *threnos*, one of the first of the funerary rituals performed in this rite, which was extremely elaborate and complicated in this period of early Greek history.

friezes of free-floating sigmas and lozenges with a centered dot.

On the shoulder panel (side A) is a *prothesis* scene, the ritualistic laying-out of the deceased prior to burial. In the middle of the scene is the deceased on a high, four-legged bier. A checkered blanket or cloth covers the dead man. This may be the shroud in which the corpse will be buried. Under the catafalque, two male figures with trian-gular bodies and small, circular heads, kneeling only for the purpose of fitting into the space the painter has reserved for them, have their arms raised above their heads, forming a semicircle. Between the figures is a shape that is difficult to discern. Is it a simple geometric motif or a piece of furniture, perhaps a *diphros*, or folding chair? On either side of the bier are two female figures, one quite large, wearing long, reticulate skirts. They also have arms raised over their heads in the shape of a semicircle, in the characteristic gesture of mourning.

Side B

This scene celebrates the aristocrat who will be buried along with this vase, and thus with this image. The scene is fixed in time, immortalizing a ritual performed only for someone of high social standing—a privilege accorded to the most noble personages—to perpetuate his memory. But those who viewed the image also saw a memorial to the funerals of the great heroes, such as those praised by Homer in the *Iliad*. The poet kept the heroes' glory alive, not only by retelling their adventures, but also by praising the magnificence and pomp of their funerals. After recovering Hector's corpse from his mortal enemy, Priam took the body of his son to Troy and *"Once inside the magnificent palace, they placed the body on a carved bier and bade sit around it singers who entoned the threnos; these sang in lamentation, and the women wailed in response. And in the midst of them Andromache, of the snow-white arms, who held in her hands the head of Hector, killer of men, began the lamentations..."* (*Iliad*, XXIV, 719–724).

The women play an essential role in our vase. In a manner similar to Andromache, Hecuba, or Helen, they are responsible for intoning the funeral lamentations, the songs of praise and farewell. Sorrow and farewell are ritualized, though not devoid of deep feeling, because they are well-earned honors to sanction once and for all the *kleos*, the glory, and the living memory of the departed. The plaint for the death of that most beautiful and noble of heroes, Achilles, son of a goddess, could be sung only by goddesses (*Odyssey*, XXIV, 44–60). Nereids and Muses, are the mythical model of those who reenact the ritual. The quality of the one who sings the lament underscores and amplifies the glory of the one in whose honor it is sung.

PROVENANCE:

Várez Fisa Collection.

PUBLICATIONS:

Museo Arqueológico Nacional 2002, 48; Cabrera 2003, no. 23.

NOTES:

1. On the development of the narrow-necked amphora in the Late Geometric: Kübler 1954, V, 1, 273f. On the significance of the narrow-necked amphora, descended from the monumental funerary vases of LGIa in the mid-eighth century: Schweitzer 1971, 47f. The narrow-necked amphoras were destined for the tombs of men, and belly amphoras for women's tombs: Simon 1976, 30, 38.

2. The style of our amphora is reminiscent of that of the Sub-Dipylon workshop as well as other workshops unfamiliar with the classical tradition. The influence of Corinth on the Attic style can be seen principally in the use of free-floating sigmas on the shoulder panel of side B and in the narrow horizontal bands on the body: Davison 1968, 65; Coldstream 1968, 56f; Coldstream 1977, 115. But there are also similarities to the Birdseed Painter style, in the use of the "hound's tooth" motif—alternating reticulate triangles—and the depiction of the mourners forming a semicircle with their arms Davison 1968, 57; Coldstream 1968, 67f.

3. On the *prothesis* rites and their iconography, see Alexiou 1974; Kurtz and Boardman 1971, 58–61, 143–144; Ahlberg 1971; Vermeule 1979, 39f; Schnapp-Gourbeillon 1982, 77–88;

Garland 1985, 23–34; Rombos 1988, 77–91; Langdon 1993, 8.

4. On the use of the geometric style for the depiction of social entities and their response to death (and the legitimization of the aristocracy's power), as well as the related changes in pottery of the LGII period: Whitley 1991, 165; Cabrera 1997.

5. On the debate surrounding the "real" or "mythic" nature of *prothesis* scenes, see Webster 1955; Ahlberg 1971, 285–291; Carter 1972, 38–51; Rombos 1988, 387; Ahlberg-Cornell 1992, 20–21.

P.C.

4. *Corinthian aryballos with serpent among flowers*

Inv. no. 1999/99/29

H: 7 cm; diameter at mouth: 2.3 cm; diameter at
base: 2.9 cm; maximum width: 7 cm

Corinth. Middle Protocorinthian
700–675 B.C.

This small, globular *aryballos* made in Corinth would probably have held scented, perfumed oil. It is remarkable for its finish, its delicacy of form, and its careful, precise decoration. The spherical body is decorated with multiple fine horizontal lines; the mouth is decorated with three concentric circles, and the neck with lines. It is unique for its shoulder decoration: an undulating serpent with spotted body slides among eight-petaled rosettes. The artist has emphasized the snake's huge and menacing open mouth, from which emerges a long, forked tongue. Its hypnotic gaze comes from a round, vigilant eye, depicted as a circle with a central point. The rosettes are placed above and below its serpentine body. A frieze of inverted triangles marks the boundaries between the shoulder and the body. Is this simply a geometric motif or a linear interpretation of vegetation, seen in the sepals of the flower from which emanates the perfume? In any case, the frieze underlines the articulation of the vase and emphasizes the symbolic space of the flowering realm over which the vigilant serpent rules.

The motif of the serpent, of ancient Mediterranean roots, follows in the tradition of the Geometric period, when in plastic form it was placed around the handles and mouths of the great funerary vessels. The demonic power of the serpent connects to the funereal and the world of death. The snake, a domestic animal that is at the same time demonic, because of its subterranean chthonic nature, accompanies the deceased in his new life. Its domestic character also has some connection with the graveyard, with the tomb, the new dwelling of the deceased. It shares an essential characteristic with other infernal, monstruous, hybrid demons: a mediating role, unifying impossible settings and universes, connecting the world of life and light with the kingdom of death and darkness, the visible and the invisible. Only its great hypnotic eyes can bore through the mists of the other world. Its knowledge of subterranean paths will be necessary to guide or accompany the deceased on the journey to Hades.

Metaphorically, the serpent also dies and is reborn. In reality, it sheds it old skin to assume a new appearance. As a metaphor of rebirth, of life in the beyond, the snake protects with its threatening power and guards with its fierce gaze this flowering field, an image of a fertile Hereafter. But, most of all, it protects the perfume, which holds the real power, just as it held the knowledge of the properties of the *pharmacon* that, in the old Cretan myth, made Glaucus come back to life. Polyidos, interred in the funerary chamber with the body of Minos's son, killed a serpent that approached the dead body, but a second snake, with an herb in its mouth,

touched the first serpent and revived it. Polyidos took the plant and rubbed it on Glaucus's body, returning him to life. (Apollodorus, *Bibliotheca* III, 3, 1, 3). Other liminal creatures also serve as vigilant guardians of the precious unguent and its secret powers. With its liminal, transforming nature, its erotic power, the perfume is a metaphor of rebirth. It represents the seduction of death. Hades made a narcissus bloom as lure for Persephone, the fragrance of which made all the wide sky and earth smile (*Homeric Hymn to Demeter*, 5–15). But it was an amorous seduction to gather the deceased to his breast and confer new life.

PROVENANCE:
Várez Fisa Collection.

PUBLICATIONS:
Cabrera 2003, no. 29.

NOTES:
1. On shape and decorative style, see Payne 1971, 5; Coldstream 1968, 104–108; and Neeft 1987, 31–86. According to Neeft's study, our *aryballos*, medium-sized and with Protogeometric traditions, would be situated in the *mu* group (Neeft 1987, 44).
2. On the funerary symbolism of the serpent, see Hampe 1960, 58. As a domestic animal and animal of the gods: Olmos 1998.
3. On the serpent as the guardian of the *pharmacon* that confers immortality, and on the myth of Glaucus in Attic imagery of the fifth century B.C., especially in Sotades, see Hoffmann 1997, 123. On its association with chthonic deities: Hoffmann 1997, 133.

R.O

5. *Protocorinthian olpe with animal frieze*

Inv. no. 1999/99/28

H: 28.2 cm; maximum width: 19 cm; diameter
at foot: 8.1 cm

Corinth. Late Protocorinthian

Circa 630–620 B.C.

The *olpe*, a jar with a circular mouth
popular in Corinthian ceramics, as
shown here, is a direct imitation of a
luxurious metallic form. Certain characteristics evoke the bronze prototypes
from the eastern Mediterranean, for
instance the triple handle finished in a
rounded shape that protrudes from the
lip. The white rosettes on the handle
and neck are reminiscent of silver
encrustations. One rosette, inside the
lip, echoes the riveting of the handle on
metal prototypes. The moulding that

separates the neck from the body resembles the articulation of bronze plates.
The elongated tongues in red, white,
and black that hang down toward the
body, in the manner of flower petals, are
also echoes of metallic decoration.

The body is articulated in friezes.
A frieze of animals, quadrupeds
proceeding to the right, surrounds the
belly of the vase. In contrast with other
vases of this style, there are no vegetal
motifs or additional ornamentation to
distract from the animal frieze. The
ivory-colored clay makes the black
figures stand out prominently. A touch
of red between the incisions highlights
the neck and front of the body of each
animal: it isolates and defines the head.
Each animal is rendered using very fine
incisions, giving them life and sense
(snout, ears, eyes, claws, tail, belly). The

final result is not so much corporeal unity as it is the sum of diverse forces.

There are six animals in the frieze. The artist drew the figures from left to right, spacing them respecting each one's place. The first three are a feline (lion or panther), a deer, and another feline. But on reaching the fourth animal (a wild goat or bearded ibex with powerful, twisted horns) the artist had to recalculate the remaining free space by squeezing the three remaining figures, even superimposing them. The male goat grazes the tail of the lion in front, and the feline that follows must contract its body and walk with its tail between its legs, the remaining room being then occupied by a last goat. There is equilibrium, based on contrasting animals, on the space that is dedicated to the diversity of nature: alternating the felines with herbivores, either goat or deer.

The animal world is conceived as a juxtaposition of individuals. Each is in its own element. No explicit aggression is apparent, nor is there any mythological narration—that would require the intervention of man. These are perceptive animals, for instance the deer is illustrated with a long neck, its eyes and muzzle attentive and ears stiffened.

In the Orientalizing period, the animal kingdom displays its immense decorative and seductive power. It awakes the visual pleasure and fantasy that lives in everyone. The large feline, an exotic animal in Greece, represents the far-away, inhospitable land in which the human footprint must never make its mark. It is also a heroic, powerful

expression of nature. Its juxtaposition to more familiar animals—goats and deer, which inhabited the mountains and were hunted regularly—amplifies the view of a varied animal kingdom, a virgin world now open to the imagination of travellers and merchants. Besides its ornamental value, the contiguity and peaceful appearance of the predator and prey alludes to a divinity who governs the reproduction and multiplication of beasts, as well as their extinction, to its will. She could be Artemis, the goddess of the beasts, who oversees both the peaceful coexistence of predator and prey and their struggles and death. The wild setting is appropriate in this symbolic vessel meant to be used by aristocrats at banquets.

PROVENANCE:

Várez Fisa Collection.

PUBLICATIONS:

Cabrera 2003, no. 30.

NOTES:

1. On shape: Payne 1931, 32 and 271–272. For classification and date: Amyx 1988; on the early Corinthian periods see also Benson 1989.
2. On the animal style: Rasmussen 1991, 72–74.
3. Lloyd 1966. On Artemis, Lady of the Beasts, see Simon 1980, 169–170.

P.C.

6. *Corinthian aryballos with komasts*

Inv. no. 1999/99/33

H: 11.9 cm; maximum width: 10 cm; diameter
   at rim: 4.9 cm

Corinth. Early Corinthian

Painter of New York *Komasts*

620–600 B.C.

The decoration on this Corinthian *aryballos* is orientalizing: a succession of tongues around the disk, along the shoulder, and on the base evokes the sepals of a flower. A metaphor seen in the perfume container, the geometric motifs are relegated to a secondary position: a vertical zigzag on the handle and a horizontal frieze that separates the shoulder from the body, on which the principal scene is painted.

Around the spherical body of the *aryballos* dance five individuals in a field of variegated rosettes. They wear short tunics, painted red over the black glaze. Bands decorated with white points belt the garments at waist and thigh. What stands out is the figures' grotesque appearance, their enlarged bellies and buttocks. Their long hair, held back with a diadem adorned with white points and placed on their foreheads, and their heavy beards accentuate their strange appearance, somewhere between comic and demonic. The artist intentionally exaggerates the contrast between the static and heavy parts of the body (stomach, buttocks, thighs) and the hands, arms, and legs (responsible for movement) that are shown as elongated, slight and flexible.

Four of these figures are shown in an orderly line, repeating the same positions and movements: oriented toward the left, the legs flexed and feet resting on the ground, they lift their right arm in front of their face and extend the left behind the buttocks. Only one figure has his left arm resting on his waist. The fifth individual faces the four others, although his head is turned completely around to contemplate an object or large rosette placed behind his back.

These are the so-called padded dancers, the "dancers of the heavy bellies," figures which are usually seen on perfume containers and drinking vessels. Very often, they are represented along with elements relating to wine (drinking horns, *kantharoi*, pitchers) and always dancing, sometimes accompanied by the music of the *aulos*. Their main activity is the dance, orderly or spontaneous, occasionally obscene. Their gesticulations are intented to emulate and propitiate the growth of the vegetation that surrounds them. Their dance is mimetic, but also represents self-abandon and transformation. A "divine" spirit has invaded them, the spirit that lives in the sacred drink, in the dance, and in the fertile activity of the germination that has taken place before them. Thus they have acquired a demonic aspect, accentuated by their grotesque appearance. They have gone beyond the limitations of the human to acquire a naturalness that is made up equally of animal and vegetative aspects, areas never radically separated in Greek thinking.

In this celebration, this feast of fertility and vegetation that the *komasts* simulate, are elements that some authors have likened to theatrical origins: the grotesque garb, the mimesis, the transformation evoked by the wine and the music, sometimes the *agon*, the competition surrounding the dance. As such, the disposition of the figures on our *aryballos* suggests a group performance directed by a leader, the

komast, at the head of the orderly line who turns his head backward, gazing intently and with wonder at the vegetative epiphany that the dance of the chorus has propitiated. What predominates in this scene is the demonic, liminal aspect of these beings. They are fused with nature, a characteristic that is not totally unkown in the theater, but that is expressed in a more immediate wild and cultural setting.

What the grotesque *komasts* on this *aryballos* also show us is that perfume, like wine, possesses a magical, transformative power that, used with wisdom, can help humans transcend mortality to reach a new life.

PROVENANCE:

Várez Fisa Collection.

PUBLICATIONS:

Cabrera 2003, no. 33.

NOTES:

1. On the Corinthian *aryballos* of the orientalizing style, and especially on the *aryballos* with "Dickbauchtänzer" or "padded dancers," see Payne 1931, 289, nos. 528–537; Amyx 1988, 441. Our *aryballos* can be attributed to Painter of New York *Komasts* (Amyx 1988, 113, pl. 47, 1 and 2) who uses the same decorative scheme and whose *komasts* are identical to those on this vase. This artist also uses the band of white points to cinch the *chitons* over waist and thigh, and the same diadem to hold back the hair. Seeberg 1971 is fundamental, especially his study on Corinthian vases with images of these grotesque *komasts*.

2. Much has been written about the significance of these figures. The initial identification of the "Dickbauchtänzer" as the precursors of satyrs

or *silenoi*—Brommer 1937, 21f; Buschor 1943—is now considered antiquated and without validity: Simon 1976, 68, no. 49. Payne 1971, 122, supposed that they were human beings enacting a ritual, and Schnabel 1910 and Webster 1970 that they were actors, because on the Dummler krater they appeared to be related to masks. For Hampe 1975 these are not masks but grotesque expressions produced as a result of imbibing wine. Other authors have thought that the activities represented, is a cultural ritual related to animal and vegetative fertility. See Payne 1971, 121; Kunze 1932, 122; Herter 1947, 10f.

3. On the dances of the grotesque *komasts*, connected to agrarian rituals, as primitive antecedents of theater and their prototheatrical elements, see Brommer 1937 who sees in them a precedent for satirical drama, or Simon 1972, 41f who sees rather, a precedent for comedy. For the identification of the dance with the *Kordax*, see Hampe 1975, 96 especially for the "Dickbauchtänzer" of the Dummler krater. On feasts and agrarian rituals, and their connection with these personages, see also Rodríguez Adrados 1983, 437f.

P.C.

7. *Corinthian alabastron with monsters*

Inv. no. 1999/99/35
H: 26 cm; maximum width: 12 cm; diameter
  at foot: 5.8 cm
Corinth. Early Corinthian
Panther-bird group
Circa 610–590 B.C.

Starting at the end of the eighth century B.C., distinct regional styles start to appear in Greek ceramics. Each

area develops its own compositions and has its own decorative schemes. It is also at this time that Greek art enters into the Orientalizing period. The Corinthian workshops are the first to develop an ornamental style greatly inspired by Near Eastern motifs that could have reached Greece through the importation of luxurious woven textiles (that are only mentioned in written descriptions). The superimposed friezes or the fillng motives like dots or rosettes that decorate these Corinthian vases could be an evocative echo of the eastern Mediterranean and Near East.

This *alabastron* follows a form that was very popular in the preceding period. In the first phase of Corinthian

vase painting, the Protocorinthian, perfume vases were very small, but our *alabastron* is large enough to have enough space for the artist to arrange the decoration in two friezes. Imaginary and real animals share the same space, but the painter has made those in the same category vertically coincide. The painter has displayed the two that are walking to the right in a row above, while the ones below turn their heads toward the viewer. Thus, on the upper part of the vase we find a duck, perhaps a swan, and in the lower frieze, an owl with large eyes; ordinary, even domestic animals. If we rotate the vase, we come upon fabulous beings from far-away lands, as exotic as the perfume that

would have been contained in this vase. On the upper part, we see a siren whose unfurled wings cover the major part of the surface of the vase. The female face gazes toward the right. Under this is seen a frontal view of a panther's face that crowns a bird's body with extended wings.

In addition to the black paint and the incision that outlines the interior detail, we find red paint in the body and the face of the siren, in the central part of the head of the panther, and in the owl, as well as red points in the neck of the swan and around the eyes of the owl. Red lines and white dots add color to the unfurled wings of the monsters. The base is filled in completely with dots and large black rosettes with incised details.

Two rows with alternating dots, like a checkerboard between painted lines, decorate the shoulder and serve to separate the two friezes. On the neck and on the base are black tongues, and a simple line of dots decorates the lip; the upper part is decorated with another frieze with projections between two bands.

PROVENANCE:
Várez Fisa Collection.

PUBLICATIONS:
Cabrera 2003, no. 34.

NOTES:
1. See, for example, a very similar vase in Amyx 1988, 93–4, pl. 43.
2. Regarding Corinthian ceramics, see, for example: Benson 1989; and Rasmussen 1991, 37–78.

C.S.

8. *Corinthian oinochoe with animal frieze*

Inv. no. 10.791

H: 19 cm; maximum width: 16 cm

Corinth. Middle Corinthian

Dodwell Painter

590–570 B.C.

The *oinochoe* with a trilobate mouth, and a wide short neck, thin elevated handle and thin base, is characteristic of the Corinthian workshops of the Orientalizing period. It belongs to the type A broad-bottomed *oinochoai*, whose origin dates back to the Geometric period, and which evolved through the seventh and sixth centuries B.C. toward thinner forms with ever-narrower necks and increasingly square shape. It retains its lid, which is adapted to the trilobate mouth and is varnished in black.

There are two friezes separated by a row of double dots, perhaps a stylized geometrical depiction of a vegetation. The frieze on the shoulder shows two swans facing each other in a heraldic posture; their necks are bent down in order to adapt to the space afforded them in the frieze. The plumage of their wings, incised, is highlighted with touches of red paint. The large round eyes and their big feet confer expressiveness to these birds. Behind them, two powerful panthers, facing forward with tails upright, complete the composition. Rosettes of various sizes occupy the space around the animals.

The frieze on the body has a row of animals immersed in a space filled with a disorderly array of rosettes. Long-horned goats and muscular panthers facing outward towards the spectator perhaps represent a peaceful state of co-existence between herbivorous and carnivorous elements, allowed by the goddess of nature, Artemis. A small bird, with its head turned backward, sits alone among the beasts. There is no violent action, only repose and a demonstration of multiple natures, each one isolated in its own sphere. What is shown here is a liminal, wild, and uncultivated world, unknown to the violent human; a world where beasts are immersed in exuberant vegetation, an expression of the infinity of life, demonstrating a powerful potential governed by the gods, and of a space and time that is sacred and fruitful.

On the lower part of the body a wide band of paint and a radiating frieze complete the decoration.

PROVENANCE:
Oriental Expedition Collection.

PUBLICATIONS:
CVA Madrid 1, IIIc, pl. 4, 6.

NOTES:

1. For the shape of the *oinochoe*, see Amyx 1988, 482–483. For the Dodwell Painter, Payne 1931, 63, 305; Amyx 1988, 205f. Amyx places another identical *oinochoe* from Madrid, M.A.N. 10.793, "close to the Dodwell Painter"; nevertheless, he does not recognize the one shown here even though it is very similar. The animal figures and the rosettes of our *oinochoe* are very representative of this artist, as are the composition and the decorative structure found in his *oinochoai* with flat bases.

P.C.

9. *Fikellura amphora with animal friezes*

Inv. no. 1999/99/40

H: 31.7 cm; diameter at mouth: 17.5 cm;
      diameter at foot: 11.4 cm

Miletos

Circa 550 B.C.

Amphora with rounded lip, narrow conical neck, flattened shoulder, ovoid body and ring base. The handles and the molding that joins the neck to the shoulder recall metallic models. The surface of the vase is covered with a creamy white slip.

The lip is decorated with a garland of ivy and alternating dots. The neck is treated differently on each side: a braided tripod cable on one side, a meander with a checkerboard pattern

divided by cross-shaped arms on the other. On the neck above the shoulder is a frieze of tongues; a necklace of vegetation, counterpoint to the vegetal frieze of flowers and lotus buds on the foot of the vase. A *guilloche* (braided cable) encircles the upper part of the body while a frieze of crescents (oriented toward the left) decorates the lower part. Small dotted bands outline the two figural friezes.

The shoulder frieze is divided into two panels by the handles. These panels have similar compositions (two sphinxes flanking a bearded wild goat, or ibex, with twisted horns), but in one case a second goat appears in the encircling band at the foot of the handles. Because of lack of space, half of the second goat figure looks as if kneeling and appears to be exhausted. Purple

On the main frieze two ferocious dogs with sharp snouts pursue their prey: the first one chases two hares, the second chases a single hare, a male goat, and two spotted deer. The sensation of terror of the prey is seen in their large round eyes, shown in silhouette. The front paws of all the animals never touch the ground, such is the urgency of the chase. A bird with large feet and unfurled wings is introduced into this violence, perhaps a crane that wants to participate in all this *agon*, or that attends, impassively, awaiting future death. Small stems and rosettes in the background, and sinuous vegetation sprouts under some of the animals indicate the wild terrain where the hunt takes place.

Both scenes introduce us to the violence of death and the tension and confrontation that governs nature. The scenes are parallel but also hierarchically differentiated. In the upper frieze the hunt takes place in the fantastic world of hybrid monsters, while on the lower frieze a real hunt is depicted.

The vases of the Fikellura style, a creation of Milesian potters and painters and heir to the decorative orientalizing style of the "Wild Goat" style, reveal the technical, stylistic, and iconographic influence of contemporary Attic black figure. Really, the influences moved in both directions. These luxurious vases were distributed by means of aristocratic commerce through the islands of the eastern Mediterranean (especially Samos and Rhodes), the central Mediterranean, and the Black Sea. Through this commerce, styles and motifs were spread and adopted by

paint adorns the hindquarters of the animals, and the shoulders and the wings of the sphinxes. On one side of the vase the two hybrid beings lift their front paws to touch the kneeling herbivore, apparently exhausted from being hunted. On the other side, only one of the sphinxes is in this position while the other moves forward. The posture of these sphinxes is, like their nature, intentionally ambiguous. Their posture is deadly as well as procreative, attacking and protecting at the same time, since these demonic beings have the power to give and take away life. In this liminal world, where the fantastic exists alongside reality, where the beasts with magic powers dominate, life and death are not total opposites. Only there, those that have been prey will become fruitful again, seed of new life. Their attitude is that of a vigilant watchman that protects this sacred place, the territory of a divinity that governs nature.

diverse production centres, for instance Athens, Laconia and Etruria, which, in the second half of the sixth century B.C., inspired by these orientalizing vases, revitalized their techniques and repertoire.

PROVENANCE:
Várez Fisa Collection.

PUBLICATIONS:
Cabrera 2003, no. 40.

NOTES:
1. The decorative scheme of our amphora is characteristic of the Lion Group defined by Cook 1933–34, 5–8. The central frieze is located on the shoulder, where normally an herbivore is attacked by carnivores or griffins. A secondary frieze of animals—dogs chasing hares, goats or deer—is depicted in the central part of the belly. The rest of the body is filled with narrow bands, some with crescents. A shoulder frieze very similar to the one here is found in other groups (E1, F2 and T4), all connected stylistically to the Lion Group.
2. The same decorative scheme for the border, neck and lower part of the vase is found in an amphora from Tarquinia: Cook 1933–34, D1. The sphinxes are very similar to ours, with the hair falling in hunks over a reserved area. The band of meander and squares that adorns the bottom part of the shoulder in the Tarquinian amphora is a linear development of the neck motif on our vase. They may belong to the same workshop.
3. Cook's study (1933–34) has been amplified by Schaus 1986, 251–295, especially as regards the work attributed to the Painter of Altenbourg and the Painter of the Running Satyrs.

P.C.

10. *Chalkidian eye cup*

Inv. no. 10.909
H: 8.5 cm; diameter: 26 cm
Chalkidian black figure
From Vulci, Etruria?
Circa 530 B.C.

The realm of Dionysos transforms cups, amphoras, and wine jugs into protective masks and strange spaces. The vessel acquires an anthropomorphic expression, or even a demonic identity. This phenomenon in the ceramic arts was well-known in the second half of the sixth century B.C. In particular, the Attic and Chalkidian workshops (the exact location of this last workshop is a matter of debate) were responsible for the spread of these cups throughout the central Mediterranean. They were frequently found in Etruscan tombs.

The two faces of this cup show a similar motif. The spatial order is identical. Two large eyes and a broad powerful Silenean nose mark the axis of this singular Dionysian transformation. A white touch for the eyelids and red on one of the concentric circles of the eye add intensity to the magical gaze.

There is an allusion to the engendering space of nature, which the cup synthesizes around the masks. Above the nose, an eagle is descending rapidly as an expression of omen, not only with the direction and turns of its flight, but also with the voice emanating from its open beak. Movement and noise are its divine signs. The serpents, mouths open wide to show fangs and forked tongues, provide a counterpoint to the sky and bird as they slither next to the eyes. The Greek *drakon*, dragon, ties in with their mythic nature. Eagle and serpent, representatives of two opposing kingdoms, are irreconcilable enemies in ancient Greek thinking. Perhaps what is being alluded to here is an imminent confrontation.

The metamorphical serpents are suspended on the strong upraised vines that grow next to the handles. The dragon is a demon that inhabits and protects the sacred tree, a motif that in Greek mythology extends to the liminal, extreme spaces of the earth. In this distant space are a bearded man and a woman, both naked, she originally painted in white. The woman is fleeing, but at the same time accepting. She raises a hand in an expressive gesture and turns her head to face her pursuer. The motif is repeated four times, with hardly any variation. However, at one point the masculine figure is a satyr, with a long tail and abundant beard. The four women have very prominent buttocks and they receive the phallus from behind. This callipygian expression underscores the generative sexuality in this marginal space that Dionysos occupies. The man's feet rest on the serpent, the woman's on the vine, a contact and physical interchange move the vegetative and animal nature of man that appears intentional.

A famous Chalkidian eye cup by the Phineus Painter, in Würzburg, is decorated in the interior with the scene of nymphs bathing as they are spied on by satyrs with erect phalluses, ready to assault them. Possibly they represent the theme that we have discussed here. In an Etruscan tomb this liminal space is also the space of death. But, unfortunately, we don't know the origin or context of our cup.

Small, reserved circle in the interior. A band in red marks the molding that separates the foot from the body. The profile of the foot, concave and open, similar to the base of an Ionic column, is characteristic of these Chalkidian cups.

The flesh-colored eyes and female forms in white applied over a black base, have disappeared; only a matte trace remains.

PROVENANCE:

Marquis of Salamanca Collection.

PUBLICATIONS:

Álvarez-Ossorio 1910, 103; Rumpf 1927, 37 no. 255, pl 44 and 183; CVA, Madrid 1, III He, pl. 2.5; Beazley Archive Database, no. 14475.

NOTES:

1. On the Chalkidian eye cup of Phineus in the Würzburg Museum, (L 164): Rumpf 1927, no. 20, pl. 40 and 44.

R.O.

11. *Laconian cup with dancing komasts*

Inv. no. 1999/99/45

H: 12.3 cm; diameter at rim: 21 cm; diameter at foot: 7.7 cm

Laconia

Hunt Painter

550–530 B.C.

Cup on a high conical foot, interior surface in the form of a flat disk, tall, convex lip, set off from the bowl at a marked angle, and horizontal handles that are slightly elevated.

The exterior decoration is quite simple in comparison with contemporary Laconian vases. The space between the handles, delimited by two painted lines, is decorated with two intertwined palms, joined at the handles by horizontal stems divided by two vertical incisions. The cup features various friezes with linear motifs, alternating bands of heavy paint and fine lines and rays in diluted glaze or in red. The foot and the handles are painted except for the interior of the foot, which is reserved save for a black band at the very bottom of both the interior and exterior of the foot.

The main decoration is in the tondo of the cup. An *auleter* presides over the scene. Standing to the right, he wears a long tunic, made of fine fabric with undulating pleats. Over it, he wears a short cloak, painted red over the black glaze. His long hair, cinched at the back of the neck, falls in sections along his back. With his right hand he holds and plays the *diaulos*, the double flute. His feet, overtaking the exergue, rest on a column. On either side of the figure, and in tune with the strident, festive music of the *diaulos*, dance two *komasts*, depicted as Attic or Corinthian "padded dancers," whose garb and gestures these figures imitate. They wear short tunics painted in red, fastened at sleeve and thigh, with exaggerated, disproportionate bellies and buttocks. Their hair, fastened with a red ribbon, falls in undulating sections. The *komast* at the left holds a flower above his head; his companion covers his face with his outstretched hand. These gestures give substance to the dance and its purpose: the celebration of a fertility divinity.

The celebration takes place within a religious ceremony and in a sanctuary. The column at the exergue, on which the flautist seems to be perched, could allude to a temple, the sacred retreat. The small birds that heraldically flank the column could be sacred to the divinity. They would also be theriomorphic symbols of that goddess who in Sparta was known as Artemis Orthia. The dance—ecstatic, grotesque, transforming, stimulated by the instrument that induces an orgiastic trance—mimes the growth of vegetation, the fertile action that this goddess governs.

In any case, the dance of the *komasts* can take place within a celebration of the ritual banquet, such as those given in honor of Hyancinth and Apollo in the *Hyakinthia* (Athenaeus, IV, 138e, 139d), or in honor of Artemis, whose festivals could have included ritual foods and orgiastic dances, elements of vegetative and fertility cults. The grotesque appearance of these dancers situates the scene in a demonic realm, a supernatural one, which is propitiated by the divinity who presides over it. The flower that one of them holds, which appears to have bloomed in his hand, is a symbol and model for all vegetative generations, of all fertile growth.

A bird flies swiftly to the left, above the *auleter* and the *komast* on the right. Is it a harbinger of good fortune or simpy a sign of the participation of all of nature in this ritualized activity?

PROVENANCE:
Várez Fisa Collection.

PUBLICATIONS:
Cabrera 2003, no 45.

NOTES:
1. The form (Stibbe's Form VIIIb), the decorative exterior scheme, and the palmettes on the handles of our cup are very similar to those used by the Hunt Painter: Stibbe 1972, 121–150, Abb. 37, nos. 227, 228, 231. The quickness of the drawing shown in the traces of face, hair and anatomical details in our figures is far from the precise style of this artist's best work. (See, for example, Stibbe 1972, nos. 220 and 227, this with *komasts*.) The birds on the exergue, however, are very similar to those of Stibbes' Cup No. 228, also on the exergue and in a similar position. We attribute the cup, thus, to the Hunt Painter.

2. The works of Lane 1933–34, Shefton 1954, and, finally the most complete and recent, Stibbe 1972, are essential to an understanding of the Laconian painters of the Archaic period.

The symposium scenes on some Laconian cups have been connected by Pipili 1987, 71f, with ritual banquets such as those held in honor of Apollo Hyakinthios and Artemis Orthia. The winged demons in these scenes had been identified as "Totenmahl," although, according to Pipili, this would not be appropriate for cups esentially destined to be temple offerings. The large majority of these cups have been found in the Heraion at Samos (Pipili 1998, 86, figs. 3 and 4; 90, note 9). The presence of *komasts* in the frieze below the symposium scene in some of these cups "makes the Totenmahl theory particulary improbable" (Pipili 1987, 72). The demons would indicate a supernatural ambience in these scenes of ritual banquets in honor of fertility deities like Artemis or Hera. They would be "fertility spirits dwelling in the sacred precincts where the symposia must have been held" (Pipili 1987, 73).

3. The scene of *komasts* dancing around a figure who plays the lyre are frequently seen in the cups painted by the Naukratis Painter, the Arkesilas Painter, the Rider Painter, even some of those attributed to the Hunt Painter (Pipili 1998, 91). Our cup is the first in which the central figure plays the *aulos*. Some have wanted to see in it a divinity, Dionysos or Apollo, but Pipili argues that such scenes, like that of the symposium, are associated with a real cultural celebration, and that because many of them have been found on Samos, this figure must be a musician playing at the festival of the Heraia (Pipili 1998, 92).

4. In the temple of Artemis Orthia lead figurines have also been found that represent musicians, both male and female, playing the lyre or *aulos*, and *komasts* performing the common gesture of beating themselves on the buttocks (Smith 1998, 79). The archaic Laconian iconography is the first and only case in which the grotesque *komasts* are used in a dedicatory function, related with the rituals and festivals in honor of Artemis (Smith 1998, 81) or Hera (Pipili 1998, 92).

5. In reference to the wardrobe of Laconian citharists, see, for example: Stibbe 1972, no. 272, 315; and Pipili 1998, fig. 12.

P.C.

12. *Lip cup with hunter and bull*

Inv. no. 1999/99/70

H: 8.8 cm; diameter at rim: 13.9 cm; diameter
    at foot: 5.9 cm

Attic black figure

The Centaur Painter

540 B.C.

Small in size, with extremely fine walls, slightly elevated handles, and a high foot, this "lip cup" is a fine and delicate example of the miniaturist style of cup painters (the so-called "Little Masters") in the middle of the sixth century B.C.

The decoration, the work of the Centaur Painter, is placed at the center of each side. On one side (side A) a young, naked hunter runs toward the left holding a large spear that he will throw at a bull shown on the other side. His other arm is raised and extended for balance when he throws. As is common in this era, head and legs are shown in profile, the torso from the back. At his waist is a sword with a black handle, hanging from a white band that crosses his chest.

On the reverse (side B), a bull faces right, toward the hunter, with its head lowered in a defensive posture. Its legs, firm and tense, are braced against the ground to receive the blow and perhaps in preparation to charge. One long lance is already buried in its neck. Spots of white paint in the form of stars cover its body. They are characteristic of its coat and a sign of the animal's quality and exceptional nature.

The scenes are to be viewed in sequence, for what begins on one side culminates on the other. The Centaur Painter uses this same device on all of his lip cups. He divides the scene into two opposing faces, making it impossible to understand the meaning in a single glance. The game of discovery and surprise, in which one has to turn the cup to scrutinize the opposite side, is appropriate in this convivial, playful setting. Which is the hunter and which is the prey?

Given the work of the Centaur Painter, this is not a banal question. As Schnapp has pointed out, the painter's vases comprise a relatively homogeneous collection of images centered on the pursuit, whether warlike or erotic, in which hunting scenes play an important role. Likewise in this hunter-hunted polarity, the artist constructs unusual narratives where the concept that the hunter of today may later become prey becomes an erotic metaphor.

However, our cup offers significant variations from the Centaur Painter's repertoire. The cup does not show a traditional hunt; the bull, a domestic animal or sacrificial victim par excellence, does not inhabit the uncivilized, wild world of deer or boars. Its territory is not the hunt, but neither the *eschatia*. Its posture is not that of the hunted, but of direct confrontation, waiting to charge the attacker. Nor does the hunter carry traditional weapons, the *lagóbolon* or stones. Instead he uses the spear and, most importantly, the sword. His weapons, his nakedness and his isolation, his solitary confrontation with the beast, which is wounded and ready to attack him, make the scene more of an *agon*, a heroic confrontation, rather than a single hunt. However, both readings are subtly united. The hunt is merely a preparatory exercise and a metaphor of more decisive, singular battles. It is an initiation through which the Athenian youth will learn the techniques of combat, in imitation of heroic

Side A

acts. Could we be looking at a mythic episode: Theseus, the hunter-hero, confronting the bull? Surely not directly—the scene does not depict the capture of the animal with his bare hands, or in direct struggle with the bull, without weapons thrown from a distance, as in heroic feats. But perhaps the metaphor and the reminiscence of the hero are a wink at the game of discovery and the identities discovered during the symposium. The cup proposes multiple readings in this game: the sacrificial animal as prey, the hunter as the adversary in combat, the hunter as hero. These identities could change at any moment, with the predator becoming prey and the prey becoming predator, which can happen in the hunt as well as in battle or in erotic relations. In a funereal context, where many of these cups were found as they were carried far afield, the role reversal could be definitive, charged with eschatological meaning.

PROVENANCE:
Várez Fisa Collection.

PUBLICATIONS:
Cabrera 2003, no. 71.

NOTES:
1. For more on lip cups, see Beazley 1932; Villard 1946, and Boardman 1974, 58.
2. On the Centaur Painter, see Beazley, ABV, 189–190, 689; *Paralipomena*, 78–79 and Jong-kees-Vos 1971, 13–21. For an updated list of works attributed to this painter, see CVA, Amsterdam 2, 67–68. Although the painter has a preference for hunting scenes and hunting pursuits, occasionally he decorates his lip cups with animals that walk or pace in tranquil manner. On one of these cups, he decorated one side with the figure of a bull, the other with that of a boar. Both figures have starred white spots on various parts of the body, a characteristic of this painter which he shares with the Tleson Painter (Heesen 1996, no. 35).
3. For an iconographic analysis of this painter's works, see Schnapp 1997, 257–261.

Side B

4. On the hunt pursuits, heroic or with youths,
   besides the essential work of Schnapp already
   cited, see, for example: Durand and Schnapp
   1984, 49–66; and Vidal-Naquet 1992, 119–148.

P.C.

13. *Band cup with hoplites*

Inv. no. 10.942
H: 18.4 cm; diameter: 28.5 cm; diameter with
handles: 38 cm; diameter of foot: 13 cm
Attic black figure
Circa 520 B.C.

The production of so-called band cups took place between 550 and 520 B.C., around the time of the so-called *komast* cups and Gordion cups. Together with the lip cups, they became extremely popular, as they were produced primarily by some of the most prestigious members of the Little Masters group, such as Tleson or the Oakeshott Painter. They are characterized by a continuous curve without any kind of edge to separate the lip from the body, as in other types of cups, and by a slightly concave lip. The walls are often a bit thicker than those of lip cups, which is why they are generally less fragile. The area of the handles, where the figures have been painted in a miniaturist style, among palmettes, is left in reserve, while the lip is covered with black paint. A reserved band marks the transition between the body and the high foot. In the interior, which is painted, one small medallion is left in reserve, with concentric circles (one in our example) and a central point.

Our example appears to be frag-mentary and was restored up to the point of the left handle. The decoration around the handles is the same on both sides: a frieze delimited by palmettes that originate next to the handles, with three pairs of hoplites that confront one another. Each pair of combatants is separated in turn by a male figure who watches the action, enveloped in a richly decorated mantle. All of them hold a spear and appear to have short hair, perhaps held back with a cord. Not especially carefully, the details are made by incisions—occasionally shaky and imprecise—and added paint, white for the shield devices, the suggestion of the interior of the shield, and the decorative motifs on the mantle. The hoplites, wearing Corinthian helmets with breastplates and cnemides, are immobilized in the movement of attack with lances at the ready. They are differentiated by the armor placed over the short *chiton* (some of the pieces of armor have incised or diluted varnish spirals to mark the pectorals over the *chiton*, though these have barely been conserved). Also the painter shows us the interior of the shields—where he has drawn the handles as well as the *episemas*, the shield devices (tripod or star surrounded by sharp lines). Only one of the hoplites wears a more elaborately designed breastplate; it is worked with fine incisions and overlaid paint. It is interesting to note the presence of small angular symbols located next to the figures that resemble letters. The custom of inscribing the names of the figures on band cups was quite common. Here the painter, who perhaps could not write, has created the illusion of writing.

The cup puts us in the masculine sphere and in one of its most typical settings, the banquet or symposium. In this aristocratic setting, the iconography surrounding the world of war and combat, either individual or multiple, was used by vase painters as a vehicle for picturing the aristocracy in a world where virtue is expressed above all in contest.

PROVENANCE:
Asensi Collection.

PUBLICATIONS:
Álvarez-Ossorio 1910, 79, 105; Leroux 1912, 131, no. 58; CVA, Madrid, 1, III HE.3, pl. 2, 2 a-b; Beazley Archive Database, no. 14.434.

NOTES:
1. Regarding black-figure cups in relation to the production of band cups, see Beazley 1932, 187f; Bloesch 1940, Schauenburg 1974; Boardman 1985, 58–62; Vierneisel and Kaeser 1990.

2. The world of war, with its distinct implications and characters, has been extensively covered by Ducrey 1985; Lissarrague 1990b; or Garlan 1999.

M.M.

14. *Amphora with Dionysian masks*

Inv. no. 10.905
H: 40 cm; maximum width: 26 cm
Attic black figure
Antimenes Painter
520 B.C.

Neck amphora with equinoidal border in black. The neck is decorated with a chain of intertwined palmettes and lotus flowers. A frieze of tongues marks the transition between neck and shoulder. On the bottom of the body are three ornamental friezes: meander, lotus buds, and radii.

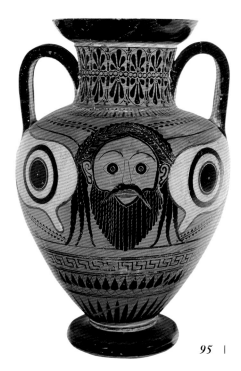

The images that decorate the body of the vase introduce us to the power of Dionysos' gaze. Four masks, all different, scrutinize from all four directions. The frontal face of the god is repeated twice, around the body of the vase, situated between prophylactic eyes. These, two on each face, with elongated tear ducts, have irises with concentric circles painted and reserved. On each face the same motif is repeated: an Archaic mask with long hair in ringlets, bound with a vine of myrtle wreaths, long beard, drawn with undulating incisions, huge almond-shaped eyes with circular irises under eyebrows drawn in an arc. The ears, shown in profile, are at attention and ready to listen. The god is crowned with a circlet of vines. From the mask jut long ivy branches of vines that extend, endlessly, along the surface of the vase.

Under the handles, in the marginal space of the *eschatia*, two satyrs' masks appear. These join the other two and construct a supplementary face, inverted and monstrous.

The multiple masks, the one of the god repeated twice, the satyrs' face, and the mask configured by the great eyes, protect the contents of the amphora, the wine that will be served at the banquet. Its consumption, sanctified by the presence of the god in the sacred liquid and in the images multiplied across the surface of the vessel, would permit and favor transformation, the fusion of he who contemplates and is at the same time contemplated by that unnerving and terribly powerful gaze of Dionysos, god of possession. The *enthousiasmos* provoked by this crossed gaze will give man the divine essence and permit him

to contemplate, risk-free, the impalpable reality of the divine. The contemplation of the god's face, whose unsupportable intensity blinds mortals, is to penetrate the otherness of Dionysos. In the ludic setting of the banquet, the multiple gazes circling the vase simulate the vertigo and hallucinations of drunkenness, opening the door to the world of otherness that the god makes incarnate. An image of the metamorphosis that takes place under the influence of drink, our amphora introduces us to the verbal, musical, and gesturing games that are characteristic of the symposium.

PROVENANCE:

Marquis of Salamanca Collection.

PUBLICATIONS:

Beazley 1956, ABV, 275, 278; CVA, Madrid 1, III HE, pl. 21, 2; Olmos and Sánchez 1988, 84–87; Beazley Archive Database, no. 320148.

NOTES:

1. On the Antimenes Painter, see Burow 1989.
2. For the Dionysian mask, see Frontisi-Ducroux 1984 and 1991.

P.C.

15. *Amphora with the marching Amazons*

Inv. no. 10.921

H: 39 cm; maximum width: 22 cm; diameter
   at rim: 19.5 cm; diameter at base: 14.7 cm

Attic black figure

End of sixth century B.C.

Neck amphora. The upper part of the mouth is reserved. In the interior only the neck is painted; on the exterior,

only the mouth, handles and foot. The neck is decorated with a chain of double palmettes interspersed with lotus flowers in silhouette. On the shoulder is a band of tongues that alternate between black and red. In the space under the handles, four large palmettes are arranged in a square, joined by stems from which lotus flowers emerge. The rest of the body is decorated with the typical radial band of tongues and, above it, an intertwined band of lotus flowers climbing upward.

The action takes place on the two faces of the vase. On each, two Amazons ride horses accompanied by dogs. Their ride is peaceful, the horses walk and the dogs stop to sniff around. These strange beings, who were said to amputate one breast to better position their bows, a belief that probably comes from an etymological study of the word *a-mazon*, without breast, are drawn as normal women, unmutilated and white-skinned.

On our vase we see combinations of different, even contradictory symbols. On the principal face an Amazon leads, armed like an Athenian hoplite. She wears armor, with a short tunic over it, a helmet with a high crest, and has two spears; from her belt emerges the pommel of her sword. Behind her marches another woman, who wears a Scythian cap, and carries a *pelta* or light shield and two spears. On the obverse face the two Amazons wear the Scythian caps, the first carrying two swords and a sheaf of four arrows, the second carrying only two spears.

Thus all types of combat are pictured on our vase, from the most heroic and honorable hopelite combat, to the mixed combat of the *peltast* and archer. There are complementary styles, such as that of the hoplite and archer, but also contrasting ones, such as that of the *peltast*. This impossible scene is here made possible because the Amazons belonged to the realm of the "other," meaning not Greek, but of the world of otherness where masculine and feminine are changeable states. The tension invoked by the mixture of all types of weapons is lessened by the calm demeanor of the women, the slow pace of their horses, the laziness of their dogs. These animals belong to the space of the *oikos*; their presence denotes domestic space, but our dogs are hunters, of the Laconian breed,

famous for their speed and sharp eyesight. Why are they in this scene?

In Archaic hunting scenes, the hunter only appears on foot, with his hunting dogs running beside him. The dogs never go along on mounted hunts. The collective equestrian hunt of the Archaic period seems to make the dog incompatible with the horse. Besides, these scenes featuring riders from the Archaic era are not really scenes of war, as it is generally assumed that special-ized cavalry did not appear in Athenian warfare before the Peloponnesian War. These images of riders were much to the liking of the aristocracy of the period, even though they are neither scenes of war nor the hunt. Our Amazons are depicted as noble aristo-crats, mounted on beautiful horses, "artistically" accompanied by valuable hunting dogs. I think the dog here does not lead us to the domestic realm of the *oikos* but rather to the world of the *aristoi*, the nobles. It is a game of appar-ently contradictory symbols, incompati-ble weapons of war, only possible in the inverted mythical world to which these noble female warriors belong.

PROVENANCE:
Marquis of Salamanca Collection.

PUBLICATIONS:
Álvarez-Ossorio 1910, 78, 104, pl. 27; Leroux 1912, 51–52, no. 75; Schnapp 1997, 243, Fig. 167; CVA, Madrid 1, III HE, 6, pl. 14, 3a-b, pl. 19, 2; Beazley Archive Database, no. 14468.

NOTES:
1. On the subject of war and the hunt: Schnapp 1997, 242f.

2. For *peltasts*, cf. Lissarrague 1990b, 151–193; Bérard and Vernant (eds.) 1984.

3. On the role of dogs in the hunt: Cook 1953, 38–42.

C.S.

16. *Hydria with women at the fountain*

Inv. no. 10.924

H: 45 cm; maximum width: 40 cm

Attic black figure

Painter of the Madrid Fountain

Circa 530 B.C.

The square proportions of this vase are characteristic of this period; in the later years of the century, the proportions tend to become more elongated. The vertical handle, which stands out from the neck, finished in small lateral disks, ends on the shoulder of the vase in an elegant palmette painted in silhouette. Both shapes recall metallic prototypes.

The central scene shows a frontal Doric fountain, with its metopes and pediment empty. The fountain, near the city limits, represents a border between country and city, nature and culture. Girls fill their *hydriae*, the same vessel on which this image is painted. The two central figures hold the vases as if they are ready to fill them, but the girl on the right has stopped herself because a child is bathing under the stream of water pouring out of a lion's head. Behind both these girls, two women walk away, carrying their filled *hydriae* vertically atop their heads. The one on the right smells a flower, while from the left another woman approaches with branches in her hand and an empty

hydria held horizontally on her head. The height of the women is varied according to whether or not they carry empty or full *hydriae*.

On the shoulder of the vase a masculine scene contrasts with the feminine scene on the body. To the left a standing man takes his leave, extending his hand to a man seated on a folding chair. The departing warrior carries a spear and his tunic over his shoulders. Behind him a charioteer enters the chariot with the *kentron* or crop in his hand. At the right another man, also seated on a folding chair, completes the symmetry of the composition.

Many theories have been advanced about the significance of these frequently used scenes on *hydriae* dating to the last third of the sixth century B.C. Some see in them images of daily life: women who seek water from a fountain, which perhaps represents (as polit-

ical propaganda) the one Pisistratus had built in Athens. That would explain why the motif disappeared circa 500 B.C. Others try to explain the fact that these women are elegantly dressed in embroidered robes, well-coiffed and carrying branches with which to adorn the fountain, as scenes of feminine rituals in the context of some Athenian festival, such as the *Anthesteria* or *Hydrophoria*. Others do not see a simple quotidian scene or a ritual but rather a type of warning about immodest behavior and the danger that awaits women in this shadowy, liminal place. There are mythical examples: Polyxena attacked at the fountain by Achilles, or the providential appearance of Poseidon at another fountain to save Amymone.

The fountain is a feminine space. In our scene a boy is bathing because children, like Troilus, belong in the female setting. Young women, elegantly dressed and coiffed like the *korai* of contemporary sculpture, play their feminine role in the lovely setting of the fountain, as young men play theirs on their way to war.

Our *hydria* shows the social values of an age group, the young, and a social group, Athenian nobles. Both scenes belong to Athenian imaginary and complement each other: the departure of the young man in a cart, which at this moment is not a war chariot but has heroic, aristocratic value in scenes of this type, and the women of gentle gestures, richly and nobly dressed, who go to the fountain for water. The scene on the shoulders is secondary. The young women occupy the visual attention of the masculine viewer of the *hydria*, who also might have gone to the *andron* during a banquet to add water to the wine.

PROVENANCE:
Marquis of Salamanca Collection.

PUBLICATIONS:
Álvarez-Ossorio 1910, 78, 104, pl. 28; Leroux 1912, 41–42, no. 66, pl. 11; Beazley 1956, ABV, 335.1; Olmos and Balmaseda 1977–78, 50–51; Beazley 1971, *Paralipomena*, 148; Olmos and Sánchez 1988, 52–54, no. 17; Carpenter, Mannack, and Mendonca 1989, 91; CVA, Madrid 1, III HE, 5, pl. 8.4, pl. 12; Beazley Archive Database, no. 301822.

NOTES:
1. On the theory of the fountain as a dangerous place: Bérard 1983, 20f.
2. For the identification and significance of the theme: Dunkley 1935-6, 142; Hannestad 1984, 252f; Manfrini-Aragno 1992, 127–148.

C.S.

17. *Hydria with wedding procession*

Inv. no. 1999/99/68

H: 35.2 cm; diameter at rim: 19.8 cm;
  diameter at foot: 13.1 cm

Attic black figure

In the manner of the Euphiletos Painter

Found in Vulci, Campanari excavations

510 B.C.

The shape of this *hydria* is a perfect example of this design, produced in the the latter years of the sixth century B.C. The shoulder is clearly separated from the body and almost flat. Two small padded rings on the border, next to each handle, maintain the tradtition of the metallic pitchers that it imitates. The lip, neck, inside and out, handles,

and foot are varnished. Rays sprout from the base like the petals of a flower from the bottom part of the vase. In the shoulder panel, there is a frieze of red and black tongues.

On the front shoulder panel is a scene that is not too clearly defined: two young naked riders astride horses that seem to rear at the sudden appearance of two strange personages: two male winged figures dressed in short tunics and animal skins. At the extreme right, a nude young man runs after one of the riders. The scene brings to mind images of Athenian young men who practice horseback riding, the athletic and equestrian exercise that is used in the hunt and in warfare, customary in these times. But, who are these winged creatures? What role do they play among the young men? Their hybrid demonic character, their dress halfway between the savage and the civilized, confers upon them the liminal means to act as mediators, as symbols that facilitate the transition from youth to maturity.

The main scene, outlined by two vertical branches of ivy, represents the *pompe*, the bridal procession that repeats a design that has, through these years, been converted into a fixed formula that barely permits variations. The artists concentrate on the procession that carries the *nymphe*, the bride, from her parents' house to her new home on her *epaulia* or wedding day. The newlyweds are on the narrow chariot that will carry them across the city, through the crowds that attend this social event, to their intended home, their *oikos*. The groom drives the chariot while holding the reins and a long riding whip. In back and partly hidden, is the bride with her head covered by a mantle, in the gesture of *aidos*; yet her virtue and modesty, her feminine charm, shine through. She holds the nuptial crown with one hand and holds on to the carriage with the other. The cortege that accompanies the procession is composed of two women and a citharist. The women carry on their heads the baskets that contain the dowry of the bride, wedding presents for the newlyweds. The long-haired citharist, almost hidden behind the horses, a human replica of Apollo, strums the strings of the instrument, which has white marble sides, with a pick, and regulates the vibrations with his open left hand resting on the strings. On the far right a woman receives the newlyweds with torches in her hands.

The scene slides subtly between the human and the divine sphere. There are no elements that define a mythical wedding ceremony, but the example of the divine weddings is evident. The ceremony celebrates the bride and groom and their betrothal, the perpetu-ation of the political and religious social order of the city under the norm fully sanctioned by the gods. But it is also a public spectacle, an exhibition of *aristeia*, of the quality and qualifications of the newlyweds to enter into the apotheosis or the initiation into a new life. As in all such performances, the *pompe* is accompanied by visual and sound effects whose real impact can only be imagined. The city is lit by torches which dispel the darkness and change night into day. The carriage, the newlyweds, the members of the cortege, dressed and adorned in their colorful finery, the magnificent horses. The wedding ritual exclamations, *Eleleu, Hymen ô Hymenai ô*, the ritual salutations to the newlyweds, the songs of the marriage ceremony accompanied by the music of the cithara or the flute, the clinking of the castanets, the dances of the young friends of the bride or the groom (*Iliad*, XVIII, 490–496; Hesiod, *Shield*, 272–280), the smell of the flaming resin of the torches, the perfume of the myrrh, the cinnamon and the incense (Sappho, Fr. 55D), the lights, the music, the perfume of the *gamos* (wedding), all are elements that affect the senses and confer upon the ceremony a profoundly religious as well as festive character.

PROVENANCE:

Várez Fisa Collection.

PUBLICATIONS:
Eisenberg 1995, No. 71, vol. VIII, 2, 9, no. 95, where the Euphiletos Painter is attributed. Beazley Archive Database, no. 44149; Cabrera 2003, no. 70.

NOTES:

1. On this painter, see Beazley 1956, 321–326. This painter specializes in Panathenaic amphoras. His other vases are part of a lower-quality series, especially his *hydriae*, many of them found at Vulci, like this example. The painter is obsessed with chariot scenes. See, for example, Boardman 1974, 112. On the wedding theme and the nuptial procession, see Bérard 1984, 94; Oakley 1995, 63; and Reeder 1995a, 126–128.

2. For the wedding as spectacle and music, see Brulé 2001, 243–275.

3. Images of the *ephebes* (youths) riding horseback in a procession or hunt can be seen in Schnapp 1984, 67–77; in athletic preparations, see Lissarague 1990b, 205–210 and 217–231, although they refer to red-figure vases.

P.C.

18. *Eye cup with Gorgon*

Inv. No. 1999/99/72

H: 11.7 cm; diameter at rim: 28.2 cm;
    diameter at foot: 11.4 cm

Attic black figure

520–510 B.C.

An eye cup of the A type takes us into the world of illusion, in the game of exchange of glances, to see and be seen, to the metaphor of the vase as a mask, and to the discovery of what those enormous eyes, which give the vase its name, must hide. These eyes decorate both sides of the vase. The eye is in the shape of an almond and the corner of the eye is only shown as a slight appendage of paint, the iris with a white and then a red circle around a black pupil. Two fine, curved lines define the eyebrows. The handles of the cup will be the ears, which, slightly lifted, lend a satirical aspect to the face.

On the other side of the vase, a gorgon runs to the right, with its arms flailing and its knees bent. Its head is a perfect circle, and it is in reality a *gorgoneion* (gorgon mask), a monstrous being with a horrible, terrifying, grotesque visage. Red and black locks of hair, separated by incisions, outline the front of the face. The dilated, round eyes have a petrifying look; the mouth, with a horizontal incision that resembles a terrifying grin; the double

row of teeth, indicated by white dots; the large red tongue; the ears seen from the front; and the bristly beard bring to mind the grotesque and monstrous one of the "Winged Three Sisters with Serpent-like Hair: The Gorgons, to the abhorrent humans." (Aeschylus, *Prometheus Bound*). Two large wings curved upward complete the monstrous image. The white, female body is covered by a short, red tunic, cinched tightly, and an animal skin. It wears what seem to be winged boots.

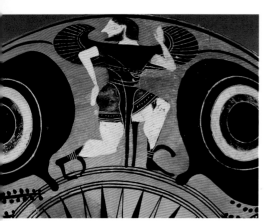

On the other side of the cup a winged, bearded demon, placed between the two large eyes, runs in the same direction. It wears the same costume and shoes as the gorgon, including the white body and the red hair and beard, but it does not look at us directly; instead, it turns its head backward. Under its arms, grapevines with clusters of white dotted grapes sprout, uncontrolled, overflowing, and fill the lower outline of the scene.

Groups of three lines and a radial frieze outlined in profile decorate the foot of the vase. A *gorgoneion*, identical to the one on the side, occupies the tondo of the cup. The wine will cover this image, creating a surprising effect. The bottom of the cup, full of the red liquid, will create a metaphoric image of a sea of wine, a circular frontier beyond which live the Gorgons, and where the gates of Hades open wide.

The gaze of the other is the theme of this cup. The winged demons, the terrible monster and the genius without a name (Death or *Thanatos*?)—of more human form but equally hybrid and because of this, liminal, or barely perceptible—preside over these images and occupy a space between prophylactic and protective eyes, eyes that are also hypnotic when one gazes directly at them. The symposiast, or drinker, will encounter multiple masks: the one of the cup which when drunk, will cover the image of his own face, or of the gorgon that runs, or awaits, hidden below the black sea of the liquid inside the cup, discovered at last in the midst of the optical vertigos and hallucinatory effects provoked by the imbibing of the "fiery liquid," gift of Dionysos. The space of the cup is also an image of otherness: the liminal geography of the underworld, traced by the flights of the gorgons "that inhabit the other side of the famous Ocean, in the limit of the night" (Hesiod, *Theogony* 275), the unnamable kingdom where lurk the hybrid beings, the monsters and the mediating spirits, the vegetal kingdom of magical fruitfulness of Dionysos, the sea of wine in the cup, the black circle of night where death's terrible face awaits. The drink will enable us to cross the limits of the mortal human condition, to explore the territory of the maximum change of the divine and beyond. The eyes will protect the one who goes there, and the demons, reminiscent of the reign of the dead and the limits that will be trespassed, will act as mediators.

PROVENANCE:
Várez Fisa Collection.

PUBLICATIONS:
Sotheby's, Antiquities, London, 12–12–1988, 83, no. 138. Cabrera 2003, no. 73.

NOTES:
1. On the Gorgon and the *gorgoneion* as a female image of transformation and death, see Vernant 1985, 79f; Vernant 1989a and 1989b.
2. On masks shown in vases and their relationship with Dionysian transformation, see Frontisi-Ducroux 1984. On the game of contemplating the Mask of the Gorgon and its association with the world of Dionysos as an aristocratic activity before death, see Díez de Velasco 1995 and 1998.

P.C.

19. *White-ground lekythos with Apollo*
Inv. no. 1999/99/78
H: 27.5 cm; diameter at rim: 5.6 cm; diameter at foot: 5.5 cm
Attic white ground
Workshop of Bowdoin Painter
First quarter of fifth century B.C.

These *lekythoi*, or perfume vessels, known for the white-ground technique, in which the surface is coated with a thick white slip over which the design is painted, were used exclusively in funerary rituals in Athens during the fifth century B.C.

Some of these small jars were decorated in the old, black-figure manner until late in the century. The two techniques coexisted for many years. Certain artists, like the Bowdoin Painter or the Painters of Diosphos and Sappho combine the two forms of painting within the same vase, in which

part of the decoration is in the black-figure technique and other parts are incised. The semi-incised technique is used in our *lekythos*.

The figure of the god Apollo is done in black paint with details incised. The god has unshorn hair and is crowned with a red branch, moving toward the right, looking behind him. His naked body is covered only with a white cloth, done in the red-figure technique, which he wears around his shoulders. He is holding in his left hand his characteristic weapon, the bow with two arrows. Ahead is an animal, probably a deer. Its head and front quarters

are completely gone. In front of the god runs a large vertical inscription containing nine meaningless letters. These inscriptions, which imitate writing and use it as a design element, give the vessel a voice and the importance and prestige of the written word. This nontextual writing guides and accentuates the path of the god.

The interior of the mouth is painted, as are the exterior of the handle, the neck, and the lip. The shoulder is decorated in the black-figure technique with caning and cauliculos. At the top of the neck are black vertical lines in tongue-like shapes. At the bottom is a very well-conserved *miltos* in the red-figure style. The bottom third of the vase and the foot are painted. Only two incised lines mark the beginning and end of the foot's molding.

The scene is framed above by a series of meanders that encircles only the front of the vase and below by a double line of superimposed red paint that surrounds the whole vase. It does not have a false bottom and, so, no firing aperture.

PROVENANCE:
Várez Fisa Collection.

PUBLICATIONS:
From the old Várez Fisa Collection Embirikos (London). Published and attributed in Kurtz 1975, 107, pl. 14, 3; *Kunstwerke der Antike: Munzen und Medaillen*, A.G. Basilea, sale catalogue 40 (13.12.1969), pl. 28, no. 82; Palagia *et al.* 1984, LIMC II, no. 67, pl. 199; Christie's, Manson and Woods, sales catalogue 28–4–1993, no. 23; J. Eisenberg, *Art of the Ancient World, Royal Athena*, sales catalogue 7.2, January 1995, no. 100;

Beazley Archive Database, no. 1434; Cabrera 2003, no. 80.

NOTES:

1. The Bowdoin Painter, named after two white-ground *lekythoi* at Bowdoin College, is also characterized by his peculiar technique of decorating his vases very simply. More than two hundred vases have been attributed to him, most of them featuring a single figure.
2. On the painter: Richter 1946, 74–5.
3. On the technique of semi-incision: Kurtz 1975, 105–6; Robertson 1992, 130.
4. On nonsensical inscriptions, see Lissarrague 1992, 196–7.

C.S.

20. *Bilingual amphora*

Inv. no. 11.008

H: 61 cm; maximum width: 37 cm

Attic black figure and red figure

Potter: Andokides. Painter: Psiax

From Vulci, Etruria

530 B.C.

This bilingual amphora is the work of two great, innovative artists, the potter Andokides, in whose workshop the red-figure style was invented, and the painter Psiax. The signature of the first, ANDOKIDES EPOESEN, is incised on the foot. The type-A amphora is characteristic of the monumental works in which the new technique was perfected. Two panels on the shoulder of each face are decorated with figures, one in black figure, the other in red figure. Friezes of stylized vegetative motifs make up the subsidiary decoration. Branches of ivy decorate the exterior of the handles, and a frieze of radiating petals the lower

part of the vase, over the foot. Under the handles are two red-figure palmettes finished in spiral tendrils.

The contrast between the two faces is due not only to the technique used, but also to the choice of iconographic themes: the transgressing Dionysian world, expressed through the magnificent epiphany of the god before his cortege, painted in the black-figure technique, and an Olympian assembly surrounding the seductive music of Apollo, in the new red-figure technique.

A static Dionysos presides over the image on side A, a symmetrical, balanced scene in which the god serves as the axis and nucleus of the composition. He wears a *himation* and a long *chiton* and his long hair is bound by a crown of ivy. His body is shown in

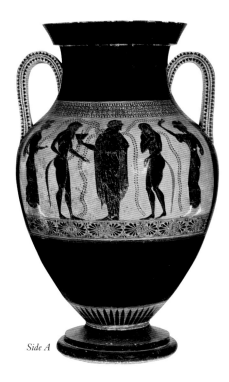

Side A

profile facing toward the right, as he turns his face back to contemplate one of the satyrs in his cortege. The god presents a *kantharos* filled with the sacred liquid to a second satyr, who contemplates, ecstatically, the marvelous contents of the vase. From his right hand surge ivy branches that, endless and fecund, extends upward and to the sides, up to the edges of the scene, inundating with immortal greenery the space of the Dionysian *parousia* and imbuing the members of the divine cortege with its renewing and generative power.

At both sides of the god are two satyrs with long tails, heavy beards and pointed, equine ears. The one on the right, shown in profile, stares at the wine the god is offering as a gift to man, instrument of Dionysian possession and enthusiasm. His gestures are fixed in the moment of contemplation; his large, fine fingers, drawn with calligraphic precision, are joined to accompany the dialogue with the god. The satyr on the left turns his frontal face toward the spectator, a face converted into a mask, whose gaze establishes an intimate connection with the viewer. This vision anticipates the transformation caused by the Dionysian ritual and the wine that this very amphora contains. In the mirror of the image, our self acquires a new identity, after submerging itself in the face of the satyr, around whom sprout the most bestial and savage aspects of our personality; such is the subversion that Dionysos and his followers make incarnate.

At the edges of the scene dance two maenads painted in white, though the paint has disappeared on the faces.

Both direct their gaze toward the god; the one on the left shakes in her raised hand the *crotala*, which mark the beat of the frenetic dance so characteristic of the Dionysian setting. Situated on the edges, these figures express the marginalization of the maenads and the feminine world.

The image introduces us to a somnolent and suspended time of the Dionysian realm, in which the marvelous ephiphany of Dionysos and the encounter with his followers has momentarily suspended the orgiastic tumult of the *thiasas*, yet is shyly recorded by the dance of one of the maenads. This contained expression of the Dionysian ritual certainly accompanies the solemnity of the Olympian scene represented on side B. Nevertheless, the two worlds could not be more opposite, as is the music that is played in both scenes: strident, festive, ecstatic in one; cultured, calm and elitist in the other.

On side B the gods hurry to this Olympian assembly, attracted by the charming sounds of Apollo's *cithara*. The god, shown as a young man with long hair gathered at the nape, model of *ephebes*, wears a long, transparent *chiton*, under which his athletic form is visible. He holds a heavily decorated *cithara* that he plays with one hand, while with his left he regulates the sound. In front of him are his mother, Leto, and Ares; at the right, behind him, is his sister, Artemis. Leto, dressed in fine transparent *chiton* and *himation*, with long hair held back with a diadem that falls in ringlets over her breast, is an image reminiscent of the contempo-

This vase presents an iconographic program surrounding two contrary religious and ritual aspects that are nevertheless essential in the cultural and social universe of the Athenian *polis*. The music, instrument of *paideia*, recalls the citizenry's *ethos* and transformation.

PROVENANCE:
Marquis of Salamanca Collection.

PUBLICATIONS:
Álvarez-Ossorio 1910, pl. 8 and 29; Leroux 1912, 63; Beazley 1963, ARV2, 1 and 7, No. 2, with bibliography; Beazley 1971, 128, 321; Olmos 1973; Carpenter, Mannack and Mendonca 1989, 77, 150; CVA, Madrid 1, III HE, pl. 23,1; 24, 1–2; 25, 1–2; 26, 1.

Side B

NOTES:
1. On bilingual vases, see Cohen 1978.
2. On Apollo playing the lyre in the presence of Artemis and Leto, see Dumas 1984; LIMC I, 261f, nos. 630–666.
3. On the Dionysian iconography, see Gasparri 1986, LIMC III, 509–512; Carpenter 1986 and 1997.
4. About the figure of Dionysos, see, especially, Otto 1960; Kérenyi 1976; Jeanmaire 1978.
5. Regarding music and musical education, see Bélis 1988; Gentili and Pretagostini 1988; West 1992.

P.C.

rary marble *korai*, in terms of the figure and drapery. Ares is dressed as a warrior, with a Corinthian helmetideally raised over his face, a great round shield, decorated with a black rooster, greaves for protecting his legs, and a short tunic. Artemis, the virgin huntress, wears a long *chiton* and drapes her shoulders with the hide of a panther, whose front feet are tied across her chest while the hind legs fall down her back, along with her quiver. The three gods, their heads inclined in rhythm with the music, looking at Apollo intently, follow the melody, snapping their fingers, subjugated by the delicious and seductive tones coming from the divine instrument.

21. *Cup with the Kottabos player*

Inv. no. 1999/99/82

H: 9 cm; diameter at rim: 24 cm; diameter
    at foot: 9.7 cm

Attic red figure

Epiktetos

Circa: 490 B.C.

Type B cup. On the upper part of the
foot is an unpainted incised line, as on
the bottom of the foot and the base.
The exterior background is painted
except for a wide band along the base
and at the cone of the foot.

The tondo represents a mature,
bearded symposiast, in the characteristic
pose of the banquet. His torso is uncovered and his *himation* rests on his hip.
He reclines on the *kline* (couch) and
rests his left elbow on a cushion. He is
crowned with a ribbon and a garland of
white flowers, of which only a trace
remains. The artist shows the symposiast with his mouth open, perhaps in
song, or shouting out the words of the
inscription described below. The
symposiast is playing a game of *kottabos*.
His index finger is laced through the
handle of a cup (filled with wine) that
he must twirl so as to toss the dregs of
wine accurately at a predetermined
target. In his left hand is another cup,
and yet a third one sits on the ground
beneath him. To the left rests a knobby
staff, attesting to the mature age of the
symposiast, and an amphora. The
amphora contains pure wine. It has
taken the place of the krater, which was
often used in the *andron* or banquet
hall. An inscription in white, now barely
legible, runs along the bottom of the

medallion. It probably reads
EGPOIESEN OIE. There are remains of
the preliminary, but uncorrected
sketches. Diluted glaze is used to mark
the muscles of the torso.

On side A, Epiktetos paints a
favorite motif: Heracles's killing a
centaur. The hero is not bearded, lacks
his lion headdress, and fights with his
sword. His image is not much different
from that of Theseus, but here an
incomplete inscription provides an
identification: ERA:::ES. On either side
of the hero, two symmetrical centaurs
with pointed ears, flat noses and long
beards approach laden with enormous
stones. In the center, Heracles, sword in
hand, fights with a centaur who defends
itself with an enormous branch, the
leaves of which have been painted in
white. The central centaur is bald, as is
his companion at right; he crouches,
poised to attack, with his front legs
firmly planted on the ground.

Both the leaves of the branch and
the garland that crowns Heracles are
painted white. The hind legs of the
flanking centaurs extend almost to the

handles. Under one of the handles is a large leaf that does not appear under the other handle.

Side B: At either end two women dressed in *chiton* and *himation* gesticulate in fear and flee from a man. In the center, behind an altar crowned with volutes, another woman runs to the right and looks behind her, toward her pursuer. She is crowned with a white ribbon and has her hair up, as does the woman on the left. The bearded pursuer runs toward her, his leg in front of the altar. The man wears a short tunic and has a sheathed sword. An inscription in red runs along the bottom of the cup. Although it is poorly preserved, the words EPOIESEN can be read. Traces of the original sketch can be seen, in which the woman's right leg is clearly visible, whereas in the final painting the leg is hidden behind the altar.

The scene probably represents the encounter between Menelaus and Helen. The man has invaded a religious place when a sacrifice was being performed, as the traces left on the altar indicate. Here is the initial moment when Helen is surprised and Menelaus has not yet unsheathed his sword, which he later drops when Helen uncovers her breast, and he is astonished by her beauty.

The two sides have a subtle relationship. On side B, Helen may be sacrificing in a domestic setting, as happens occasionally. This contrasts with the wild scene on the other face, appropriate to an encounter with centaurs. Menelaus and Heracles are the two heroes who combat evil, treachery, gluttony. The centaurs violate the hospital-

ity that Pholos had offered Heracles, just as Paris violated Menelaus's hospitality in Sparta. The centaurs, monstrous beings (half-animals, bald, and flat-nosed), cannot be contained when the wine is uncorked and its aroma wafts through the forest. Possibly wine is the red liquid in side B that still flows off the altar and which had been drunk by the women—in this case sacred drink. Wine can make one wild, as it did the centaurs, if it is drunk in its pure state, just as it flows from the amphora of our symposiast in the central medallion of the cup.

Side A

Side B

PROVENANCE:

Várez Fisa Collection.

PUBLICATIONS:

Cahn 1995, No. 14; Cabrera 2003, No. 86.

NOTES:

1. See a very similar cup painted by Epiktetos, with the centaur and Heracles, in Boardman 1975, no. 72 (although here the hero carries a club and not a sword).

2. On Epiktetos see Robertson 1992, 17 and 18.

3. Regarding the encounter between Menelaus and Helen, see, for example, Boardman 1975; Kahil and Icard 1988; LIMC IV, 463–563; Hedreen 2001, 57f.

4. On the *centauromchia*, see, for example: Vollkommer 1988; Dubois 1994.

5. On the *kottabos*, see, for example: Sparkes 1960, 202–207.

6. On images of symposiasts with incriptions, see, for example: Lissarrague 1987, 119–137.

7. Regarding the inscription of the medallion upon which a man plays at *kottabos*, the inscription ETPOIESEN OIE has been read, or, otherwise, ETHOIESEN AIE. I would like to thank Professors Ricardo Olmos and Adolfo Domínguez Monedero for their help in reading this complex inscription. As well, Professor Alberto Bernabé has helped me with his understanding of it and has made some very valuable suggestions. So, ETPOIESEN could be the aorist tense of the verb EKPOIEW, which means, among other things, "it is finished" or "he completed it," or "it was sufficient." Professor Bernabé suggests that the inscription does not so much refer to the potter or painter, so much as if refers to the *kottabos* player. In other words, the meaning would be that the symposiast received enough points, that he played well. His performance is what is celebrated with words. The inscription here would

therefore refer to the points gained. The following word, if it were AIE, could be the vocative of a divine god. Or, there is another possibility: the imperative of the aorist of AEIAW "have fear" "begin trembling," but I think it is more probable that it is an exclamation, a cry. OIE, EUAI. and EIAI have been documented, according to Professor Bernabé as Bacchic exclamations; not OIE, but as Bernabé points out, exclamations do not necessarily follow the rules. In our vase the exclamation referred to the moment of joy at the triumphant end of the game.

C.S.

22. *Nolan Amphora with warriors*

Inv. no. 11.118

H: 34 cm; maximum width: 18 cm; diameter at rim: 12.7 cm; diameter at base: 8.8 cm

Attic red figure

Berlin Painter

Circa 480 B.C.

The Nolan Amphora is a type of amphora that is small and sparely decorated. It is totally glazed except for two small reserved lines that mark the molding that separates the body from the foot. Our vase has been decorated by one of the best and most prolific painters of the red-figure technique, the Berlin Painter, to whom almost three hundred vases have been attributed. This artist belongs to the generation following that of the so-called "pioneers" at the end of the sixth century B.C., and his favorite forms are kraters and amphoras, which he decorates with simplicity and grace, renouncing the elaborate decoration

Side A

Side B

familiar to the black-figure technique. His figures, realistic down to the last detail, often appear isolated, drawn over the black surface of the vase, sometimes without even a ground line.

On our amphora only one figure is shown on each face, and ornament is confined only to the ground line, a small and careful continuous meander. The action continues from one face to the other, something frequently seen in the work of the Berlin Painter. Side A shows a bearded man who has unsheathed his sword, which he lifts over his head, attacking toward the right. His body is represented from the front, with one foot in profile and the other foreshortened. He is nude, and

his *himation* hangs from his left arm, which, extended, holds the sheath of his sword. On side B, another adult, bearded man defends himself from the attack of the aggressor. This man has his back toward the viewer, with his right leg flexed as if he had spun around suddenly to repel the attack. In drawing the figure, the painter has made a major error, as he has shown the left leg from the front, as in the man on face A, which is impossible for a figure not facing forward. This warrior still wears his *himation* and holds, in his extended left hand, like his attacker, the sheath of his sword. Both wear laurel garlands, highlighted with red paint that is also used in the bands around the sheaths.

Lines are shown in relief, and the anatomical details have been drawn with diluted varnish. Side A has had more attention and is drawn in more detail than the obverse face. In the case of the attacker, the muscles of the left arm are drawn, his nostrils are visible on his face, and the preliminary sketch of the leg which is not shown drawn under the mantle is more precise.

Beazley identified these figures as Ajax attacking Odysseus in the celebrated dispute over the armor of Achilles. But there is no indication in the image that would allow us to make a positive identification. There are neither weapons nor inscription, only the isolated figures of the two adult men who are shown in the instant previous to the violent confrontation. This preoccupation with the selection of the precise instant, the details of the musculature, the attitude and posture of our figures attacking with wide-legged stance and the weight over the flexed leg, vividly recall contemporary sculptures, particularly the group of the tyrannicides, created during the same time by Kritios and Nesiotes in substitution for the old Antenor group stolen by the Persians. The warrior on A is drawn in the same position as Aristogiton, and the movement of his arm, with the threatening blade, recalls the aggression of Harmodius. The tyrannicides were located in the Atenían Agora, to be seen in profile, as the figures on our vase, and the sculpture was converted into the public space of the square as a visual remembrance of Athenian heroism and the triumph of its excellent form of government,

democracy. So it is that the posture of the tyrannicides is repeated over and over in Greek art, from the metopes of the Parthenon to the Altar of Zeus at Pergamon, a posture connoting heroic success and triumph over the forces of disorder, victory, and liberty.

PROVENANCE:
Asensi Collection.

PUBLICATIONS:
Álvarez-Ossorio 1910, 83, 113; Leroux 1912, 103–104, no. 185; Beazley 1963, 200; Kurtz 1983, pl. 44, nos. 18, 19, Beazley's drawings on pl. 9; CVA, Madrid 2, III IC, 11, pl. 22.1a-b, pl. 26.2; Beazley Archive Database, no. 201860.

NOTES:
1. This painter was recognized by Beazley in one of his first works, 1911, 276–295. Here the scholar first laid out his analytical method for attributing vases to painters. Also see Beazley 1930 and 1964; more recently, Kurtz 1983.
2. On the tyrannicides, their later version and the connotations of the "heroic posture," see Bérard 1983, 5–37.

C.S.

23. *Nolan Amphora with the sphinx*

Inv. no. 11.106
H: 34 cm; diameter at rim: 14.5 cm; diameter
   at base: 9 cm
Attic red figure
Loeb Painter
Circa 480 B.C.

Beazley attributes this amphora to the Loeb Painter, a minor artist who moved in the circle of the Achilles Painter's

Side A

Side B

workshop, around the time of the works in his first period, and the Phiale Painter. All of these painters are characterized by their preference for medium-sized shapes, as in the Nolan amphora and the *lekythos*.

Nolan amphoras are Attic vases whose production occurred between 490 and 430 B.C. They owe their name to the fact that more than half of the 800 examples documented to date were found at Nola, near Naples. Most of these types of vases have been found in Italy; examples from Greece and Attica are particularly scarce, which seems to indicate that their production was principally intended for export.

This is a neck amphora, small in size, with a simple mouth and a simple disk foot. Three periods have been

identified in the production of these amphoras according to their morphology. Our example is from the developed phase (480–460 B.C.), characterized by the presence of triple-molded handles and an oval body, with a refined mouth and flat lip; the interior of the mouth is concave. The disk base is relatively short.

One common characteristic of this type of vase is the small number of figures represented on each face, situated over a frieze, typically meander, and standing out from the black paint. Our example is decorated with a sphinx on the obverse (side A), over a roughly drawn frieze of meander, and a female figure on the reverse (side B), over a frieze of meander and crosses. The sphinx, in profile and facing right, is seated on the top of a Doric column, with its heavily plumed wings half-open. It wears a diadem decorated with five leaves and pendants. On the other face appears a young woman with her hair tied low on her neck, wearing *chiton* and *himation* with rectilinear pleats and with a more somber appearance than the sphinx. Oriented toward her right (viewer's left), she extends her right arm forward with an open hand. This gesture serves to connect both sides of the vase and also signals the *thauma*, the apparition of the sphinx.

This hybrid being, which appears here in its canonical form, with the body of a lion, face of a woman, and wings, appears for the first time in Hesiod's *Theogony* (326). The sphinx, which the Greek imagination conceives as female, is a creature born of the union of chthonic beings tied to the untamed forces of the earth. Ancient writers have described her as daughter of Echidna and Orthos or of Typhoeus and the Chimaira. From the end of the sixth century B.C. the image of the sphinx assumes a determinedly female form, something which will be accentuated after the fifth century B.C., with the ever-more generalized presence of breasts, although that is not the case in our vase. The sphinx, a creature of complex nature, appears tied in the Greek context to Theban legend, but also serves as the guardian of tombs, a funerary and apotropaic symbol. It is probably in the last sense that it should be understood here: the painter is echoing the funerary Attic stelae of the Archaic period, which would have been crowned by a sphinx.

PROVENANCE:
Marquis of Salamanca Collection.

PUBLICATIONS:
Álvarez-Ossorio 1910, 74, 112; Leroux 1912, 101, no. 179; Beazley 1963, 1005.2.; Carpenter, Mannack and Mendonca 1963, 314, Beazley attributes eight Nolan amphorae to Loeb Painter; CVA, Madrid, 2, III I c, pl. 21.6 a-b and 26.1–2; Beazley Archive Database, no. 214084.

NOTES:
1. On the morphology and phases of the Nolan amphora, see Richter and Milne 1935; Euwen 1986, 142.
2. On the iconography of the sphinx, see Moret 1984; Kourou 1997, with bibliography.

M.M.

24. *Column krater with utensils of the symposium*

Inv. no. 1999/99/96

H: 36.8 cm; diameter at rim: 30.6 cm; diameter at foot: 16.9 cm

Attic red figure

A Late Mannerist painter

Circa 460 B.C.

On side A is a banquet scene: two youths are enjoying the music of an *auleter*. The three unbearded symposiasts recline on cushions on *klinai*. The two on the left are on the same couch. Their naked torsos and the cloths covering hips and legs are typical of the symposium. The middle youth rests his back against two cushions while playing the double flute. The youth on the left watches him and gesticulates, while the

Side A

one on the right rests on his left elbow and lifts his right arm in a gesture that indicates that he is listening intently. The moment represented here is the symposium, when the food has been removed and the drinking begins. On the back wall of the banquet hall hang a cup on the left and an empty stippled leather sack. Below, instead of the traditional small, three-legged tables, the artist has drawn a collection of drinking vessels. These are, from right to left, an *olpe* or jar, a *skyphos*, a *pelike*, a column krater and two *skyphoi*.

Our scene emphasizes that song is inseparable from wine, just as the wine is inseparable from the drinking vessels. But the containers lined up in order along the bottom also symbolize the city dweller's common, moderate drinking. Our banquet is exemplary and these tranquil symposiasts, who have not yet picked up drinking cups, will not reach the extremes described

ironically by the comic poet Eubulus in the *Atheneum*:

> "I only mix three kraters for those who are moderate, the first is for health, and is the one drunk first. The second is for love and pleasure, and the third is for sleep. When this last has been drunk those who would be judicious go home. The fourth krater is no longer ours but belongs to *hybris*, the fifth to uproar, the sixth to a procession of drunks, and the seventh to the black eye. The eighth is for the tribunals, the ninth to bile and the tenth for craziness and throwing furniture."
>
> (*Atheneum*, II, Epitome 36 c)

On side B one of the youths commonly found in these types of scenes is supplanted by a woman. Thus, the gathering becomes a scene of heterosexual seduction. The figures are posi-

Side B

tioned as they commonly are in masculine scenes. The woman who takes the place of the *eromenos* stands passively in the center, totally enveloped by her *himation*. Two men gesticulate toward her, their hands extended, the left hand resting on their staffs. The three wear white bands in their hair. The drawing is less careful than on the principal side, and diluted glaze is used for some of the folds in the mantles. Traces remain of the preliminary sketches, which show the legs under the mantles.

Is the woman being courted a *hetaira* or a virtuous woman? The first hypothesis would tie together both faces of the vase, given that the *hetaira*, the "companion," was the only woman who participated in the male symposium. However, nothing in this woman's aspect would lead us to think that she is a *hetaira*, other than her free companionship with men. Perhaps, as has been suggested with other red-figure vases, she is a *hetaira* "disguised" as an virtuous woman. Well covered, demure, and even engaged in the domestic task of weaving, a *hetaira* could be more desirable and thus increase her stature and price.

PROVENANCE:

Várez Fisa Collection.

PUBLICATIONS:

Christie's, Antiquities, London, 10–7–1992, 20, fig. 340 and J. Eisenberg, *Art of the Ancient World*, no. 71, Jan. 1995, vol. VIII, part 2, 22, fig. 109; Cabrera 2003, no. 103.

NOTES:

1. On the banquet, see, for example: Dentzer 1982.

2. On the iconography of the banquet, see, for example: Lissarrague 1987.

3. On *klinai*, see, for example: Boardman 1999, 122–131.

4. On courting scenes, see, for example: Schnapp 1997, 318f.

C.S.

25. Column krater with satyr libating in Dionysian procession

Inv. No. 1999/99/97

H: 39.7 cm; diameter at mouth: 31.3 cm; diameter at foot: 16 cm

Attic red figure

Middle of the fifth century B.C.

The column krater, which the Greeks called a Corinthian krater, was a very popular shape among red-figure vases

Side A

of the late Archaic period, when some artists specialized almost exclusively in decorating this elegant shape. By the middle of the fifth century B.C. kraters were still being painted by good artists, but the form would quickly fall into disuse and would be abandoned completely before the end of the century.

The interior of the vase is covered with a dilute glaze. The outsde of the lip is decorated with animals, perhaps boars and felines. Stylized as to be unrecognizable, they are painted in the black-figure technique, in silhoutte but without incised detail. They may echo the hunting motifs that were favoured by the Archaic aristocracy.

The decoration of chained lotus blossoms on the neck is restricted to the principal face. On the shoulders are bands of vertical tongues, and flanking the figural scenes are double lines of points. On the right side of side A the

double line of points becomes a double line of leaves. The foot is painted, except for a reserved groove. The external surface of the foot is reserved.

On side A is a Dionysian scene. In the center, is the god, bearded (with a longer and bushier beard than those of the satyrs) and festooned with a garland of ivy leaves. He wears a fine long *chiton* and *himation*. He walks to the right holding a staff and two branches with white leaves. In his right hand he holds a *kantharos* extended toward the satyr behind. The satyr, also garlanded with ivy leaves, carries an *oinochoe* from which he will fill the god's drinking cup. At the head of the line, another bearded satyr plays the *aulos*. The difference between the two satyrs, who are otherwise similar, is that the one behind, who makes the ritual act of libation, is infibulated. This practice of supporting the genitals is common with athletes and, therefore, for city dwellers. Our satyr is civilized here and is in charge of the ritual act, unlike the *auleter* who begins the procession. Much preliminary sketching and relief lines are evident.

The scene on side B runs contrary to the usual pattern of reverses that show three cloaked youths. In this case the central male is replaced by a woman. She is substituted for the *eromenos*, creating a heterosexual courting scene out of what is normally a homosexual scene. On the left a youth wearing a *himation* gesticulates with his arm, addressing the woman in the center of the scene, who repeats the same gesture. On the right another youth enveloped in a *himation*, resting on his staff in the classic *erastes* posture,

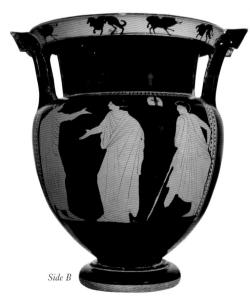

Side B

watches them. Above is a sketched element, perhaps a discus, which indicates the gymnasium scene. Women are not normally included in these Dionysian scenes. However, the artist seems to have corrected that omission by including, in the masculine homosexual courtship on side B, a woman in place of the *ephebe*.

PROVENANCE:
Várez Fisa Collection.

PUBLICATIONS:
Cabrera 2003, no. 105.

NOTES:
1. Regarding ritual libation, see, for example: Lissarrague 1995b, 126–144.
2. For Dionysian scenes on red-figure vases, see, for example: Carpenter 1997.
3. For the *thyasos*, see, for example: Schöne 1987.
4. About infibulation, see, for example: Lissarrague 1990a, 59–60.

C.S.

26. *Cup showing contest between Pelops and Oinomaos*

Inv. no. 1999/99/85

H: 6 cm; diameter at rim: 20.4 cm; diameter
at foot: 11.2 cm

Attic red figure

Hippacontist Painter

Circa 420–410 B.C.

Outstanding form and decoration grace this beautiful short-footed cup of the Delicate Class with a marked interior lip. The many ridges of the concentric circles that decorate the base of the foot bring to mind a metal vase. The interior is covered with a complex floral motif incised on the black background.

Sides A and B are decorated in a miniaturist style with exquisite calligraphy. In both scenes are figures in chariots pulled by two horses. On side A the horses ascend into the air, their front and back legs already off the ground. The chariot is driven by a youth wearing a *chiton* or tunic, with extremely fine folds, that leaves his arms uncovered. He holds the reins and a crop, bending at the waist, lips half open and expectant, hair flowing loose in the wind. His companion, a warrior, holds onto the edge of the chariot. He wears a bronze cuirass over a linen shirt or tunic. In his left hand he carries a shield and spear; placed carefully on his head is a Corinthian helmet which does not cover his face. Under it we can see two bands of leather over the temples, indicating that he is wearing a cap of Oriental type. Between the point of the crop and the horse's head runs a minute inscription written left to right, in the same direction as the cart. Although difficult to read, it is clear what it says: OINOMAOIS, Oinomaos, in the nominative.

On side B the chariot is borne by winged horses (the area showing the wings has been mostly lost). It shows the exact moment of ascent, when the horses still have their back legs on the ground and the travelers are preparing to fly. The guide here is a young warrior. He carries neither lance nor shield, but he does have a sword hanging from his waist. His long hair hangs in ringlets over his shoulders, which emphasize his youth and beauty. He holds a woman with both arms. She trusts in him, her left arm placed on his shoulder. She wears a tunic and a mantle that covers one arm. A diadem holds back her hair, as if she were a bride. The inscription, still almost completely visible on the horses' heads, alludes to the hero: (P)ELOPS.

The two faces of the cup tell the tale of Pelops' struggle to win the hand of Hippodamía. The lovers are being persued by Hippodamía's father, Oinomaos, in the chariot driven by his charioteer Myrtilos. This story was told, with certain variations, in the Hesiodic poem of the Megalai Ehoiai: thirteen illustrious youths died. Later the tale was recounted by Pherekides and other authors. The mythic epítome of Apollodoros (2, 4–9) resumes the story. In the last decades of the fifth century, Sophocles and Euripides both related the story in plays named *Oinomaos*.

The king Oinomaos posed a chariot-race challenge to suitors of his youngest daughter, Hippodamía. The purpose of the challenge was to ensure that Oinomaus, by winning the race and killing the suitor, would be able to escape the prophesy that his future son-

Side A

Side B

in-law would kill him. Many pretenders competed in vain, dying in the attempt, but Pelops would be victorious, thanks to the gold chariot pulled by indefatigable winged steeds, a gift of the god Poseidon, who had answered Pelops' plea. (Pindar, *Olympian* I, 87). Pelops was also able to win through trickery. It was said that Pelops himself, or Hippodamía, who fell instantly in love with the youth, coerced the charioteer Myrtilos to improperly adjust the linchpins of her father's chariot, or, in another version, to substitute the metal spokes with ones made of wax. The effect was dramatic. In the middle of the race, Oinomaos' chariot disintegrated, dragging the king, who was tangled in the reins, behind it. Thus Oinomaos was unable to avoid his destiny.

On the east pediment of the Temple of Zeus in Olympia is shown the moment just prior to the action, imaging the excitement and tension before the denouement. In contrast, the artist of this cup has elected to portray the act itself. The race is a nuptial abduction, welcomed by a smitten Hippodamia, seduced "by the special brightness in his eyes" (Sophocles, *Oinomaos*, Athenaeus 564 B), who allows the beautiful Pelops to take her away without resisting. Oinomaos pursues them.

The tragedies of Sophocles and Euripides influenced the myth. In Sophocles's drama, the exotic horses would be brought on stage and as a chorus sang expectantly of the race's outcome. "I wish I were a high-flying eagle, thus to elevate myself above the brilliant expanse of the sea" (fr. 476). Our cup, which follows precisely the sketch of the chest of Kypselos (Pausanias V, 17, 7) and Pindar's version, might be an echo of the Sophoclean chorus.

Nothing has happened yet. It is the beginning of the chase, but the prophesy appears to be unfolding. Certainly, Oinomaos is not the bearded father found in other representations. Rather he is a youthful competitor, almost like Pelops, thus possibly suggesting the ambiguity of father as lover. All is exquisite and subtle in the ideal and ambiguous world of this very special, delicately illustrated cup.

PROVENANCE:

Várez Fisa Collection.

PUBLICATIONS:

Sothebys'-Parke-Bernet, New York, sale catalogue, 31.5.1997, no. 77; Beazley Archive Database, no. 21845; Cabrera 2003, no. 114.

NOTES:

1. On cups of the Delicate Class, see, for example, Sparkes and Talcott 1970, 102–105.

2. About the compex variants of the myth, see Gantz 1993, 540–542. Testimony of the *Megalai Hoiai*: Merkelbach and West 1967, no. 259 (= Pausanias, VI, 21, 10f).

3. For the imagery of the Pelops chariot race, see Triantis 1994b, LIMC VII, 282–287, no. 25f; and Lacroix 1976, 327–341. On the image of Pelops' winged horses on vases, see, for example, the Attic black–figure *lekythos*: Triantis 1994a, LIMC VII, 19–23, 20, no. 5 = 284, no. 12 (s.v. Pelops). On the vase-painting tradition and the pediment of Olympia, see Säflund 1970. For the chest of Kypselos: Splitter 2000, 23–24. The competition is documented in South Italian ceramics (Apulia). See, for example: Trendall and Cambitoglou 1983, 151, 21a, for instance the volute krater of the Baltimore Painter. For the acceptance of the kidnapping and Herodotos, see, for example, Harrison 1997, 185f.

4. The attitude of acceptance by Hippodamia in the chariot (see the contemporary bell krater by the Oinomaos Painter, Naples Museum inv. No. 2200; Boardman 1989, fig. 351) is similar to other kidnapped brides. For Oinomaos and his possible reflection in Sophocles and Euripides, see, for example: Séchan 1967, 447f, ch. 22. For Apulian images, see, for example: Giuliani 1995, 118f.

5. For the leather cap worn under Oinomaos's helmet, see, for example, the copy of Myron's Athena in Hamburg, as well as the parallels with warriors and, mainly, amazons depicted in Attic red-figure vases. On this theme, see, for example: Knauer 1986, 121–126, especially 123 and notes 28–31.

6. In this period, incriptions referring to personages in Attic ceramics are in the nominative.
   They generally follow the direction of the
   figure they accompany, as in this case.

R.O.

27. *Hydria with hetairai*

Inv. no. 11.129

H: 29.3 cm; maximum width: 27.3 cm; diameter
   at rim: 13 cm

Attic red figure

The Painter of Tarquinia 707 (Later Mannerists)

Circa 440 B.C.

The *hydria* adopts a continuous profile
between shoulder and belly; it is the
variant called a *kalpis*, popular in Attic
pottery of the fifth century B.C. Wide
proportions and style–the second gener-
ation of mannerists that transform and
stylize previous formulas—place the
vase in the third quarter of this century.

A continuous frieze over the shoulder of the vase, marked by two horizontal bands of stylized grape vines,
borders the scene. This is articulated in
relation to a central axis; on the opposite side of the vertical handle, in the
center of the front panel, is a double
window, with three pilasters and floral

capitals—in red—under which a young
acrobat arches her nude body to the
rhythm of music. Two *heterai* mark the
beat with *krotala* to the left, and a
woman to the left plays the *diaulos*,
seated on a *klismos*, an elegant chair
with a back from which hangs the
mottled leather sack for the instrument.
Behind the musician, a youth, who has
just arrived, leans on his staff and
participates in the feast, with his hand
extended. On this side, the composition
is completed by a woman dressed in
tunic and mantle, with her hand resting
on her hip. She has entered and
observes the scene from a distance.

Two different settings are
contrasted. To the right is the realm of
the nude female in movement. A stool
holds the pile of clothes shed by the
hetaira, whose hair is completely unrestrained. To the left is the strictly regu-
lated space of Greek dress and the
traditional female hairstyle, as well as of

repose and interested contemplation. The young women respond to the arrival of the Athenian youth who observes them. Two contrasting kingdoms, then, whose relation is established by the window with crowns as an allusion to interior and exterior spaces and an indication of a feast.

The ambiguous significance of these scenes has been discussed before by scholars. The *hydria* or *kalpis* is a vase associated with the female world and the nuptial feast. It is connected with Aphrodite. On other examples of this type we see the musical instruction of high-class women in the interior of the *gynecium*, *paideia* of the lyre and the poetic song that brings them nearer to the Muses. But in this and other similar vases, the female, musical world adopts a different air. We approach the erotic realm of Aphrodite from the *ethos* or character of the sharp music of the *aulos* and *krotala*, from the nudity of the adolescent women, and the unrestrained movement of their contorted bodies. This is all very far from the relaxing music of a domestic interior. Even though it is an apparently female vase, the arrival of the youth allows us a look through his—the male—perspective, as he is introduced or initiated into a house of *hetairai*. Behind him the dressed woman keeps herself slightly apart: she has completed her function as intermediary. But the young man lacks a purse of coins, which would certify the erotic interchange. Thus the ultimate purpose of the visit remains somewhat unknown.

Everything, then, is ambiguous, even the crowns, which Aphrodite likes.

The nuptial crown (*stephos galeion*) could be at the same time funereal (*stephos necron*). Our *hydria* could well have been part of the furnishings of a tomb.

Diluted glaze is used to indicate the loose hair of the *hetairai*.

PROVENANCE:
Marquis of Salamanca Collection.

PUBLICATIONS:
Álvarez-Ossorio 1910, 84, 113; Leroux 1912, 119, no. 199; Beazley 1963, 1112, 1703; CVA, Madrid 2, III–ID pl. 6–2, pl. 7 1, 2–3; Beazley Archive Database, no. 214707.

NOTES:
1. On the visit of a youth to a brothel on Attic vases, see Reinsberg 1989, 120–125. For the other *hydriae*, with women and the musical *paideia*, see Kaufmann-Samaras 1997, 285–295.

R.O.

28. *Glauxs with the image of Athens*
Inv. no. 11.432
H: 8 cm; maximum width: 8 cm; diameter at mouth: 8.1 cm; diameter at foot: 5 cm
Attic red figure
Last quarter of fifth century B.C.

This small drinking cup is decorated with an owl, or *glaucous*, which gives the vase its name. It is in the shape of a *skyphos*, but one of its horizontal handles is twisted around to be vertical, which perhaps is intended to evoke the beak, while the other handle represents the bird's tail.

The vase is painted in the interior and exterior, except for the foot, whose base and bottom are reserved, although covered with reddish miltos.

In our owl *skyphos* the same image is repeated on both sides, an owl that fixes its wide, fascinating, vigilant eyes on the spectator. The huge pupils are one of the most characteristic marks of these owls. Our bird is between two olive branches. In classical art spatial representation is reduced to a suggestion. The tree on which the owl would be perched is indicated only by two small vertical branches, one on each side of the bird. Owl and olive are the favorite animal and plant of Athena, patron of Athens. Silver Athenian coins contain the same design. It is the invisible presence of the goddess. Owl and olive become the emblem of the city, in the image of Athens.

Most of the owl *skyphoi* date to the second and third quarters of the fifth century B.C., even though ours is dated somewhat later. This coincides with the most brilliant moment in the Athens of Pericles, when the structures that would change the look of the city were built:

the Parthenon and Propylaeia on the Acropolis; when the economy was healthy; and the city reached its maximum commercial expansion. Emblem of the imperialism of Athens, image of the city, the owl that looks at us through olive branches is diffused in ceramic form and on silver coins as Athenian nationalist propaganda throughout the Mediterranean.

PROVENANCE:
Marquis of Salamanca Collection.

PUBLICATIONS:
Álvarez-Ossorio 1910, 126; Leroux 1912, 151, no. 259; Olmos and Sánchez 1988, 11, no. 1; Beazley Archive Database, no. 3364.

NOTES:
1. On these vases, see Johnson 1955, 119–124, pl. 38, fig. 42.

C.S.

29. *Cup with feats of Theseus, signed by Aison*

Inv. no. 11.265

H: 14.2 cm; maximum width: 45.7 cm;
    diameter at rim: 45.7 cm

Attic red figure

Aison

Circa 420–410 B.C.

The large size of this vessel and its decorative complexity transcend the simple drinking cup and turn it into an exceptional commemorative and symbolic object. It transports its owner to an ideal realm, a different symposium.

On the black exergue of the medallion, under the main scene, Aison left his signature, which is hard to read today: AISON EGRAPSEN, "Aison painted (me)." Through his name and his action, the artist himself is incorporated in the illusion of the scene and the heroic memory of the poets and artists to whose long creative tradition this painter legitimately belongs. Present here with his name, Aison is a privileged witness to what he recounts. It is not a new story. Aison follows and commemorates an old mythological and iconographic tradition.

The entire cup, on both external faces and in its central medallion, exalts the quintessential Athenian hero, Theseus. The succession of images and accumulated inscriptions–painted in red–refer exclusively to Theseus and his feats. In each case, the written word, alluding to each of the characters, gives testimony of the heroic act. The powerful palmettes under the handles, a pictorial wonder, lend vegetative exuberance to this vase. Its greenery forms an integral part of the composition and history.

Theseus is the model aristocratic Athenian youth who must travel an initiatory path of incalculable difficulty

Side A

Side B

throughout Attica and, finally, through-out the sea routes. In his solitary jour-ney he is confronted by bandits and monsters, whom he defeats with his strength and intelligence, with the learned words and fine education he gained at the palaestra. As in all initia-tory journeys, the hero goes in search of his true identity: he seeks to be recog-nized by his father, Aigeus, mythical king of Athens, because the father's name is essential for an Athenian youth in the Classical period. The name and fame confer collective support to his exceptional value.

After reaching puberty, Theseus wanted to take the land route on the obligatory journey from Troizen–where he was born and passed his infancy—to Attica, traversing inhospitable and dangerous regions. By liberating the land of the existing dangers he looks to reestablish justice, or *dike*, for the community of Athenian citizens. On the two exterior faces, the painter continually narrates the feats on this journey. The images do not occur in strict chronological order, and some scenes overlap others, creating on the surface of the vase an extraordinary spatial illusion that always exalts the nude body of Theseus.

On side A, from left to right, Theseus battles first with Sciron, a local hero who guarded a narrow path near the sea, in the Gulf of Saronica, between Megara and the Isthmus. This inhospitable giant would force travelers who passed that way to wash his feet. Then he would quite calmly and care-lessly throw them off the cliff into the sea. There, a huge turtle would devour them. Using a scheme to trick Sciron, Theseus takes his footbath, the *poda-nipter*, and manages to grab the giant's hair to throw him into the sea. We see the turtle peering between the rocks: it is a well-deserved end to the transges-sor; we look forward to his destiny. There follows the episode with Krom-myon's wild sow in the forest. The old and disquieting white-haired wet nurse, Krommyon, lives there and protects the ferocious beast, which Theseus kills immediately with his sword. With *chlamys* extended, the hero looks for protection from the fangs of the sow. Krommyon pleads in vain. The branches of the forest tremble, because the scenery participates, in this and other images, in the dramatic tension of the encounter. Third, Theseus fights with Sinis, also known as Pityokauptes, the Pine Bender. Sinis lived next to his tree, a flexible and powerful pine, at the entrance to the Corinthian Isthmus. Sinis would tie his victims to the tree, and the pine, once doubled back all the way to the roots, would suddenly jut forward and slam its victims against the earth. But now Sinis, at the hand of the young Theseus, will himself become a victim of his own arrognace or *hybris*. He extends his arm, pleading in vain. Theseus is deaf to his pleas.

We continue the initiatory journey on side B. Theseus has managed to reach the terrible bull of Marathon, who laid waste to the fields of Attica. He grabs him by one horn and ties his legs with a red lash because he must deliver the bull alive to the Acropolis in Athens to be sacrificed to the gods. The raised club will tame him. There follows the episode with Prokroustes, the Beater, who inflicted innumerable sufferings on travelers, after forcing them to lie on his immense bed of torture. With an enormous hammer Prokroustes would beat the body of the unfortunate traveler until he made him fit the size of the horrible bed. Taking advantage of an unwary moment, Theseus raises the two-bladed hammer, the *sphyra*, and hits the giant with it. Now his solitary bed shall be his tomb. Finally, a nude Theseus does battle with Kerkyon at Eleusis, whom he defeats with a wrestling trick. He holds him in his arms, picking him up, and soon he will toss him to the ground. The spear, the *pilos*, or conical cap, and the *chlamys* sit on a rock. We await again the immediate triumph that, as in the other cases, our attention awakes. Theseus is the incarnation of athletic wisdom, the *paideia* of the young Athenian fighter. Myth and reality are both intertwined and enriched in each of these scenes.

The medallion, culmination of the vase, relates the triumph of Theseus over the Minotaur. The optical illusion reaches its peak here. The hero with arched torso stands out against the dark, shiny interior of the vase. The end of Athena's spear goes beyond the circular boundary and increases the three-dimensional sensation. It is almost an epiphany. Theseus escapes the labyrinth of King Minos in Crete—whose palace is alluded to in the section with vertical checkerboard-meander, steps, and the two Ionic columns on the building at the back—dragging the dying body of the Minotaur, a humanized monster, given that his forelegs are here inert

arms. Minos–not Minotauros—is his written name here. The escape of Theseus from the labyrinth represents his triumph over death, his victorious surging forth from the underworld. Athena's attentive presence and her admiring face represent the sacred recognition of the city. Theseus is the chosen youth and protected by the gods, thus reaching immortality. His nudity is proper for a victor and an athlete.

The Aison cup suggests a political version of the myth, centered on Theseus and the ideal of Athenian masculinity. Ariadne, who helped the ingrate hero in Crete, is completely absent. The model of a triumphant and pacifying Theseus is a political message for the Athenian citizen in those years of hopes and doubts that marked the Peace of Nikias, during the disastrous Peloponnesian War.

Restored in antiquity with staples (see two orifices on face A).

PROVENANCE:
Marquis of Salamanca Collection.

PUBLICATIONS:
Álvarez-Ossorio 1910, 76–77, 119, pl. 33; Leroux 1912, 110–113, no. 196; *CVA*, Madrid, 2, III I D, pls. 1–5 and 15; Beazley 1963, 1174, 1; Carpenter, Mannack and Mendonca 1989, 239, with bibliography; Simon 1976, pls. 221–223; Olmos 1992, 9–50; Beazley Archive Database, no. 215557.

NOTES:
1. On the ceramic shape of this Type B kylix, see Lezzi-Hafter, in Olmos 1992, 57–73.
2. On Aison and his times, see Wehgartner, in Olmos 1992, 75–96.

R.O.

30. *Lekythos with tomb offering*

Inv. no. 19.497

H: 35 cm; diameter at shoulder: 11 cm

Attic white ground

The Inscription Painter

Circa 470–460 B.C.

White-ground *lekythoi*, so called because of the color of the slip that covers their surface, are perfume vessels used in funerary rituals. The color white has a dual symbolic sense here: it is an immediate allusion to *tymbos*, or a pile of dirt covered with lime under which lies the cadaver, as well as the anticipation of the white, blinding light that bathes Elysium, the heavenly afterworld.

The scene offers us a clear and direct image of the ritual and the funereal space: the visit to the tomb. Two young women approach with gifts. From the back of the scene (the white-washed wall of the cemetery?), hang two offerings: a *lekythos* and a *phormiskos*, a receptacle. One of the women goes to deposit an egg, perhaps made of clay and filled with perfume, a customary offering at tombs, charged with eschatological symbolism. The second woman holds the ribbons that will serve to adorn the monument, funerary ribbons that, in a more profound and subtle reading of the image, could allude to wedding ribbons, a loving gift for the bride. In many funeral scenes, hidden under the appearance of the commonplace, we find, in a metaphorical sense, a close relationship between death and weddings. For the woman, the transition must be completed, if not in life,

then after death. In the kingdom of shadows the bridegroom awaits. He is Hades, god of the Inferno, who will marry the young women who have died unwed. For the bride, her tomb will be her marriage bed: *Oh, tomb, nuptial bed, subterranean living space forever vigilant, to where I journey beside my own...."* (Sophocles, *Antígone*, 892).

The sacred, ritual action of the offering at the tomb is part of the cult of the dead. But, above all, it is an act of piety, a religious duty for family members. The offering tries to salve the immense abyss and the radical otherness of death that those who remain must confront. Not only does one approach the border between one world and another, in the vertiginous attraction of the afterlife, but stretches out a hand to death to make it closer.

In the image on this vase, the funerary monument is customary in Athenian cemeteries in the first years of the fifth century B.C.: a stele raised over three steps. The monument is crowned by a *kantharos* with high handles, the vase of Dionysos. Tied closely to his cults, this is a hero-making vase from which drink heroes like Heracles. Perhaps its position on top of the stele is meant to indicate that the interred is an illustrious man, emulator of heroes. However, it could also allude to an initiate into the cult of Dionysos. Contemporary Athenian tombs topped by *kantharoi* are never found; the typical arrangement is a stele garlanded with a large palmette, a motif that superseded around 530 B.C. the archaic, more sumptuous images of lions, sphinxes, and sirens—psychopomps, guardians of the tomb. The image of the ritual vase here has, thus, symbolic value: it is an allusion to the transforming power of the sacred liquid the *kantharos* often contains, and the transition of the deceased to a new life.

On the upper part of the stele, markings that imitate letters become the epitaph of the deceased, the song of praise and farewell, glory, and memory.

PROVENANCE:
Stützel Collection.

PUBLICATIONS:
Álvarez-Ossorio 1910; Leroux 1912, 299; Beazley 1963, 748, no. 1; Kurtz 1975, 20, 45, 86, 153, pl. 19; Olmos 1980, 63–68, figs. 50–56; Beazley Archive Database, no. 209238.

NOTES:
1. On the ritual of death in the Greek world, see Vermeule 1979; Garland 1985.
2. Regarding the cult of the dead and religious ideology surrounding death, see the definitive work of Rohde 1894.

P.C.

31. *Lekythos with deceased smelling a flower*

Inv. no. 11.192
H: 56.5 cm; maximum diameter: 15.2 cm
Attic white ground
The Triglyph Painter
Circa 415 B.C.

This white-ground *lekythos* allows us to peer into the funeral space and landscape of death by way of the scene that decorates it. A woman is seated on a tomb consisting of two high steps, a wide stele, a frieze of triglyphs, and a cornice topped with acanthus leaves that sprout alongside a floral element, a suggestion of the acanthus trees that grow around the tombs in cemeteries. The woman, who is the deceased, rests in a relaxing attitude while holding a small flower, whose perfume she smells. Near the tomb, which is adorned with ribbons on the stele and steps, are the visitors: a man to the right, leaning on a staff, and a woman to the left, wearing a transparent *chiton* and a mantle whose folds she holds in her left hand, while she holds an offering in the right. At the extreme left of the scene stands a tree with violet leaves and brown branches.

The scene configures an idealized space, at once real and symbolic. On one hand, there is the immediate

The gesture and attitude of the deceased woman also allude to an easy and well-omened world. The woman shows herself to us in the splendor of her beauty and youth. The flower, a sensitive element, is a metaphor for her grace and enchantment, the attribute of goddesses. Her posture, lying indolently on the steps of the tomb, is that of a woman who receives the visit to her new home of those who accompanied her in life. An atmosphere of idealized serenity, and at the same time melancholy, submerges the figures in a nostalgic dream that tries to perpetuate the beautiful, joyous moment. Death is a time for remembering and a time for forgetting. Remembering is the prerogative of the living. The dead must drink the water of forgetting, the water from the River Lethe—inhale also the amnesiac perfume of a flower?—to get to the kingdom of shadows or the paradise of the fortunate.

suggestion of an Athenian cemetery: arranged in terraces, sprinkled with white stelae raised over steps, adorned with ribbons, sculptures, and reliefs among vegetal elements, various plants and trees. On the other, it is also an imaginary and idyllic space. In this setting, in which both worlds are juxtaposed, the scenery could be that of Elysium, the realm of the fortunate dead described by Pindar: "...*and among fields of purple roses, the outskirts of the city are overflowing with dark forests of incense and trees of golden fruit....A delicious odor is dispersed throughout that place....*" (*Threnody* VIII, frag. 129).

Both living and dead share the same space, but the radical distance, separation, and solitude, is made evident in these images in the last years of the fifth century B.C., expressing a new way of representing the relationship of man and death, charged with *pathos*, with melancholy, even pessimism. It is a reflection of the sober atmosphere that dominated Athens during the Peloponnesian War. The preoccupation now is not with the community as a whole, but with the individual and his destiny. Hope and good fortune are found after death, in a happy and comfortable afterlife. What appears in this image is a profound reflection on the condition and destiny of man, on death and the pain of separation, on inexorable and fugitive time, sentiments that would come to a peak in contemporary tragedy.

PROVENANCE:
Expedition to the Orient Collection.

PUBLICATIONS:
Álvarez-Ossorio 1910, 92; Leroux 1912, no. 319; Olmos 1980, 121–124, no. 31; Beazley Archive Database, no. 3366.

NOTES:
1. For the Triglyph Painter and white-ground *lekythoi*, see Kurtz 1975.
2. For the reconstruction of the fragmented figure of the man: Lullies 1955, no. 82, pl. 43; Beazley 1963, 1385, 10; Webster 1965, pl. 18, fig. 91.
3. On cepotaphs, gardens or funerary plantings: Cumont 1949, Motte 1973.
4. Plato (*Laws*, VII, 171) gives rules regarding the planting of trees alongside tombs.
5. About iconographic changes at the end of the fifth century B.C. in white-ground *lekythoi*: Kurtz 1975; and Olmos 1980.

P.C.

32. *Volute krater with siren playing a cithara*

Inv. no. 1998/92/1
H: 94 cm; maximum width: 55 cm; diameter at rim: 43.5 cm; diameter at foot: 23.2 cm
Apulia, red figure
The Baltimore Painter
340–320 B.C.

The *volute* krater is one of the vessels used in Magna Graecia as a grave good, or even as a funereal monument. The

numerous ornamental motifs, such as oval shapes at the rim, wavy lines below, laurel branches and rosettes on the neck, tongues on the shoulder, oval shapes and meander outlining the scenes, underline the complex architectural composition of this vessel.

Decorating the back of the vessel (side A) is a characteristic funerary scene: in the center we find a *naiskos*, or white temple with two Ionic columns supporting an architrave with a triangular gable. The corners are finished off with three palmette-shaped acroteria. The *naiskos* stands on a podium decorated with scrolls. In the interior of the *naiskos* we see the deceased, a warrior in armor, wearing a Corinthian helmet with its horsehair plume situated over

Side A

his head, and his sword, lance, and round shield placed at his feet. Directly in front of him is another warrior in similar military attire. Both of them are in white, with armor, shield and helmets painted in red. There are four figures around the sides of the temple: a naked male, two females, and Eros. The humans have mirrors and branches or garlands in their hands. They are the officiates of the heroic cult that celebrates the passing of the warrior and the witnesses to the beyond. Eros is a necessary presence as a guide on this last journey and to grant to the deceased a fruitful new life in eternity.

The scene on the reverse complements the previous one. We again see the participants in the funerary ritual

Side B

who bring offerings to place in front of a stele. The monument has now been converted into a pillar that is decorated with black and white ribbons, raised to a podium which is decorated with spirals and topped by a large cup with high handles; a *kantharos*, heroic vessel of the Dionysian world, that contains sacred liquid in its purest form, a ritualistic object, pregnant symbol of the power that wine and Dionysos represent. The objects that these personages carry—wreaths, boxes, mirrors and branches—allude to the festive, fruitful, and beatific atmosphere of the Hereafter.

The image that covers the neck of side A surprises one for the apparent strangeness of the fruitful and verdant scenery. This scene is presided over by a siren dressed in a short tunic, situated over a large floral chalice, strumming the strings of a *cithara* with one hand and holding a pick in the other hand. Her expression of profound melancholy, full of pathos, reminds us that her song is one of death, a chant for the deceased whose image is celebrated in the *naiskos* below. Eros and a swan flutter around in this paradisaic garden where tendrils and buds of flowers and spirals of vegetation sprout incessantly to form a fruitful metamorphosis. They show us that we are in the Garden of Aphrodite, a transitory space, a paradise where the deceased warrior will be welcomed. As a funereal creature, the siren, Muse of the Hereafter, whose song is knowledgeable and prophetic, awaits the deceased who is going to start the journey and to whom she communicates privileged understanding, the knowledge necessary to achieve immortality. Eros guarantees the necessary fruitful cosmic action: the creation of a new life.

On side B a large palmette is surrounded by medium-sized palmettes and verdant sprouts, synthesizing and expressing creative action of a new life. Four swan heads, molded perfectly and painted in black, sprout from the sides of the neck over the shoulder. The female heads, shown in relief, that decorate the circular medallions of the volutes, are white with golden hair. They are frontal masks of the Gorgon or Medusa of the idealized or beautiful type, guardians of paradise that safeguard with their apotropaic power the underworld and beyond. Under the handles is a complex array of palmettes that are superimposed. Numerous touches of white and golden paint adorn the figures, the objects and the vegetation.

PROVENANCE:
Acquired from Günter Puzhe.

PUBLICATIONS:
Kunst der Antike, Galerie Günter Puzhe, Katalog 12, no. 212; Schauenburg 1989, 21–76.

NOTES:
1. For the Baltimore Painter, see Trendall and Cambitouglou 1982, 856f; Todisco 1983; Schauenburg 1984; Schauenburg 1994a, 543–569; and 1994b.
2. For the scenes with *naiskos*, see Lohmann 1979.
3. On the divine garden, an image of a paradisaic thereafter, see Cabrera 1998, 76–85.
4. On the siren playing the *cithara*, "The Muse of the Hereafter," see Buschor 1944; Ensoli 1996.

P.C.

33. *Leutrophorous with the abduction of Persephone*

Inv. no. 1998/92/2
H: 94 cm; maximum width: 36 cm; diameter
   at rim: 27 cm
Apulia, red figure
The Baltimore Painter
340–320 B.C.

This monumental vase, designed for the funerary ritual, is characteristic of Apulian production of the second half of the fourth century B.C. The pedestal, cylindrical and with a molded foot, is an independent piece. It has the characteristic trumpet-shaped mouth, the narrow and high neck, protruding shoulder,

Side A

and cylindrical body with two convex moldings on the top and bottom that connect it to the body and the foot.

As is characteristic of the adorned Apulian style, a profusion of vegetal and geometric elements decorate the subsidiary parts of the vessel: a frieze of oval figures in the lip, palmettes and network of rhomboidal forms in the upper part of the neck, rays in the lower part, friezes of ovals and central rosettes in the neck, a band with laurel branches and rosettes in the center between the neck and the shoulder, and a frieze with a meander and a cross and a row of waves in the lower molding of the foot.

Side A has a typical funerary scene:

Side B

on the inside of a white *naiskos*, or funerary temple, is seen the heroic image of a deceased woman, who stands and leans over a basin. In her hands she holds a fan of yellow feathers and a box adorned with white paint and little balls, surely containing wool, the symbol of feminine labors and the domestic virtues of the deceased woman. To the sides of the *naiskos*, four feminine figures complete the image; they are the deceased woman's friends who bring offerings to the tomb. They repeat the image of the feminine virtues that ennoble their companion. The vase thus images a new *gynaikeion* for her in the Hereafter, a beatific space that the woman will enter after death.

The two images that decorate both faces of the shoulder allude directly to this essential moment of the journey. On side B, the face of a winged female is seen in three-quarter view, all in white, sprouting from a large chalice in the midst of a verdant explosion of floral tendrils, buds, spirals and flowers. On side A, a feminine face is seen in profile, sprouting from this verdant space. Both images of this *anodos*, or upward passage represent the journey, across this marvelous garden, to the blessing realm of the Hereafter.

The iconographic discourse, contained in the idea of the journey and the triumph over death, culminates magnificently in the scene on side B, where the abduction of Persephone is narrated. The abduction is shown in two scenes separated by a perspective meander. In the upper frieze, Hades has descended from his chariot and walks toward the girl, who is terrified and tries to escape. The god of the Under-world, with his mace in his hand, appears suddenly. His charioteer awaits him, trying to control the horses that are already preparing to fly upwards to the three star rosettes overhead—an allusion to the celestial voyage, the heroic "ascent." A large flower in the front could be an allusion to the narcissus, *"flower of prodigious brilliance which surprised everyone who saw it...."* (*II Homeric Hymn to Demeter v.* 10–11), which Hades grew and used as bait to lure Persephone.

In the lower frieze, the goddesses Artemis and Athena, fully armed, run to prevent the abduction of their sister and playmate. Behind Athena, a feminine figure (Demeter? an Oceanid?) runs, frightened by the impetuous reaction of the goddesses and the violence; and at the end of the scene are Eros and Aphrodite. The scene clearly illustrates the version of the myth that is verified in the second *Homeric Hymn to Demeter* (vv. 419–426) and in the *Helena* of Euripides (vv. 1301–1319), wherein we note the actions of Athena and Artemis to prevent the abduction, and the final intervention of Zeus to allow the neces-sary act so that the entrance of Kore into the Underworld could transpire. Literary and theatrical references, ritu-als and precise religious writings confirm the message conveyed by these scenes, a model image to those who are starting their voyage to their last abode.

PROVENANCE:
Acquired from Günther Puzhe.

PUBLICATIONS:
Kunst der Antike, Galerie Günther Puzhe, Katalog 12 no. 213.

NOTES:
1. For the Baltimore Painter, see Trendall and Cambitouglou 1982, 856f; Todisco 1983; Schauenburg 1984; 1994a 543–569, and 1994b.
2. For the scenes with *naiskoi*, see catalogue no. 32.
3. On the image of the *anodis* that sprouts among the flowers, see Jucker 1961, 199f; Lohmann 1979, 54–69; Schaenburg 1957, 198; 1984, 127–160; 1989, 39–44.
4. On the abduction of Persephone, see Zunt 1971; Richardson 1974; and Lindner 1984.

P.C.

34. *Calyx krater with Io's initiation*

Inv. no. 1999/99/121

H: 46.5 cm; maximum width: 43.2 cm

Apulia, red figure

Berlin-Branca Group

Circa 340 B.C.

This *calyx* krater is decorated with a garland of flowering laurel, a frieze of palmettes and lotus blossom, and a border. On side A three figures walk hurriedly toward the left, guided by a hermaphroditic Eros. They are on a meadow (a white ground of flowers; ahead is blooming vegetation; behind, a palmette). It is a blossoming, well-omened place that these elegant beings traverse with their light step, almost as if they are dancing.

A woman leads the procession. She wears a bow in her hair and plays the *diaulos*. She has her face turned toward

Side A

the woman who follows quickly behind. That woman's hair is festooned with many white spots (flowers?). Two resplendent horns emerge from her forehead. She is Io of the cows' horns (*kerastis*), fugitive and wandering the farthest confines of the earth, "wanderer of many wanderings." She is completely enveloped in her tunic and mantle, which hides both arms. Her garment is decorated with small white circles or eyes, like the inescapable gaze of Argos, "of infinite eyes" that follows the unfortunate woman wherever she goes. She carries the *narthex*, the palm of the initiate, adorned with a ribbon. She returns the inquisitive look of the naked youth who follows behind, carrying a branch or *narthex* and a double-handled *situla*. He could be a young satyr, the acolyte of Dionysos who accompanies the young woman. Eros gambols above Io, with fabulous wings and the ritual bands of the newlywed. Other bands and a garland hang from

the bottom. Who is Eros accompanying on his journey? Io began her never-ending journey by divine oracle, a journey that took her to the ends of the earth and the Orient. The god Zeus desired her, a groom for an impossible wedding. But on our vase the love of Zeus is shared by Dionysos. Io reaches the end of her journey, where a new god awaits her as she approaches death. Under the watch of Eros the mediator, she will exchange the pain of human love for effortless good fortune. At last she fulfills her destiny.

Aeschylus's *Prometheus Bound* made the story of Io famous. Io on her journey enters the scene and hears from the lips of Prometheus, who is tied to the rock of Caucasus, that her future is to wander the earth. This motif was transmitted through theater, where her shape would be human rather than a heifer, as in Aeschylus; a mask with horns characterized her. A South Italian *skyphos*, Lucanian, from Metaponto, pictures Io sitting on a rock and contemplating her transformed face. The mirror in her hand shows her the horns, and the young woman will witness her metamorphosis. Eros accompanies the young Io on a red-figure *rhyton*. On other contemporary vases, Io becomes a divinity and is transformed into a flowering tree. The South Italian world seems to have changed the terrible destiny of the errant young woman into a fortunate initiation. Frontal masks of Io, with white carnations and golden hair, decorate the medallions of the volutes that garland the great Apulian kraters. Her melancholy look reflects the destiny of one who wandered the earth endlessly

Side B

and is now a permanent model on the funerary vessels.

On side B three youths with staffs enveloped in mantles converse amiably. They wear white bands in their hair. In the background, there is a spatial indication of a high window, suggesting a public building or home. The youths in the middle, and left look at each other. A partly-conserved painted incription appears above. The tablet shows writing, an allusion to the *paideia*, the education of the aristocrat. Or does it have a funerary, oracular meaning? The letters H.IHIWIO seem to be merely a simple succession of vowels. However, among them we see featured the letters IO, which could refer to the heroine of the anverse face or the similar cry of lamentation, where the words Io, Ie, Ió, Io are repeated, something like, "Oh, Io! Oh, Io!" Apart from the conventional scene,

the scene alludes to the endless conversation of the youths in the afterlife. Are they discussing Io's destiny?

PROVENANCE:
Várez Fisa Collection.

PUBLICATIONS:
Cabrera 2003, no. 130.

NOTES:
1. I think this vase could be part of the Berlin-Branca Group, among the predecessors of the Darius Painter, a group that anticipates the ornate style of the Apulian ceramics and the tendency toward scenes with mythological content. For the two *calyx* kraters attributed to the Branca Painter, see Trendall 1989, figs. 192–3, and 87; Trendall and Cambitoglou 1982, 476–478, pl. 169. They employ the same ornaments in sides A and B: "The ornamental patterns on the two kalyx-kraters are almost identical—berried-laurel above, lotus and palmette below on the obverse, with meanders and enclosed quartered squares on the reverse" (Trendall and Cambitoglou 1982, 478).

2. Furthermore, Prometheus tied to the rock is the theme on the principal face of the *calyx* krater of Berlin 1969.9: "a remarkable 'Liberation of Prometheus.' The Branca Painter is a bold draughtsman, fond of putting a halo of curly hair above the faces of figure in three-quarter view, and of treating his themes in a novel way" (Trendall, 1989, 87). A third theme of a bell krater by this painter, in Gothenburg, shows that the punishment of Actaeon suggests a theatrical inspiration as well, a theme covered by the *Toxotides* of Aeschylus (Trendall and Cambitoglou, 1991–1992, 477). The myth of Io is also represented on the back of a volute krater by the Darius Painter, along with Zeus, and Hermes, who attacks Argos. (See, for

example Trendall and Cambitoglou 1983, 76 and 78, no. 63 — "once American Market").

3. Icard-Gianolio 1978, LIMC V, 661–676, nos. 63–64: "divinitization of Io. Io in a vegetative decoration." On Io, shown in the medallions of the great *volute* kraters of the Apulian red-figure ceramics, ibid, no. 95, with many examples. On the Io for the South Italian Aeschylus drama, see, for example, Kossatz-Deissmann 1978, 131–132 and note 756, with bibliography. In Apulian ceramics, see, for example, Io on the Berlin hydria F 3164, The Group of Moscow Pelike (Trendall and Cambitoglou 1983, 170, No. 34): Io seated at the feet of the statue of Artemis, with Hera, Argos, Zeus, Aphrodite and Eros, above.

4. On the Lucanian vessel with Io, Metaponto 20150, see: Trendall 1970, 84 b, pls. 1, 2. There is in Pompeii a painting of Io (Schefold, SB III 136f, fig. 178), perhaps a copy of the late classical original by Nicias (Pliny, *HN* XXXV, 27).

5. The infinite eyes -*myriopón*- of Argos: Aeschylus, *Prometheus Bound*, 568. "wandering of multiple wanderings," Prometheus Bound, 584.

of Italy and Sicily called *phlyax* (cf. no. 34). The main character is no less than Zeus, the father of the gods, who is at stage center and stumbles and trips as he walks with his cane between two companions. He is dressed in the costume of the *phlyaxes* (with long sleeves and pants), a leather phallus, and a protruding belly.

On the costume he wears a short tunic with embroidered edging, befitting his high rank. His crown appears to be a small, short basket, like the ones worn by the *karpophoros* Demeter, on which appears a wreath with small white dots that may simulate tiny pieces of fruit. The white branch (that is barely preserved) shown on the front of the mask alludes to the restless and festive character of Zeus as a pilgrim. The mask has straight and unruly hair and an unkempt beard. The raised eyebrow shows displeasure. The hidden

R.O.

35. *Calyx krater with phlyax scene*

Inv. no. 11.026
H: 31 cm; maximum width: 28 cm
Campania, red figure
The Dirce Painter
380–370 B.C.

The *calyx* krater has connections to Dionysian celebrations and to the atmosphere of the theatre. The scenes on both sides are related.

The main scene (side A) condenses the acting of a burlesque farce, of the theatrical genre so popular in the south

Side A

hand of the god holds the winged bolt of lightning, his attribute and symbol.

Zeus is accompanied by two servants. The one in front carries a ritual basket with offerings, or *kanoun*, on his head, on which appear pieces of bread or white cakes, and offerings, and holds in his right hand a vessel, an *askos* with a circular mouth that doubtless contains the wine. The servant turns to his hobbling master. The wide-open mouths of the two characters suggest a shouted conversation.

Zeus marches to the beat of the *dialous*, in white, of the second servant, who wears *phlyax* theatrical attire, with the tunic, or *exomis*, commonly worn by servants, gathered at the shoulder and with a large dangling phallus. The cord, tied around the foreskin, which squeezes the phalluses of both servants who accompany Zeus, can barely be seen. Can this be a comical allusion to the Greek practice of infibulating the

sexual organs of young men, or is it connected to the limitation of the sexuality of these shameful personages? All of this is not sufficient reason for this musical servant to wear a cap, or *sakkos*, in the feminine manner, as it could be the role of the *auleter*, or the feminine flautist, who beats the rhythm in the festive processions. The farce permits this confusion of sexual roles with the hilarity of the phallus scene combined with the feminine cap of the servant. It is not hard to imagine where the ill-humored god is going: to a party given by Dionysos, a god of another sphere, with a different sense of humor and whom he cannot stand. So many times Dionysos has made him angry and disgusted!

On the reverse side, two youths in robes tied with ribbons, surely complement the meaning of the vase. One of them holds the *narthex* or knotted rod crowned with ivy that converts it to a Dionysian thyrsus. He is the initiate, a *thyrsophoros*. His lively companion, carrying a walking stick, shows him the way.

Allusions to a Dionysian atmosphere of initiation with funerary connotations are customary in South Italian pottery of this period of the fourth century. The burlesque farce belongs to this sphere of the Dionysian world and is not foreign to the representation of death. The two elegant youths shown in the back of the krater, appropriate the theatrical transformation, which provokes and prolongs hilarity and prophylatic laughter in the hereafter.

The foot is decorated with a wide cross painted in *miltos*.

Side B

PROVENANCE:
Marquis of Salamanca Collection.

PUBLICATIONS:
Álvarez-Ossorio 1910, 80, 108, pl. 39; Leroux 1912, 223–224, no. 388; Trendall 1970, 204, no. 30.

NOTES:
1. On the world of the *phlyaxes*, see bibliography in cat 36.

R.O.

36. *Bell krater with phlyax scene*

Inv. no. 1999/99/122

H: 28.3 cm; diameter at rim: 31.6 cm;
    diameter at foot: 14.1 cm

Apulia, red figure

Second quarter of fourth century B.C.

On side A three *phlyaxes*, two youths and a woman, act upon a wooden stage. The two males, with shameless penises, wear a tight-fitting wardrobe of pants and sleeves (which represent nakedness)

Side A

with an *exomis* on top. The hanging sack of leather ends in a shameless prepuce. An inflated stomach characterizes his grotesque appearance. The woman, doubtlessly played by a male actor, wears a shirt with tight sleeves and over it an *exomis* belted at the waist. They are all barefoot.

The grimacing masks worn by the actors feature protruding eyes and wide, shouting mouths. The three animated *phlyaxes* are officiating at the gift of perfumes to a god. The one on the left holds a small box filled with aromatic grains (incense) that he sprinkles into a tall bronze incense burner. His companion pleads with him blatantly as he anticipates the powerful fragrance of a badly measured aroma or, perhaps, one that is too sparingly prepared. The woman also interferes, with a lively hand. A sacred, spitted band hangs from the back of the stage. The solemn ritual—which as all offerings to gods, should be perfomed seriously—is in this instance filled with mockery. The hieratic tension of the divine clashes with the grotesque nature of the scene and the stylized masks. It is a cathartic transgression that transcends life: the parody would delay its effectiveness and prolong its effects in death. These are vases found in tombs.

In the South Italian ceramics of this period, scenes shown on a *logeion* or improvised wooden stage, in the open air, are common. Such stages could be quickly installed in agoras or squares and in the theaters of Magna Graecia. The stage was a simple wooden platform, resting on boards or on knotted wooden supports, raised just a few feet

Side B

off the ground. The actors were itiner-
ant, with their own repertoires or
stories adapted from the dramas of the
Old and Middle periods of the Attic
Theater period (400–320 B.C.). The
characters were comic stereotypes,
using the gestures and grimaces familiar
from farce. Some have made analogies
to the Baroque *Commedia dell'Arte*.
However, any realism is hidden behind
the unreal and exaggerated masks.

The fragmentary side B reunites
three characters commonly seen in
South Italian ceramics. A woman, in the
center, would have held a Dionysian
staff in her left hand, now missing, in a
resting position. She speaks with a
youth totally enveloped in his mantle.
Another young person appears behind
them, though only traces remain, and
creates a symmetrical relationship with
the woman holding the staff, the
protagonist in this case. The reign of
the *phlyax* on side A is associated with
the reign of Dionysos shown on side B.
The krater of wine establishes this link
between two different worlds.

A garland of laurel or olive branches
appears below the lip. Palmettes are
painted under the handles.

PROVENANCE:
Várez Fisa Collection.

PUBLICATIONS:
Cabrera 2003, no. 128.

NOTES:
1. For an exellent synthesis on the theater and
   the iconography of plays, see Simon 1982. The
   mixture of the mythic and quotidian in the
   burlesque of the *phlyaxes*, see Beare 1964,
   335–339 (who also addresses the limitations of
   these images on vases as testimony or reflection of the play, "evidence for staging").
2. On the most famous of the *phlyax* authors,
   Rhynton of Syracuse, active in Taranto, half a
   century after our vases, and his influence on
   farce, see Gigante 1971, pl. 9, a bell krater from
   the National Museum of Bari, which shows a
   woman between two *phlyaxes*, on a stage.
3. On spacing for the performance and theatrical
   architecture, see, for example, Todisco 1990,
   103f, especially 122–124.

R.O.

37. *Tarantine rhyton showing the death of Actaeon*

Inv. no. 1999/99/130
H: 20.5 cm; width: 15 cm; diameter at rim: 8.5 cm
Apulia, Taranto, red figure
350–330 B.C.

Rhyta are based on an originally Near
Eastern form. Their ritual character is
inspired by metallic vases. A *rhyton* is a
drinking vessel, a type of deep cup often
shaped like the head of an animal. Like

its metallic prototype, the *rhyton* has neither support nor foot. It can be left lying on its side or upside down when empty, or even hanging from its single handle. Ceramic *rhyta* are fundamentally different from their metallic models in that they are not ritual vessels, but rather are votive or funerary offerings found in sanctuaries or tombs. In the metal *rhyton*, the mouth of the animal is perforated so the liquid libation may flow through it; the ceramic pieces have no holes.

The production of animal-headed plastic *rhyta* appears to be a specialty of the south Italian city of Taranto. Our vase is one the oldest examples, carefully constructed and without engraving, derived from the Attic *rhyta* of the end of the fifth century B.C. In this example the only engraved details are the whiskers indicated with three lines on either side of the nose.

This *rhyton* is in the shape of a Laconian dog's head. This breed was particularly prized by the Greeks because of its speed and sharp eyesight. The sharp senses of this dog are evident in this cup: the eyes are wide-open, the ears held slightly back, indicating that the animal is alert.

The decoration is restricted to the obverse of the neck. The mythological theme selected is especially appropriate to our vase and does not appear on other Tarantine *rhyta*: the death of Actaeon, attacked in this scene by the same Laconian dog that forms the vase. The cause of the hunter's horrible death, devoured by his own hounds, differs according to the specific versions of the myth. According to some, it was

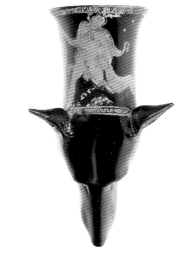

Zeus who caused his death because he tried to win the love of Semele. However, most authors agree that the death was a punishment for surprising Artemis in her bath.

On our cup the conventional scene is depicted. Actaeon is naked save for an animal pelt over his shoulders and boots. He tries to defend himself with a spear from a dog that attacks him and has already bitten his thigh. The metamorphosis has begun. From his forehead sprout two deer horns in white and gold. Beneath some reserved circles and white branches, the rocks and plants of a wild landscape setting are depicted. To the right rises a sun in white paint, which is almost undetectable.

The rest of the vessel is almost completely glazed, both inside and out, except for the eyes, which are indicated with two painted circles, and the interior of the ears. The rim of the vase and the transition between neck and head are articulated with egg-and-dart friezes; a palmette, surrounded by a reserved band and petals, decorates the neck on either side of the figured scene. The piece is very well preserved.

PROVENANCE:

Várez Fisa Collection.

PUBLICATIONS:

Cabrera 2003, no. 132.

NOTES:

1. For a similar example: Hoffmann 1966, 46, no. 258, pl. 28. On the iconography of Actaeon in South Italian vases, see: Aeellen 1994, 44f, pls. 20–21.

C.S.

38. *Lebes Gamykos*

Inv no. 11.445

H: 27.5 cm; maximum width: 15.5 cm; height of lid: 12.5 cm; diameter of lid: 10.5 cm

Paestum, red figure

Asteas group

360–320 B.C.

Lebes with oval body, marked shoulder and vertical handles, topped with molded cones. At either side of the handles, female plastic faces, wearing Phrygian caps, with long hair and long, fine-featured faces. The shoulder appears decorated by two stems that share a central flower with four petals

in added white and yellow paint, which is very characteristic of the work of Asteas. The same can be appreciated, for example, in the *aryballic lekythos* in Naples (2873).

The figure scenes are bordered above and below with a frieze of tongues and one of waves and marked by two thin vertical bands in reserve that separate them from the decoration under the handles. Tronco-conical foot, with a number of moldings. The vase is topped with a central cylindrical shape crowned by a small *lekanis* that is missing its lid.

The *lebes gamikos* is a receptacle associated with nuptial rituals in the Attic world, though ours is from a South Italian context. The iconography is not circumscribed exclusively to the preparations for the wedding. In fact, it

Side A

would probably be more accurate to relate it more broadly to rituals surrounding the initiation into sexuality, as the iconographic repertoire would seem to suggest.

Our example, extraordinary for the richness of its decoration, is filled with detail. On side A we see a scene with two young women before a washbasin. This bath scene, far from being merely anecdotal, introduces us to the ritual thanks to the presence of Eros, standing on the edge of the bath, the real focal point of the action. At the foot of the bath an *alabastron* is placed to one side and two oval objects to the other. The young woman to the right of the god leans over the tub, a posture shown often in Paestan ceramics. Partially nude and with loose hair, only a mantle held on her left forearm covers her thighs. She extends her right hand toward Eros, presenting a small, round object (an egg? fruit?). Her gaze meets the god's, turned toward her, winged and covered with a small purple mantle that covers part of the genitals and is rolled up in his left arm. Eros, as are the two women in the scene, is shod. The god, whose hair is gathered in some type of *korymbos*, holds in his right hand an *oinochoe*, pointed down, as if to make a libation, and in his left a phiale.

From the other side of the tub, a young woman seated on a floral stem turns her body to observe the scene that is occurring behind her. Partially nude like her companion, with a mantle covering her legs, she holds what is probably a mirror in her right hand and a hollow *phiale* that holds small, round objects, and a string of beads in her left.

The scene is completed by a bird looking through a window in the left upper corner of the vase scene, with its feet bound by a cord, or *tainia*. The scene is enormously vivid and minutely detailed, not only in the attentive manner in which the bird, perhaps a partridge, watches the scene from the window, or for the turned body of the young woman who is surprised by the appearance of the god, or for the necklaces, bracelets and earrings with which the women are adorned, but for the *alabastron* the painter has shown half-full, placing the viewer in the exact instant that the action is taking place.

On the reverse (side B), a youth with long hair restrained with a garland, shod and adorned with a necklace of beads around his chest and bracelets, holds a mirror in his right hand and a ribbon in the left. He is infibulated, behind him is a *tainia*. In front of the ephebe, a young woman seated on a stem—which, as on side A places the scene outdoors—richly dressed and jeweled, holds in her right hand, behind her, a mirror; in the left she carries a *phiale* with small round objects that she presents to the youth. The dialogue between the characters is accentuated by the mutual gaze.

Under each of the handles has been drawn a bird on a palmette from which emerges an exuberant flower—the so-called *Asteas flower*, which is very typical of this painter. Both motifs appear oriented toward the scene of the youth and the seated woman. Under the handle, behind the woman, is probably a partridge that appears to be taking a libation while, behind the youth, a

Side B

hoopoe with its characteristic crest has been drawn with an insect in its beak.

Everything on this vase leads us to the world of sexuality, initiation and sacred. The presence of Eros brings us into the world of the divine, making the scene sacred; the *phiale*, receptacle in which the communication between human and sacred realms is materialized, and the mirror, reflection of otherness, give a good account of this dialogue. The youth on side B, who may perhaps be seen as a satyr, or even Dionysos himself, reinforces this meaning.

In this *lebes*, nature is not only exuberant, a constant element in the vase painting of South Italy, but alive. It is enough to remember the extraordinary presence of the birds that, far from being static, participate in the action,

and the scene on the lid, where a young mottled feline stalks a partridge.

PROVENANCE:
Marquis of Salamanca Collection.

PUBLICATIONS:
Álvarez-Ossorio 1910, 90, 127, pl. 41; Leroux 1912, 433; Trendall 1936, no. 87, 52, pl. 13a; Olmos 1973, 89, figs. 43, 90 and 92, fig. 44; Hermary et al. 1986, 654 (j); Trendall 1989, 202, fig. 365.

NOTES:
1. For the offerings in this type of vases and the plastic heads on the shoulder, with examples, see Schneider-Herrmann 1976.
2. On Eros, see Hermary et al. 1986; other examples of the floral decoration on the shoulder, see Trendall 1989, no. 351. Other examples of birds at the window in the South Italian context very similar to our example: Apulian *pelike* from the Museum of Matera; a rendering of the hoopoe very similar to that on our vase, see Trendall 1989, fig. 363, a ring *askos* attributed to Asteas from the Museum at Paestum, no. 26635.
3. On the Italian *lebes*, see Cassimatis 1993.

M.M.

39. *Situla showing banquet of the gods*

Inv. no. 1999/99/133
H: 26.3 cm; diameter at rim: 21.9 cm; diameter at foot: 12.5 cm
Apulia, red figure
Dublin Situlae Group
Circa 350–330 B.C.

On this *situla* (side A), a vessel used in Dionysian settings, we see three

Side A

symposiasts resting on one couch, under a leafy pergola weighted down with enormous branches, leaves, and grape vines. To the right, a long-haired Dionysos, identified by his characteristic attribute, the *narthex*, holds in his right hand a pomegranate, the fruit of immortality. Next to him is seated Hermes, with the *caduceus* in one hand, and the *kantharos*, the heroic vessel characteristic of Dionysian ritual, in the other. Hermes appears to be conversing with Dionysos. At the far left of the couch a figure holds a laurel branch while raising his face to the sky. He is Apollo, transfixed, in the bachannalian sense, that is, "possessed" by the sound of music. The three gods have garlanded their heads with refreshing and sacred laurel wreaths. In front of the couch, we see a small table loaded with fruit and white cakes, and a krater with figures painted in white. Near the edge of the couch, on a carpet repre-

sented in perspective, appears Pan, who participates marginally in this banquet. The hybrid god, with goat's horns and legs, does not share the couch with the gods, given that his sphere is not of the civilized world, of the *kline* or the table, but rather of the wild and natural settings on earth. However, in this case, the *stromata*, or rug, decorated with a trim of meander and angles that simulate fringe and figures of animals in white imitating a textile pattern, lends an exotic, luxurious and coloristic touch to his "couch." A rich tapestry of Oriental origin reminds us that the god, companion of Dionysos, came with him and his staff from the east. Two separate spaces are depicted here, the seminatural *skias*, with the shadowy bower, and the rug, whose borders and bright colors lent luxury and pleasure to the symposium. Pan addresses the *pais*, the young pourer who extends a drinking vessel to him while holding a jug in the other hand, instruments used in the ritual libation of the symposium. At the far right of the scene, an *auleter* imbues the magical ambience of this divine banquet with the sounds of the double flute.

Tendrils, leaves and vines configure a sacred space for the triple divine epiphany, a fragrant place, eternally youthful and renewed, a garden refreshed by the shadowy bower, on which delicious fruits ripen. Dionysos presides over this garden of never-ending delights. He also presides over the gathering and feast celebrated there. His companions are Hermes, the messenger god who knows the hidden and subterranean paths; Apollo, with whom he shares the sanctuary at Delphi and who has allowed himself to be seduced by the Dionysian pleasures; and Pan, member of his staff and the incarnation of the bucolic enchantment of the bacchic paradise. This is the heroic banquet that, as a promise for the future, is offered to the sight of mortals, the eternal symposium in which the *mystai* can participate in the blissful life offered as a recompense after death.

Side B takes us to the most bucolic scene of the god's encounter with his *thiasos*. It is a mountainous setting indicated by small white points, for the most part now erased, at various levels. The long-haired Dionysos, seated upon a mound of earth, holds the *alabastron* that contains the perfume of immortality. A maenad, holding the *narthex* adorned with white bands, offers him the crown of triumph. A young satyr,

seated on a higher plane, with an animal skin tied around his neck, holds a flaming torch decorated with a band of white pearls. A second maenad holds the *narthex* in one hand and a white garland—now lost—in the other. An *oinochoe*, a platter with white fruit, and a *situla* at the feet of the god are the equipment for the future celebration of the symposium. The rosettes in the background allude to the fecundity of this initiatory space. The scene depicts the supernatural plenty of the *bakkhoi*, the followers of Dionysos, and exudes the beatific peace of the meeting with the god in a happy afterlife.

PROVENANCE:
Várez Fisa Collection.

PUBLICATIONS:
Trendall and Cambitouglou 1991–92, Sup. II, 105, no. 15/35b, pl. XXII 1; Sotheby's, *Antiquities*, London, 3–12–1991, 116–117, no. 199; Cabrera 2003, no. 140.

NOTES:
1. On Apulian *situlae*, see Schauenburg 1981.
2. On the theme of the heroic banquet in the hereafter, see Cumont 1949, 255–256; Vernant 1986, 291–293; Burkert 1987, 105; Versnel 1990, 150f; and Cabrera 1998.
3. On the figure of Pan, see Boardman 1997; LIMC VIII, 923–940; and Bourgeaud 1979.
4. On the carpet, W.H.G., *RE*, 398, s.v. "Stromata." The images of carpets are frequent in symposium scenes.

P.C.

Side B

40. *Lepaste with multiple lids*

Inv. no. 1999/99/145

H: 19.2 cm; maximum width: 29 cm; diameter at
foot: 9.6 cm

Paestum, red figure

Painter of Naples 1778

Last quarter of fourth century B.C.

This vessel is a *lepaste*, or dressing-table
box. However, on lifting the lid of our
box we find not one receptacle but four,
each protected by is own little lid perforated with two openings through which
a cord could be laced.

The lid, whose interior is not
glazed, has a border covered with undulating waves that break toward the
right. The main handle is surrounded
by two reserved lines and a border of
double lines of triglyphs and white
points. In the center is the frontal view
of a woman's white face with loose hair
adorned with red bands. On the top of
the lid the figures are depicted without
ornamental interruptions, as occurs in
the Apulian models. Many elements of
the scene were painted in white, superimposed, and only traces now remain.
The principal figure is a woman seated
on a white *klismos*. In one hand she
holds a platter with offerings and a
garland. Her left hand holds a mirror.
At her feet lies a bird that Eros
approaches with extended hands,
perhaps in a propitiating gesture. His
hair is bound over his forehead, and his
skin and wings are white. Behind the
god and in the center a swan, represented by a line of white points, drinks
from a vessel. At the left a naked
woman approaches with *kekryphalos* and

rests a hand on the basin, while holding
in the other a string of white beads.
Under her is an *aryballos*. This is the
bathing theme that explains the naked
female figure and the vessel of perfume
at her feet. Behind her, on the ground,
a bird serves to conclude this part of the
scene. There follows a standing feminine figure on foot. She holds a white
garland and the same string of beads as
the previous figure, which Trendall
called a "skewer of fruit," although it is
actually an object whose symbolism is
unknown. In the other hand the female

figure holds a white mirror. In front of her proceeds a small Eros who walks toward the right and extends his hands toward a bird on the ground. Ahead, an unbearded satyr is positioned similarly, with hands extended. His right wrist is tied with thick red bands that hang down. His ankles are bound with white bands. On the left thigh and on his chest are bands of points that represent amulet holders. Ahead, a nude woman holds a mirror while advancing toward the left, but she turns her head to look behind her. Ahead a very young satyr with his hair over his forehead, like the first Eros, approaches her with something in his hand, represented by a white point. As with the other satyr, he wears white bands on his ankles and one wrist and the same bandolier of white points lies across his chest.

The interior lids are matched pairs, set across from each other. Two are decorated with women seated in the same position as the principal figure on the exterior, although here they are seated on rocks. Behind them are vegetal elements, reserved or in white paint. They hold in their hands the string of beads and white bands. The other two little lids depict a young, naked but shod youth, his body leaning forward, in a posture characteristic of Paestan ceramics. He makes an offering at an altar. In his right hand he holds the string of white beads, and in the other a white line. On the altar are white points, possibly offerings, and behind the youth are yet more vegetal motifs.

Without a doubt, woman is the central theme of this feminine vessel.

We have already seen her image atop the lid. In the interior, we see women surrounded by plants and seated on rocks, attended and received by a male figure. The small, inner lids are placed so that in both cases the woman and man meet each other's gaze. The same female figure appears on the lid: standing and seated, at one point in a chair, and at another in a festive environment, surrounded by nude women, a young satyr, a boy, two winged demons, birds, garlands and mirrors. This is an image of paradise as suggested by a funerary inscription from Macedonia: "*Reanimated, you live among the flowered pastures, where, in the satyrs' cortege, the mystai of Bacchus, marked by the sacred seal and the basket-bearing Naiads, so that you can join the festive party behind the torch.*"

This little box is a characteristic example of the religious environment of South Italy in the fourth century B.C., where there is, from the end of the fifth century B.C., strong evidence of Dionysian rituals in relation to life and death. Our images take us to a world of death-initiation symbols, in the context of the satyrs and the Dionysian Eros, alluding to a blissful afterlife under the protection of Dionysos.

PROVENANCE:
Várez Fisa Collection.

PUBLICATIONS:
Cabrera 2003, no. 149.

NOTES:
1. For Naples Painter 1778, see Trendall 1989, 206.
2. For Paestan vases, see Trendall 1987.

3. For the funerary significance of the Dionysian cult: Cole 1993, 276–296; Cabrera 1998, 61–87, with bibliography.

4. The inscription from Macedonia is explained by Cumont 1949, 255.

C.S.

41. *Orientalizing Etruscan olla with mythical animals*

Inv. no. 1999/99/152

H: 31.6 cm; diameter at rim: 7.3 cm; diameter at foot: 11.9 cm; maximum width: 43 cm

Etruria, Impasto

Last quarter of seventh century B.C.

This globular vase has a somewhat shiny surface. From the widest part of the body of the vase extend two horizontal handles in the form of palmettes sprouting from two opening shoots. Inside the mouth and around the neck are etched tongue friezes, imitating metallic prototypes.

The decoration of the body, incised deeply and profusely, is divided into four areas. In the upper band, a procession of mythological animals marches to the left. The variety of the mythical universe is herein accumulated in the characteristic orientalizing manner: the lion or panther with its large mane, which turns its head threateningly toward the spectator, is shown twice, as well as the winged lion and the sphinx with curved wings. And finally, the centaur, is shown in its most archaic manner, that is, with a complete human body to which is attached the hindquarters of a horse. The long-haired human part is naked, and the sexual organ is

well defined (and duplicated in both parts of this fecund hybrid being). In its right hand the centaur holds a long branch on its shoulder that bestows upon him its savage nature. The branch is flowery and fruitful, verdant. It is the centaur itself, with its demonic and savage nature, who fertilizes it. Its presence in this frieze shows us the magic and savage nature of the centaur rather than the later representation of the civilized half-man half-beast warrior-hunter dressed in a short tunic and with a sword.

Two rosettes with four flowers are also included in this area, one under the abdomen of the sphinx, filling in the space as is customary, and the other larger one is placed above the tail of one of the felines that faces out, as an intentional living association between the power and ferociousness of the animal and the vegetation. A tall tree, in front of the winged lion, appears from

Side A

the lower frieze and opens its branches under the mouth of the winged lion whose teeth and long tongue are showing. It evokes the extended orientalizing motif of the mythical animal protector of the tree of life. This tree surges above one of the handles (which also could be considered vigorous vegetation), and therefore could suggest the beginning and end of the era of the procession of monsters.

The second band is decorated with alternating rosettes and four-leafed flowers in a row. This ornamental band is more lightly incised.

The third frieze is divided into two parts by the handles, and the decoration is thus arranged differently. The animal procession is now replaced by a composition of animals facing a vegetable element, the tree of life. We see two long-bodied birds with thin, long necks, each one in front of their own palm tree that surges to sprout like a stylized flower that evokes in us a memory of an Aeolic column. Lateral branches sprout from the stalk. This is a live flourishing plant, in which birds nest, but it is also a kind of column that brings to mind an edifice, a holy entrance.

The motif is varied slightly on each side. On one side the birds have their wings tucked in (side A), while on the other side the wings are flapping.

In the wide band that surrounds the vase are the usual petals of orientalizing style that were introduced to Etruria through Protocorinthian prototypes at the beginning of the seventh century B.C., a profusion of lines that distinctively mark each petal of our vase, itself conceived as a flower.

Side B

The Etruscan aristocracy appropriated an eclectic repertoire of mythical beings. The influences are multiple and from all types of media: bronzes, ivories, ceramics, ostrich eggs, etc., a way of appropriating the symbolic world that identifies and distinguishes the princes of the Mediterranean. The Phoenician influences (for example, the Aeolic column) co-exist with a bestiary of the Greek eastern Mediterranean to which is added the powerful Greek figure of the centaur. All is intermingled. The exuberant decoration of the fabulous bestiary is an essential part of the imagination of a powerful elite that is capable of appropriating the totality of space and images.

PROVENANCE:
Várez Fisa Collection.

PUBLICATIONS:
Cabrera 2003, no. 36.

NOTES:
1. For the Orientalizing period, see Colonna 2000, 55–66. Also Menichetti 1994, 24–75 and

46–47 on the Etruscan appropriation of the centaur, and the polarity between human/animal and human, an expression of a very stratified social context "ove i gruppi dominanti possono sbandierare una cultura esemplata sulle forme ellenizzanti rispetto a coloro che vengono invece rappresentati alla stregua di un uomo-animale e fermi allo stato di natura." For the typology of the Archaic centaur, see Schiffler 1976; for the Etruscan centaur in bucchero and impasto ceramics, see, for example, Cristofani 1993, 77–84; Gran-Aymerich 1999a, 383–404, especially 397f for "le centaure à l'épée et le centaure aux rinceaux."

2. Griffin protomes, with buttonlike protrusions on the head, decorate Orientalizing bronze vessels and the local Etruscan imitations. See, for example, *AA*. 2000, no. 79: griffin protomes from Tarquinia.

3. The inclusion of rosettes on the bodies of animals, as an ornamental feature or envigorating them, is found on contemporary Italo-Corinthian ceramics. For example, amphora of Tarquinia, *AA*. 2000, no. 234 (Pittore dei Cappi).

4. For the symmetrical decoration and the tendencies that encompass syntactic and compositive language, see, for example, Harari 1995, 111f, cited by Gran Aymerich 1999a, 403, from whom I have taken the quoted phrase in my text.

R.O.

42. *"Pontic" oinochoe with banquet scene*

Inv. no. 1998/55/4
Height: 28 cm; maximum width: 16.5 cm
Etruscan, Archaic
Circa 525–520 B.C.

The lip, handle, and conical foot are painted black. The handle rotelles are decorated with eyes. A half round molding separates the lip from the neck, which is decorated with two meanders decorated with X's. Between the meanders is a frieze of dotted X's, all loosely painted. At the bottom of the vase, flaring from the foot, is a ray pattern, surmounted by a frieze made up of a sinuous wreath of lozenge or spear-shaped petals; the spine of the wreath is decorated with dots of added white; the row of upper petals is separated by red dots. The main decoration of the vase is made up of a frieze of banqueters on the shoulder and a frieze of fantastic animals on the belly. The spacing is

sometimes awkward; the front wing of the first sphinx encroaches on the rear of the second feline.

The animals are shown in profile, moving from right to left. Beginning under the handle, the first animal is a large-winged bird with its prominent beak agape. There follow a feline with frontal face; a griffin, a female sphinx (added white for the face), another feline with frontal face, and a second female sphinx. Incision is used for the feathering and anatomical details of the animals. Remarkable is the careful handling of the beautiful profiles of the sphinxes which contrasts markedly with the loosely-painted frontal felines whose ears are strikingly out of proportion. Loose rosettes are placed under the animals.

The upper frieze is made up of four *klinai* or couches on which recline groups of banqueters. The frieze moves from left to right; all the banqueters are shown with body facing the viewer's left, gesticulating in that direction as

well. To the right of the first couch, starting from the handle, is a standing nude male figure, possibly a young boy, a servant or slave. He touches the first couch with his right hand. This first couch has three figures reclining on it; the three other couches only support two figures. The couches are shown with added white; the serving tables in front of them in black; and the drapery on the upper part of the couch is red. The figures are all in black silhouette with incised detail. Added white and red is used for the hair or head coverings, but no added paint is used for the faces, even for the middle figure on the first couch who is clearly indicated as female by her costume and headdress. None of the figures is bearded.

Although initially dubbed "Pontic," this class of vases is clearly of Etruscan origin, probably produced at one of the major south-Etruscan centers. This jug is one of a pair, probably by the same painter and from the same Etruscan grave group, formerly in the Hirschmann Collection. While this vase shows a lively banquet, the other vase depicted a drunken dance, the inevitable result of the feasting that takes place on our example. This type of scene is common in Etruscan art, and the banquet is ubiquitous in both funerary and non-funerary iconography. Unusual about this scene is the couch with three figures on it. Also of note is the fact that the painter fails to use added white to differentiate women from men, even though one of the figures is clearly female.

PROVENANCE:

Acquired from Royal Athena Gallerie.

PUBLICATIONS:

Bloesch 1982, no. 17, 42–43 and 98.

NOTES:

1. The painter of this vase clearly worked in the ambit of the Paris Painter, the major painter of "Pontic" Vases. It has been suggested that the animal frieze resembles the work of the Tityos Painter while the banquet is closer to the hand of the Silen Painter, both followers of the Paris Painter: Bloesch 1982, 98. The animals and other figures are very close to a vase in Basel (Antikenmuseum Inv. No. Zü 211), attributed to the Silen Painter. See Hannestad 1976, no. 61, p. 63. It is possible that the friezes were painted by different painters, as suggested by Hannestad 1976, 59, for instance, for an amphora in the Biblothèque Nationale, Paris.

2. For Etruscan banquets, which unlike the Greek symposium, would normally include female banqueters: Small 1994b. For Pontic vases: Dohrn 1937, Ducati 1968.

G.W.

43. *Etruscan black-figure amphora*

Inv. no. 10.928

H: 42.4 cm; maximum width: 18.8 cm

Etruscan black figure

From Tarquinia

Second half of the sixth century B.C.

Neck amphora with vertical handles and concave offset lip. The outside of the lip is reserved and decorated with a tongue pattern. The outside edge of the foot is also reserved. The bottom of each of the two figural registers is delineated by a broad horizontal band surmounted by a thin horizontal band that serves as the ground line for the register.

The areas between the handles are reserved and treated as separate panels that depict human-animal and animal combats. On the principal side (side A) is a siren pursuing a running male figure. Both figures move from right to left. The siren holds a long club behind her in her left hand and gestures or

Side A

reaches out to the running youth with her right. The youth is nude and runs vigorously with his left arm forward and his right arm behind him (bent at the elbow with palm turned down). Large vegetal motifs intrude on the scene: two plants or flowers between the figures and another plant on the far left. On the other side (side B) the panel between the handles shows two large birds, most likely swans, fighting. Details of wings and feathering are indicated by incision.

The scene on the belly of the vase is continuous and shows three nude males and three horses running from right to left. The youths are all moving vigorously in a pose similar to that of the youth pursued by the siren on the neck panel; the feet are far apart, the right arm is extended forward, and the left arm is thrown back (bent at the elbow with down-turned palm). Vegetal motifs are again prominent. Flowers or plants hang from the top of the register between man and horse on side A, and a plant protrudes from under the horse on side B. A large flower or plant blooms between horse and man in the center of side A.

The scenes on this amphora are characteristic of the repertoire of Etruscan painting in the second half of the sixth century B.C. Of note is the combination of human, vegetal, and animal elements, depicted as equally important. The human element in this case is subsumed into the forces of nature, forces that can be benign (plants) or threatening (the siren), forces that evoke response from the nude, in this case also naked, human figures. Also worth noting is the

Side B

Etruscan painter's reliance on outline, volume, or silhouette. Only rarely is incision used for detail, mainly in the subsidiary scenes on the neck panels.

PROVENANCE:
Asensi Collection.

PUBLICATIONS:
Álvarez-Ossorio 1910, 104.

NOTES:
1. Compare the shape of the vase and zones of decoration, including the offset foot and the tongue pattern on the lip, to an amphora in Tarquinia, inv. no. 858: Spivey 1987, 32, pl. 34c. Spivey suggests that Tarquinia 858 may belong to the Micali Painter. This amphora also shows running youths on the belly, but the outline of the figures is handled with more assurance, and the details of the figures are indicated with sure incision. Also, the decoration of the neck panels is quite different from the Madrid amphora. Our amphora should thus be considered a product of the workshop of the Micali Painter.

G.W.

44. *Faliscan column krater*

Inv. no. 1999/99/160

H: 31.8 cm; diameter at rim: 21.5 cm; diameter at
    foot: 12.6 cm; maximum width: 30 cm

Faliscan

Last quarter of fourth century B.C.

The column krater of elongated
proportions evolved from South Italian
and Attic forms common in the fifth
and fourth centuries B.C. The Etruscan
aristocracy incorporated this form, in
many cases connected to the funerary
world, as a means to attain prestige, as a
sign of appropriation and identification
of status, and in our example, to give
the form an ornamental and symbolically renovated meaning.

The wide space of the belly, or the
body of the vase, is reserved for the
decoration and the inscription. Image
and inscription mutually define the
decorative space. The artistic process
seems to be as follows: a row of ten
masks was painted first, and then,
below, the inscription was painted from
right to left without inter spaces:
CAVIOSFRENAIOSFACED: "Cavios
Frenaios made me." The inscription is
written in Faliscan, an Italic language
spoken in that part of Eturia. The word
"faced" would thus be equivalent to
"fecit," like the *epoiesen* on Greek vases.
There is a wide horizontal band
between the inscription and the masks
that ends in serpentine feet and four
tails on the right side and a phallus at
the opposite end. It seems, in this fashion, that a table or stage (or a strange
anthropomorphic and demonic
diagram) has been constructed, very

unusual and almost dynamic. In this
way, the row of masks and faces become
a dedication, an offering or *anathema*
that ratifies the testimony of the writer
of the inscription.

The masks facing us are grotesque
and simply reflect a complex theatrical
group of individualized personages and
semi-human demons and satyrs, a group
of individualized characters. The two
central characters, with four companions at either side, stand out by their
size and by the heavy outlines of their
faces; they seem to be the main actors.
Each face is different: one of them (the
third from the right), perhaps bearded,
has only three-fourths of the face showing. The companion, to the right, above
the raised eyebrows, shows a bald spot
or mottled skin. Another, (fourth from
the right) has a pointed beard like the
paniskoi. The round faces (first from the
right) are a colorful contrast to the other

long and thin ones. The last one on the far left is associated with the large erect phallus. The characterization (individual or typical) corresponds to the tradition of the new drama or to the contemporary South Italian *phlyaxes*; the tails allude to the demonic and semi-animal world of satyrs.

To whom does the inscription "*Caviso Frenaios made me*" refer? To the artist maker of the vase, as on the Attic vases, or to the local personage who had the vase made, or to the owner of the krater, as on *Genucilia* plates, or even as on the controversial *Manios* fibula from Palestrina? The first option seems unlikely. The system of using two names is not in keeping with the social standing of a mere artisan. It is unthinkable that the name of the artisan should appear on our vase!

It must be the second possibility. The local aristocracy, emulating the prestigious Greek society, could intro-

duce fables and theatrical companies in the Etruscan-Latin or Faliscan world of the later fourth century B.C. The name would refer to a local promoter who sponsored theatrical presentation and paid for the masks and costumes. The word "*faced*" would then be the equivalent of "*faciendum coerauit*," the producer or impresario, if the modern transposition is used; the *choregus*, or *evergetes* sponsor, if we transpose to the Greek language. If this were the case, the promoter would then be the sponsor of all the masks, who celebrates the performance with this sort of Dionysian krater.

Little is known of the rich and heterogeneous tradition, which in the Italic world, with its heritage and mutations, would lead to the origins of the Roman theatre, and of the appearance of Plautus in the final years of the third century B.C. The play has many facets, as the grammarian Donatus might say (*de comoedia* VI, I): "*comoedia autem multas species habet.*" In its juxtaposition of species, Donatus speaks of the comedies of the countryside, and of the "*Rhintonics*" which were named for the famous Rhinton of Syracuse, who was active at the end of the fourth century B.C. and to whom are attributed the *phlyaxes*. There is also the incipient and difficult to comprehend *satura* that has little to do with the satyrs. Also there were the *tabernaria*, of an unpretentious style and plot, and the *palliata* and *crepidata* which the Latins associated with the Greek theatre. Our group of individual masks could be related to the *phlyax* tradition and with some of the new styles of the theatre, which in the Greek tradition used masks in farces for caricatures, for ridiculous scenes of everyday life, or for the sacred context of Dionysos and the satyrs. There is also room for a mixture of diverse theatrical worlds.

The ten faces or characters, along with the phallus and demonic-satirical beings, could be the expression of those insolent personages, heirs of the ancient *komos*, ready and willing to intercede and joke with the spectators.

They look at us, unveiled. Each individual mask, as in the Latin comedies, would have its name. The krater, ancient vessel of Dionysos and wine, could be used to celebrate the success of a theatrical performance. The local Italian world is appropriating with new vitality the ancient Greek farce. The philhellenic people of *Falerii*, or in Etruria, can add the Etruscan tradition of the Dionysian world to the cultural, religious, and commercial world of Magna Graecia at the end of the fourth century B.C. The promoter who proudly displayed his name and the masks that he had paid for, on this wine krater might have been a local patrician.

PROVENANCE:
Várez Fisa Collection.

PUBLICATIONS:
Cabrera 2003, no. 155.

NOTES:

1. The inscriptions painted on the vase with antroponimics in Latin or Faliscan would find a contemporary parallel in the plate of *P(oplia) Genucilia* in Rhode Island, which Del Chiaro attributes to Caere, and other authors to Falerii. See Del Chiaro 1957, vol 3, no. 4, 243f; Del Chiaro 1974, 64 for additions to the *Genucilia* Group. See the discussion of this inscription, painted before the pot was fired and situated under the foot, in Beazley 1947, 10 and 175, pl. 38, figs. 17–19; also *JHS* 53, 312. For discussion of the manufacture, Caeretan or Faliscan, see Ashmead and Phillips 1976, 91.

2. For the controversial gold fibula of Praeneste (Palestrina), see *AA.* 2000, no. 440, 326–327, with previous bibliography.

3. For Greek theatre and iconography, see Simon 1981. On the legacy and transmission of the Rhinton theater to the comedy of the first Roman epoch, see the excellent synthesis by Gigante 1971, 133–135. Beare 1964, appendix D, 264–266: "*crepidata, palliata, tabernaria, togata;*" Bieber 1961; Grimal 1978, ch. 6, "La naissance du théâtre à Rome." Also, Paratore 1957, 11f; Frassinetti 1953, 15f; Blänsdorf 1997, 152–153, with extensive bibliography. On the names of the masks, see, for example, Bonfante 1967, VIf. and Kerényi 1970, 98f.

R.O.

Bibliography

AA. 2000. *Principi etruschi tra Mediterraneo ed Europa.* (1 ottobre 2000 –1 aprile 2001), Comune di Bologna. Museo Civico Archeologico. Venice.

Aellen, C. 1994. *À la recherche de l'ordre cosmique. Forme et fonction des personnifications dans la céramique italiote.* Zurich.

Ahlberg, G. 1971. *Próthesis and Ekphorá in Greek Geometric Art.* Studies in Mediterranean Archaeology 32. Göteborg.

Ahlberg-Cornell, G. 1992. *Myth and Epos in Early Greek Art. Representation and Interpretation.* Studies in Mediterranean Archaeology 100. Jonsered.

Alberti, L.B. 1976/1435–6. (J.R. Spencer, trans.) *On Painting.* New Haven.

Alexiou, M. 1974. *The Ritual Lament in Greek Tradition.* Cambridge.

Álvarez-Ossorio, F. 1910. *Vasos griegos, etruscos é italo-griegos, que se conservan en el Museo Arqueológico Nacional.* Madrid.

Amyx, D.A. 1988. *Corinthian Vase-Painting of the Archaic Period.* Berkeley.

Anderson, W.D. 1994. *Music and Musicians in Ancient Greece.* Ithaca.

Andronikos, M. 1968. *Totenkult von Manolis Andronikos. Archaeologia Homerica,* vol. 3 W. Göttingen.

Arafat, K. and C. Morgan. 1989. "Pots and Potters in Athens and Corinth: A Review." *Oxford Journal of Archaeology,* 8: 311–346.

Ashmead, A.H. and K.M. Phillips, Jr. 1976. *Catalogue of the Classical Collections. Museum of Art. The Rhode Island School of Design.* Providence, Rhode Island.

Bal, M. 1985. *Narratology: Introduction to the Theory of Narrative.* Toronto.

Bal, M. 1991a. *On Story-Telling: Essays in Narratology.* Sonoma, CA.

Bal, M. 1991b. *Reading Rembrandt.* Cambridge.

Barthes, R. 1982. "Introduction to the Structural Analysis of Narratives." In *A Barthes Reader,* edited by S. Sontag, 251–295. New York.

Bažant, J. 1980. "Classical Archaeology and French Nineteenth Century Realists." *Listy Filologicke* 103: 193–201.

Bažant, J. 1981. *Studies on the Use and Decoration of Athenian Vases.* Prague.

Beard, M. 1991. "Adopting an Approach II." In *Looking at Greek Vases,* edited by T. Rasmussen and N. Spivey, 28–35. Cambridge.

Beare, W. 1964. *The Roman Stage: A Short History of Latin Drama in the Time of the Republic.* London.

Beazley, J.D. 1911. "The Master of Berlin Amphora." *The Journal of Hellenic Studies* 31: 276–295.

Beazley, J.D. 1930. *Der Berliner Maler.* Mainz.

Beazley, J.D. 1932. "Little-Master Cups." *The Journal of Hellenic Studies* 52: 167–204.

Beazley, J.D. 1946. *Potter and Painter in Ancient Athens.* London.

Beazley, J.D. 1947. *Etruscan Vase-Painting.* Oxford.

Beazley, J.D. 1956. *Attic Black-Figure Vase-Painters.* Oxford. (=ABV)

Beazley, J.D. 1963. *Attic Red-Figure Vase-Painters.* 2nd edition. Oxford.

Beazley, J.D. 1964. *The Berlin Painter.* Melbourne.

Beazley, J.D. 1971. *Paralipomena. Additions to Attic Black-Figure Vase-Painters and to Attic Red-Figure Vase-Painters.* 2nd edition. Oxford.

Beazley, J.D. 1986. *The Development of Black-Figure.* Rev. ed. Berkeley.

Benson, J.L. 1989. *Earlier Corinthian Workshop: A Study of Corinthian Geometric and Protocorinthians Stylistic Group.* Amsterdam.

Bentz, M. 1998. *Panathenäische Preisamphoren: Eine athenische Vasengattung und ihre Funktion vom 6.–4. Jahrhundert v. Chr.* Basel.

Bérard, Cl. 1983. "Iconographie-iconologie-iconologique." *Etudes de Lettres* 4: 5–37.

Bérard, Cl. 1984. "L'ordre des femmes." In *La Cité des images. Religion et société en Grèce antique.* Institut d'Archéologie et d'Histoire Ancienne, Lausanne, Centre de Recherches Comparées sur les Sociétés Anciennes. 85–104. Paris.

Bérard, Cl., C. Bron, J.-L. Durand, et al. 1989. *A City of Images: Iconography and Society in Ancient Greece.* Princeton.

Bérard, Cl. and J.P. Vernant, eds. 1984. *La Cité des images. Religion et société en Grèce antique.* Institut d'Archéologie et d'Histoire Ancienne, Lausanne, Centre de Recherches Comparées sur les Sociétés Anciennes, Paris.

Bianchi Bandinelli, R. and A. Giuliano. 1973. *Etruschi e Italici prima del dominio di Roma.* Milan.

Bieber, M. 1961. *The History of Greek and Roman Theatre.* Princeton.

Bienkowski, P. 1899. "Dos ánforas áticas de la colección de Madrid." *Revista de Archivos, Bibliotecas y Museos* 3: 604–611.

Blänsdorf, J. 1997. "Atellana fabula." *Der Neue Pauly* 2: 152–153.

Bloesch, H. 1940. *Formen Attischer Schalen von Exekias bis zum Ende des Strengen Stils.* Bern.

Bloesch, H. 1982. *Greek Vases from the Hirschmann Collection.* Zurich.

Blundell, S. 1995. *Women in Ancient Greece.* Cambridge.

Boardman, J. 1952. "Pottery from Eretria." *Annual of the British School at Athens,* 47: 1–48.

Boardman, J. 1957. "Early Euboean Pottery and History." *Annual of the British School at Athens,* 52: 1–29.

Boardman, J. 1974. *Athenian Black Figure Vases. A Handbook.* London.

Boardman, J. 1975. *Athenian Red Figure Vases. The Archaic Period.* London.

Boardman, J. 1980. *The Greeks Overseas.* 3rd ed. London.

Boardman, J. 1984. "Image and Politics in Sixth Century Athens." In *Ancient Greek and Related Pottery,* edited by H.A.G. Brijder. Allard Pierson Series, vol. 5. Amsterdam.

Boardman, J. 1985. "Image and Politics in Sixth Century Athens." In *Ancient Greek and Related Pottery,* edited by H.A.G. Brijder. Allard Pierson Series, vol. 5. Amsterdam.

Boardman, J. 1987a. "Amasis: The Implications of His Name." In *Papers on the Amasis Painter and His World,* edited by M. True, 141–152. Malibu.

Boardman, J. 1987b. "Silver is White." *Revue archéologique:* 279–295.

Boardman, J. 1989. *Athenian Red Figure Vases. The Classical Period.* London.

Boardman, J. 1990. "Symposion Furniture." In *Sympotica. A Symposium on the Symposion,* edited by O. Murray, 122–131. Oxford.

Boardman, J. 1992. "Kaloi and other names on Euphronios' Vases." In *Euphronios: atti del seminario internazionale di studi, Arezzo, 27–28 maggio 1990,* edited by M. Cygielman, M. Iozzo, F. Nicosia, and P. Zamarchi Grassi, 45–50. Florence.

Boardman, J. 1994. *The Diffusion of Classical Art in Antiquity.* Princeton.

Boardman, J. 1997. "Pan." In *Lexicon Iconographicum Mythologiae Classicae,* vol VIII, 923–941. Zurich.

Boardman, J. 1998. *Early Greek Vase Painting, 11th – 6th Centuries BC.* London.

Boardman, J. 2001. *The History of Greek Vases.* London.

Boedeker, D. and K. A. Raaflaub. 1998. *Democracy, Empire, and the Arts in Fifth-Century Athens.* Cambridge.

Bonamici, M. 1974. *I buccheri con figurazioni graffite.* Florence.

Bonfante, G. 1967. "La lingua delle Atellane e dei mimi." In *Fabula Atellana: saggio sul teatro popolare latino,* edited by P. Frassinetti. Genova.

Boss, M. 1997. "Preliminary Sketches on Attic Red-figured Vases of the Early Fifth Century B.C." In *Athenian Potters and Painters,* edited by J. Oakley, W.D.E. Coulson, and O. Palagia, 345–351. Oxford.

Bourgeaud, P. 1979. *Recherches sur le Dieu Pan.* Rome.

Bowditch , L.P. 1976. "The Role of Redundancy in Cohesion and Evaluative Functioning in Narrative: A Grab for the Referential Hierarchy." *Rackham Literary Studies* 7 (Winter):19–37.

Braun, K. 1981. *Das Kabirenheiligtum bei Theben,* vol. IV. Berlin.

Brilliant, R. 1984. *Visual narratives: Storytelling in Etruscan and Roman Art.* Ithaca.

Briquel, D. 1987. "Regards étrusques sur l'au-delà." In *La Mort, les morts et l'au-delà dans le monde romain,* edited by F. Himard: 262–277. Caen.

Brisson, L. 2002. *Sexual Ambivalence: Androgyny and Hermaphroditism in Graeco-Roman Antiquity.* Berkeley.

Brock, R. 1994. "The Labour of Women in Classical Athens." *Classical Quarterly,* 44: 336–346.

Brommer, F. 1937. *Satyroi.* Würzburg.

Brulé, P. 2001. "Hyménée sonore: la musique du *gamós.*" In *Chanter les dieux. Musique et réligion dans l'Antiquité grecque et romaine,* edited by P. Brulé and C. Vendris, 243–278. Rennes.

Bruns, G. 1940. *Das Kabirenheiligtum bei Theben,* vol. I. Berlin.

Bruschetti, P. and P. Zamarchi Grassi. 1999. *Cortona etrusca. Esempi di architettura funeraria.* Cortona.

Bryson, N. 1991. "Semiology and Visual Interpretation." In *VisualTheory:Painting and Interpretation,* edited by N. Bryson, M.A. Holly, and K. Moxey, 61–73. New York.

Buitron-Oliver, D. 1995. *Douris: A Master-painter of Athenian Red-figure Vases.* Mainz.

Burkert, W. 1985. *Greek Religion.* Cambridge.

Burkert, W. 1987. *Ancient Mystery Cults.* Cambridge.

Burn, L. 1991. "A Dinoid Volute-Krater by the Meleager Painter: An Attic Vase in South Italian Manner." In *Greek Vases in the J. Paul Getty Museum,* vol. 5, 107–130. Malibu.

Burow, J. 1989. *Der Antimenesmaler.* Mainz am Rhein.

Buschor, E. 1943 *Satyrtänze und frühes Drama.* Munich.

Buschor, E. 1944. *Die Musen des Jenseits.* Munich.

Cabrera, P. 1997. "Imagen y poder en el proceso de formación de la polis griega." In *Arte y poder en el Mundo Antiguo,* edited by C. Sánchez and A. Domínguez Monedero, 61–79. Madrid.

Cabrera, P. 1998. "Dioniso en un jardín: el espacio de la iniciación en la iconografía de los vasos apulios." In *En los límites de Dioniso,* edited by C. Sánchez and P. Cabrera, 61–87. Actas del Simposio celebrado en el Museo Arqueológico Nacional (Madrid, 20 de junio de 1997). Murcia.

Cabrera, P., ed. 2003. *La colección Várez FISA en el Museo Arqueológica Nacional.* Catálogo de la exposición celebrada en el Museo Arqueológica Nacional (septiembre – noviembre 2003). Madrid.

Cahn, H.A. 1995. *Kylikes. Trinkgefässe der griechischen Welt.* Katalog 7, Basilea.

Calatayud, M. A. 1888. *Pedro Franco Davila y el Real Gabinete de Historia Natural.* Madrid.

Calimach, A. 2002. *Lovers' Legends: The Gay Greek Myths.* New Rochelle, New York.

Campbell, J. 1982. *Grammatical Man: Information, Entropy, Language, and Life.* New York.

Canciani, F. 1978. "Lydos, der Sklave?" *Antike Kunst* 21: 17–20.

Cantarella, E. 1987. *Pandora's Daughters: the Role & Status of Women in Greek & Roman Antiquity.* Baltimore.

Cantarella, E. 1992. *Bisexuality in the Ancient World.* New Haven.

Carpenter, T.H. 1983. "On the Dating of the Tyrrhenian Group." *Oxford Journal of Archaeology* 2: 279–293.

Carpenter, T.H. 1984. "The Tyrrhenian Group: Problems of Provenance." *Oxford Journal of Archaeology* 3: 45–56.

Carpenter, T.H. 1986. *Dionysian Imagery in Archaic Greek Art. Its development in Black-figure Vase Painting.* Oxford.

Carpenter, T.H. 1989. *Beazley Addenda: Additional References to ABV, ARV2 and Paralipomena.* 2nd ed. Oxford.

Carpenter, T.H. 1991. *Art and Myth in Ancient Greece.* London.

Carpenter, T.H. 1997. *Dionysian Imagery in Fifth-Century Athens.* Oxford.

Carpenter, T.H., T. Mannack and M. Mendonca. 1989. *Beazley Addenda: Additional references to ABV, ARV2 and Paralipomena,* vol. II. Oxford.

Carter, J. 1972. "The Beginnings of Narrative Art in the Greek Geometric Period." *Annual of the British School at Athens* 67: 25–58.

Cassimatis, H. 1993. *Le lèbes à anses dressées italiotes àtravers la collection du Louvre.* Napoli.

Castellanos, B. S. 1847. *Apuntes para un Catálogo de los objetos que comprende la colección del Museo de Antigüedades de la Biblioteca Nacional de Madrid.* Madrid.

Castriota, D. 1992. *Myth, Ethos, and Actuality: Official Art in Fifth-Century B.C. Athens.* Madison.

Catalina, M. 1872. "Urnas cinerarias con relieves del Museo Arqueológico Nacional." *Museo Español de Antigüedades* 1: 511–539.

Catálogo del Museo Nacional de Arqueología que se publicó siendo director del mismo el Excmo Señor Don Antonio García Gutiérrez. 1883. sec. 1, vol. 1. Madrid.

Chatman, S. 1978. *Story and Discourse.* Ithaca, New York.

Cohen, B. 1978. *Attic Bilingual Vases and their Painters.* New York.

Cohen, B. 1991. "The Literate Potter: A Tradition of Incised Signatures on Attic Vases." *Metropolitan Museum of Art Journal* 26: 49–95.

Cohen, D. 1993. "Consent and Sexual Relations in Classical Athens." In *Consent and Coercion to Sex and Marriage in Ancient and Medieval Societies*, edited by A.E. Laiou, 5–16. Washington, D.C.

Cohen, B. 2000a. "Man-killers and Their Victims: Inversions of the Heroic Ideal in Classical Art." In *Not the Classical Ideal: Athens and the Construction of the Other in Greek Art*, edited by B. Cohen, 98–131. Leiden.

Cohen, B., ed. 2000b. *Not the Classical Ideal: Athens and the Construction of the Other in Greek Art*. Leiden.

Coldstream, J.N. 1968. *Greek Geometric Pottery*. London.

Coldstream, J.N. 1977. *Geometric Greece*. London.

Cole, S.G. 1993. "Voices from beyond the Grave: Dionysus and the Dead." In *Masks of Dionysus*, edited by T.H. Carpenter and C.A. Faraone, 276–296. Ithaca, New York.

Colonna, G. 2000. "La cultura orientalizzante in Etruria." In *AA.VV.: Principi etruschi tra Mediterraneo ed Europa*, 55–56 (1 ottobre 2000 –1 aprile 2001), Comune di Bologna. Museo Civico Archeologico. Venice.

Cook, R.M. 1933–34. "Fikellura Pottery." *Annual of the British School at Athens* 34: 1–98.

Cook, R.M. 1953. "Dogs in Battle." *Festchrift A.Rümpf*. Krefeld: 38–42.

Cook, R.M. 1971. "'Epoiesen' on Greek Vases." *Journal of Hellenic Studies*, 91: 137–138.

Cook, R.M. 1997. *Greek Painted Pottery*. 3rd ed. London.

Corbett, P.E. 1965. "Preliminary Sketch in Greek Vase-Painting." *Journal of Hellenic Studies*, 85: 16–28.

Courbin, P. 1966. *La céramique géométrique de l'Argolide*. Paris.

Cristofani, M. 1983. *La scoperta degli Etruschi*. Rome.

Cristofani, M. 1993. "Da selvaggio a incivile." *Prospettiva* 71: 77–84.

Csapo. E. and M. Miller. 1998. "Towards a Politics of Time and Narrative." In *Democracy, Empire, and the Arts in Fifth-Century Athens*, edited by D. Boedeker and K.A. Raaflaub, 87–125. Cambridge.

Cumont, F. 1949. *Lux Perpetua*. Paris.

Daumas, M. 1984. "Apollon. Die apollinische Trias." *Lexicon Iconographicum Mythologiae Classicae* II, 261 ss., no. 630–666.

Davidson, J.N. 1997. *Fishcakes and Courtesans: The Consuming Passions of Classical Athens*. London.

Davison, J.M. 1968. *Attic Geometric Workshops*. Rome.

Davison, J.M. 1991. "Myth and the Periphery." In *Myth and the Polis*, edited by D.C. Pozzi and J.M. Wickersham, 49–63. Ithaca.

Darcque, P. and J. Poursat, eds. 1985. *L'iconographie Minoenne. Bulletin de correspondance hellénique* supplement 11, Paris.

Del Chiaro, M.A. 1957. *The Genucilia Group: A Class of Etruscan Red-Figured Plates*. University of California Publications in Classical Archaeology, vol 3. Berkeley.

Del Chiaro, M.A. 1974. *Etruscans Red-Figure Vase-Painting at Caere*. Berkeley.

Denoyelle, M. 1997. "Attic or non-Attic?: The Case of the Pisticci Painter." In *Athenian Potters and Painters*, edited by J. Oakley, W.D.E. Coulson, and O. Palagia, 395–405. Oxford.

Dentzer, J.M. 1982. *Le motif du banquet couché dans le Proche-Orient et le monde grec du VIIème au IVème siècle avant J.-C.* Rome.

DeVries, K. 1997. "The 'Frigid Eromenoi' and their Wooers Revisited: A Closer Look at Greek Homosexuality in Vase Painting." In *Queer Representations: Reading Lives, Reading Cultures*, edited by M. Duberman, 14–24. New York.

Diehl, E. 1964. *Die Hydria*. Mainz am Rhein.

Díez de Velasco, F. 1995. *Los caminos de la muerte. Religión, rito e imágenes del paso al más allá en la Grecia antigua*. Madrid.

Díez de Velasco, F. 1998. "Dioniso y la muerte: Gorgo en contextos dionisíacos en la cerámica ática." In *En los límites de Dioniso*, edited by C. Sánchez and P. Cabrera, 41–60. Actas del Simposio celebrado en el Museo Arqueológico Nacional (Madrid, 20 de junio de 1997). Murcia.

Dohrn, T. 1937. *Die shwarzfigurigen etruskischen Vasen aus den zweiten Hälfte des sechsten Jashrhunderts*. Berlin.

Dover, J.K. 1978. *Greek Homosexuality*. London.

Dubois, P. 1994. *Centaurs and Amazons: Women and Pre-History of the Great Chain of Being*. Ann Arbor.

Ducati, P. 1932. *Pontische Vasen*. Rome.

Ducrey, P. 1985. *Guerre et guerriers dans la Grèce antique*. Paris.

Dummer, J. 1977. "Realität des Lebens und Realitatsschwund in der Vasenmalerei." In *Beitrage zum antiken Realismus*, edited by M. Kunze. Schriften der Winckelmann-Gesellschaft 3, 57–62. Berlin.

Dunkley, B. 1935–1936. "Greek Fountain Buildings before 300 a.C." *Annual of the British School of Athens*, 36, 142.

Durand, J.L. and A. Schnapp. 1984. "Boucherie sacrificielle et chasses initiatiques." In *La Cité des images. Religion et société en Grèce antique*, 49–88. Institut d'Archéologie et d'Histoire Ancienne, Lausanne, Centre de Recherches Comparées sur les Sociétés Anciennes. Paris.

Eisenberg, J. 1995. *Art of the Ancient World*. New York.

Eisman, M.M. 1974. "A further note on EPOIESEN signatures." *Journal of Hellenic Studies* 94: 172.

Elston, M. 1990. "Ancient Repairs of Greek Vases in the J. Paul Getty Museum." *Journal of the J. Paul Getty Museum*, 18: 53–68.

Engelmann, H. 1987. "Wie nie Euphronios." *Zeitschrift für Papyrology und Epigraphik*, 68: 129–133.

Ensoli, S. 1996. "Le sirene omeriche e le sirene musicanti di età classica." In *Ulisse. Il mito e la memoria*, edited by B. Andreae, 96–107. Rome

Fehr, B. 1990. "Entertainers at the Symposion." In *Sympotica: a Symposium on the Symposion*, edited by O. Murray, 185–195. Oxford.

Ferrari, G. 2002. *Figures of Speech. Men and Maidens in Ancient Greece*. Chicago.

Ferrari, G. 2003. "Myth and Genre on Athenian Vases." *Classical Antiquity*, 22, 1: 37–54.

Frassinetti, P. 1953. *Fabula Atellana: saggio sul teatro popolare latino*. Genova.

Frel, J. 1983. "Euphronios and his Fellows." In *Ancient Greek Art and Iconography*, edited by W.G. Moon, 147–158. Madison.

Froning, H. 1988. "Anfange der Kontinuierenden Bilderzahlung in der griechischen Kunst," *Jahrbuch des Deutschen Archäologischen Instituts* 103: 169–199.

Frontisi-Ducroux, F. 1984. "Au miroir du masque." In *La cité des images. Religion et société en Grèce Antique*, 147–161. Institut d'Archéologie et d'Histoire Ancienne, Lausanne, Centre de Recherches Comparées sur les Sociétés Anciennes. Paris.

Frontisi-Ducroux, F. 1991. *Le dieu-masque. Une figure du Dionysos d'Athènes*. Rome.

Gantz, T. 1993. *Early Greek Myth, A Guide to Literary and Artistic Sources*. Baltimore.

Garlan, Y. 1999. *La guerre dans l'Antiquité*. Paris.

Garland, R. 1985. *The Greek Way of Death*. London.

Gasparri, C. 1986. "Dionisos." In *Lexicon Iconographicum Mythologiae Classicae*, vol. III, 413–514. Zürich.

Gebhard, E. 1969. "Actors and Acting." In *The Muses at Work: Arts, Crafts, and Professions in Ancient Greece and Rome*, edited by C. Roebuck, 250–269. Cambridge.

Gempeler, R.D. 1973. *Die etruskischen Kanopen*. Eisiedeln.

Gentili, B. and R. Pretagostini, eds. 1988. *La musica in Grecia*. Rome-Bari

Gericke, H. 1970. *Gefässdarstellungen auf griechischen Vasen*. Berlin.

Gigante, M. 1971. *Rintone e il teatro in Magna Grecia*. Naples.

Giuliani, L. 1995. *Tragik, Trauer und Trost. Bildervasen für eine apulische Totenfeier*. Antikensammlung staatliche Museen zu Berlin Preussischer kulturbesitz. Berlin.

Goldhill, S. and R. Osborne. 1994. *Art and Text in Ancient Greek Culture*. Cambridge.

Gombrich, E.H. 1960. *Art and Illusion: A Study in the Psychology of Pictorial Representation*. New York.

Gombrich, E.H. 1984. *The Sense of Order: A Study in the Psychology of Decorative Art*. Oxford.

Götte, E. 1957. *Frauengemachbilder in der Vasenmalerei des fünften Jhs*. Munich.

Gran-Aymerich, J. 1999a. "Images et mythes sur les vases noirs d'Étrurie (VIII–VI siècle av. J.-C)." In *Le mythe grec dans l'Italie antique. Fonction et image*, edited by F.-H. Massa-Pairault, 383–404. (Rome Nov. 1996) Rome.

Gran-Aymerich, J. 1999b. "Vases grecs et vases étrusques: les services mixtes." In *Céramique et peinture grecques. Modes d'emploi*, edited by M.-C. Villaneuva Puig, F. Lissarrague, P. Rouillard, and A. Rouveret, 449–453. Paris.

Grimal, P. 1978. *Le théâtre antique*. Paris.

Guía Histórica y Descriptiva del Museo Arqueológico Naciona. 1917. Madrid.

Halliday, M.A.K. and R. Hasan. 1975 (1989 reprinting) *Cohesion in English*. London.

Halperin, D.M. 1990. *One Hundred Years of Homosexuality and Other Essays on Greek Love*. New York.

Halperin, D.M. 1996. "Homosexuality." In *The Oxford Classical Dictionary*, 3rd ed., edited by S. Hornblower and A. Spawforth, 720–723. Oxford.

Halperin, D.M. 2002. *How to do the History of Homosexuality*. Chicago.

Hannestad, L. 1974. *The Paris Painter: an Etruscan Vase-painter*. Copenhagen.

Hannestad, L. 1976. *The Followers of the Paris Painter*. Copenhagen.

Hannestad, L. 1984. "Slaves and the Fountain House Theme." In *Ancient Greek and Related Pottery*, edited by H.A.G. Brijder, 252–55. Amsterdam.

Hampe, R. 1960. *Ein Frühattischer Grabfund*. Mainz.

Hampe, R. 1975."Dickbauchtänzer und Diebe auf Korintischen Krater. *Jahrbuch des Deutschen Archaologisches Institut* 90: 85–99.

Harari, M. 1995. "Ipotesi sulle regole del montaggio narrativo nella pittura vascolare etrusca." In *Modi e funzioni del racconto mitico nella ceramica greca, italiota ed etrusca dal VI secolo VI A.C.*, (*Actas del Coloquio de Vietri sul Mare*), 111. Salerno.

Hardee, A. and F. Henry. 1990. *Narratology and Narrative*. Columbia.

Harrison, T. 1997. "Herodotos and the ancient idea of rape." In *Rape in Antiquity*, edited by S. Deans and K. F. Pierce, 185. Chippenham.

Harvey, F. 1988. "Painted Ladies: Fact, Fiction and Fantasy." In *Proceedings of the 3rd Symposium on Ancient Greek and Related Pottery*, edited by J. Christiansen and T. Melander, 242–54. Copenhagen.

Haxthausen, C.W., ed. 2002. *The Two Art Histories: The Museum and the University*. Williamstown.

Haynes, S. 1985. *Etruscan Bronzes*. London.

Hedreen, G.H. 1996. "Image, Text, and Story in the Recovery of Helen." *Classical Antiquity* 15: 152–184.

Hedreen, G. H. 2001. *Capturing Troy. The narrative Functions of Landscape in Archaic and Early Classical Greek Art*. Ann Arbor.

Heesen, P. 1996. *The J.L. Theodor Collection of Attic Black-Figure Vases*. Amsterdam.

Hemelrijk, J.M. 1984. *Caeretan Hydriae*. Mainz.

Hemelrijk, J.M. 1991. "A closer look at the potter." In *Looking at Greek Vases*, edited by T. Rasmussen and N. Spivey, 233–256. Cambridge.

Hermary, A. et al. 1986. "Eros." In *Lexicon Iconographicum Mythologiae Classicae*, vol III, 850–942. Zürich.

Herter, H. 1947. *Vom dionysischen Tanz zum komischen Spiel, die Anfänge der attischen komodie*. Iserlohn.

Himmelmann, N. 1994. *Realistische Themen in der griechischen Kunst der archaischen und klassischen Zeit*. Berlin.

Hoffmann, H. 1966. *Tarentine Rhyta*. Mainz.

Hoffmann, H. 1977. *Sexual and Asexual Pursuit: A Structuralist Approach to Greek Vase Painting*. London.

Hoffmann, H. 1989. "Rhyta and Kantharoi in Greek Ritual." In *Greek Vases in the J. Paul Getty Museum*, vol. 4, 131–166. Malibu.

Hoffmann, H. 1997. *Sotades: Symbols of Immortality on Greek Vases*. Oxford.

Holliday, P., ed. 1993. *Narrative and Event in Ancient Art*. Cambridge.

Hübner, E. 1862. *Die antiken Bildwerke in Madrid*. Berlin.

Icard-Gianolio, N. 1978. "Io." In *Lexicon Iconographicum Mythologiae Classicae*, vol. V, 661–676. Zurich.

Immerwahr, H. 1990. *Attic Script: A Survey*. Oxford.

Iozzo, M. 1993. *Ceramica "calcidese." Nuovi documenti e problemi riproposti*, Atti e Memorie della Società Magna Grecia, Series 3, vol 2. Rome.

Iozzo, M. 2003. "L'acqua e le donne ad Atene." In *L'acqua degli Dei: Immagini di fontane, vasellame, culti salutari e in grotta*. Siena.

Jahn, O. 1967. "Kottabos auf Vasenbildern." *Philologus* 26: 201–40.

Jannot, J-R. 1998. *Devins, Dieux et Demons. Regards sur la religion de l'Étrurie antique*. Paris.

Jeanmaire, H. 1978. *Dyonisos. Histoire du culte de Bacchus*. Paris.

Johnson, F.P. 1955. "A note on owl skyphoi." *American Journal of Archaeology*, 59: 119–124.

Johnston, A.W. 1979. *Trademarks on Greek Vases*. Warminster.

Jongkees-Vos, M.F. 1971. "The Centaur Painter." In *Varia Archaeologica*, 13–21. Utrech.

Jordan, J.A. 1988. *Attic black-figure eye-cups*. Diss. New York University. Ann Arbor.

Jucker, H. 1961. *Das Bildnis im Blätterkelch. Geschichte und Bedeutung einer römischer Porträtform*. Lausanne.

Kaempf-Dimitriadou, S. 1979. *Die Liebe der Götter in der attischen Kunst des 5 Jahrhunderts v. Chr.* Basel.

Kahil, L. and N. Icard. 1988. "Helene." In *Lexicon Iconographicum Mythologiae Classicae*, vol. 4, 463–563. Zurich.

Kanowski, M.G. 1984. *Containers of Classical Greece, A Handbook of Shapes*. St. Lucia.

Kassaplogou, E., ed. 1992. *L'image en jeu: de l'antiquité àPaul Klee*. Yens-sur-Morges.

Kaufman-Samara, A. 1997. ""Ouk apomouson ta gynaikon" (Eurip. Med., 1089). Gynaikes mousikoi sta attika aggeia tou 5ou ai. p X." In J. H. Oakley, E. D. Coulson and O. Palagia, *Athenian Potters and Painters.* Oxford Monographs 67, 285–295. Oxford.

Kennedy-Quigley, S. 2001. "Visual Representations of the Birth of Athena/Menrva: A Comparative Study." *Etruscan Studies* 8: in press.

Kerényi, K. 1970. "Satire und Satura." In *Die römische Satire*, edited by D. Korzeniewski, 238. Darmstadt.

Kerényi, K. 1976. *Dionysos. Archetypal Image of Indestructible Life.* Princeton

Keuls, E.C. 1985. *The Reign of the Phallus: Sexual Politics in Ancient Athens.* Berkeley.

Keuls, E.C. 1988. "The Social Position of Attic Vase Painters and the Birth of Caricature." In *Ancient Greek and Related Pottery*, edited by J. Christiansen and T. Melander, 300–313. Copenhagen.

Kilinski, K. 1986. "Boeotian Trick Vases." *American Journal of Archaeology* 90: 153–158.

Kilinski, K. 1990. *Boeotian Black Figure Vase Painting of the Archaic Period.* Mainz.

Kilinski, K. 1992. "Teisias and Theodoros: East Boiotian Potters." *Hesperia* 61, 2: 253–263.

Kilinski, K. 1994. "Contributions to the Euboean Corpus: More Black Figure Vases." *Antike Kunst* 37, 1: 3–20.

Kilinski, K. 1998. "Greek Masculine Prowess in the Manifestations of Zeus." In *Myth, Sexuality and Power: Images of Jupiter in Western Art*, edited by F. Van Keuren. *Archaeologia Transatlantica* 16: 29–50.

Kilmer, M. 1993. *Greek Erotica on Attic Red-Figure Vases.* London.

Kinkel, G. 1877. *Epicorum graecorum fragmenta. Collegit, disposuit, commentarium criticum adiecit.* Lipsiae.

Knauer, E. 1986. "Still more light on old walls. Eine ikonographische Nachlese." *Studien zur Mythologie und Vasenmalerei. Festschrift für Konrad Schauenburg,* 121–126. Mainz.

Kolb, F. 1977. "Die Bau-, Religions- und Kulturpolitik der Peisistratiden." *Jahrbuch des Deutschen Archäologischen Instituts* 92: 99–138.

Kossatz-Deismann, A. 1978. *Dramen des Aischylos auf Westgriechischen Vasen.* Mainz.

Kourou, N. 1997. "Sphinx." In *Lexicon Iconographicum Mythologiae Classicae* vol. VIII, 1149–1165. Zurich.

Kübler, K. 1954. *Kerameikos. Die Nekropole des 10. Bis 8. Jahrhundert*, Deutsches Archäologisches Institut. Berlin.

Kübler, K. 1970. *Kerameikos VI. Die Nekropole des späten 8. Bis frühen 6. Jahrhunderts.* Deutsches Archäologisches Institut. Berlin.

Kunisch, N. 1998. *Ornamente geometrischer Vasen : ein Kompendium.* Cologne.

Kunze, E. 1932. "Eine attische schwazfigurige Vasengottung und die Darstellung des Komos in 6. Jahrhundert." *Gnomon* 8: 120–124.

Kurke, L. 1990. "Pindar's Sixth *Pythian.*" *Transactions of the American Philological Association* 120: 85–107.

Kurke, L. 1997. "Inventing the Hetaira: Sex, Politics, and Discursive Conflict in Archaic Greece." *Classical Antiquity* 16, 1: 105–150.

Kurke, L. 1999. *Coins, Bodies, Games and Gold: The Politics of Meaning in Archaic Greece.* Princeton.

Kurtz, D.C. 1975. *Athenian White Lekythoi. Patterns and Painters.* Oxford.

Kurtz, D.C. 1983. *The Berlin Painter.* Oxford Monographs on Classical Archaeology. Oxford.

Kurtz, D.C. 1984. "Vases for the Dead: an Attic Selection 750–400 B.C." In *Ancient Greek and Related Pottery*, edited by H. A. G. Brijder, 314–328. Amsterdam.

Kurtz, D.C., ed. 1985. *Beazley and Oxford.* Oxford University Committee for Archaeology, Monograph no. 10. Oxford.

Kurtz, D.C., ed. 1989. *Greek Vases: Lectures by J.D. Beazley.* Oxford.

Kurtz, D.C. and J. Boardman. 1971. *Greek Burial Customs.* London.

Labov, W. 1972. *Language in the Inner City.* Philadelphia.

Lacroix, L. 1976. "La légende de Pélops et son iconographie." *Bulletin de Correspondance Hellénique* 100: 327–341.

Lane, E.A. 1933–34. "Lakonian Vase-Painting." *British School of Athens* 34: 99–189.

Langdon, S., ed. 1993. *From Pasture to Polis. Art in the Age of Homer.* Columbia, Missouri.

Laumonier, A. 1921. *Catalogue de Terres Cuites de Musée Archéologique de Madrid.* Paris.

Leach, E. 1974. *Claude Levi-Strauss.* New York.

Leroux, G. 1912. *Vases Grecs et Italo-Grecs du Musée Archéologique de Madrid.* Paris.

Lewis, S. 2002. *The Athenian Woman: an Iconographic Handbook.* London and New York.

Lezzi-Hafter, A. 1997. "Offerings Made to Measure: Two Special Commissions by the Eretria Painter for Apollonia Pontica." In *Athenian Potters and Painters*, edited by J. Oakley, W.D.E. Coulson, and O. Palagia, 353–369. Oxford.

Lindner, R. 1984. *Der Raub der Persephone in der Antiken Kunst.* Beiträge zur Archäologie 16, Wurzburg.

Lissarrague, F. 1987. *Un flot d'images. Une esthétique du banquet grec.* Paris.

Lissarrague, F. 1990a. "The Sexual Life of Satyrs." In *Before Sexuality: the Construction of Erotic Experience in the Ancient Greek World*, edited by D.M. Halperin, J.J. Winkler, and F.I. Zeitlin, 53–81. Princeton.

Lissarrague, F. 1990b. *L'autre guerrier: archers, peltastes, cavaliers dans l' imagerie attique.* Paris.

Lissarrague, F. 1990c. *The Aesthetics of the Greek Banquet: Images of Wine and Ritual.* Princeton.

Lissarrague, F. 1990d. "Around the Krater: An Aspect of Banquet Imagery." In *Sympotica. A Symposium on the Symposion*, edited by O. Murray, 196–209. Oxford.

Lissarrague, F. 1992. "*Graphein:* écrire et dessiner." In *L'image en jeu: de l'Antiquité à Paul Klee*, edited by C. Bron and E. Kassapoglou, 186–197. Yens-sur-Monges.

Lissarrague, F. 1995a. "Women, Boxes, Containers: Some Signs and Metaphors." In *Pandora, Women in Classical Greece*, edited by E. Reeder, 91–101. Princeton.

Lissarrague, F. 1995b. "Un rituel du vin: la libation." In *In vino veritas*, edited by O. Murray and M. Tecusan, 126–144. Rome.

Lissarrague, F. and A. Schnapp. 1981. "Imagerie des grecs ou Grece des imagiers?" *Le temps de la reflexion* 2: 275–97.

Lloyd, G.E.R. 1966. *Polarity and Analogy: Two Types of Argumentation in Early Greek Thought.* Cambridge.

Lohmann, H. 1979. *Grabmäler auf unteritalischen Vasen. Archäologische Forschungen*, vol. 7. Berlin.

Lonsdale, S.H. 1993. *Dance and Ritual Play in Greek Religion.* Baltimore.

Lullies, R. 1955. *Eine Sammlung griechischen Kleinkunst.* Munich.

Lund, J. and A. Rathje. 1988. "Italic Gods and Deities on Pontic Vases." In *Ancient Greek and Related Pottery*, edited by J. Christiansen and T. Melander, 352–368. Copenhagen.

Mackay, E.A., ed. 1999a. *Signs of Orality: The Oral Tradition and its Influence in the Greek and Roman World*. Leiden.

Mackay, E.A., et al. 1999b. "The Bystander at the Ringside. Ring-composition in Early Greek Poetry and Vase-Painting." In *Signs of Orality: The Oral Tradition and its Influence in theGreek and Roman World*, edited by E.A. Mackay, 115–141. Leiden.

Madrazo, P. 1872. "Vasos Italo-Griegos del Museo Arqueológico Nacional." *Museo Español de Antigüedades* 1: 293–324.

Malinowski, B. 1953. "The Problem of Meaning in Primitive Languages." In *The Meaning of Meaning*, edited by C.K. Ogden and L.A. Richards, 296–336. London.

Manakidou, E. 1992. "Athenerinnen in schwarzfigurigen Brunnenhausszenen." *Hephaistos* 11: 51–91.

Manfrini-Aragno, I. 1992. "Femmes a la fontaine: realite et imaginaire." In *L'image en jeu: de l'antiquite a Paul Klee*, edited by C. Bron and E. Kassapolgou, 127–48. Yens-sur-Morges.

Mannack, T. 2001. *The Late Mannerists in Athenian Vase-Painting*. Oxford.

Marcos Pous, A. 1993. *De Gabinete a Museo: tres siglos de historia. Museo Arqueológico Nacional Abril-Junio de 1993*. Madrid.

Marinatos, N. 1993. "Some Reflections on the Rhetoric of Aegean and Egyptian Art." In *Narrative and Event in Ancient Art*, edited by P. Holliday, 74. Cambridge.

Martelli, M. 1979. "La ceramica greca in Etruria: problemi e prospetiva di ricerca." In *Secondo Congresso Internazionale Etrusco* 2, 781–811. Rome.

Martelli, M. 1997. *La Ceramica degli Etruschi*. Novara.

Matheson, S.B. 1995. *Polynotos and Vase Painting in Classical Athens*. Madison, Wisconsin.

Mélida, J. R. 1901. "Donación Stützel. Barros griegos." *Revista de Archivos, Bibliotecas y Museos* 5: 559–566.

Mélida, J. R. 1922. "Adquisiciones del Museo Nacional de Arqueología 1920." *Revista de Archivos, Bibliotecas y Museos, Año* 26I: 163–172 and 341–353.

Menichetti, M. 1994. *Archeologia del potere. Re, immagini, e miti a Roma e in Etruria in età arcaica*. Milan.

Merkelbach, R. and M.L. West. 1967. *Fragmenta Hesiodea*. Oxford.

Meyer, J.C. 1980. "Roman History in the Light of the Import of Attic Vases to Rome and Etruria." *Analecta romana Instituti Danici* 9: 47–68.

Mora, G. 1980. *Un relieve funerario helenístico procedente de Ilion en el Museo Nacional de Arqueología*. Madrid.

Moret, J.M. 1984. *Oedipe, la Sphinx et les Thébains. Essai de morphologie iconographique*. Institut Suisse de Rome. Genève-Rome.

Morgan, L. 1985. "Idea, Idiom, and Iconography." In *L'iconographie Minoenne*, edited by P. Darcque and J. Poursat, 5–19. Paris.

Morgan, L. 1988. *The Miniature Wall-Paintings of Thera*. Cambridge.

Morris, I. 1992. *Death-Ritual and Social Structure in Classical Antiquity*. Cambridge.

Morris, S.P. 1984. *The Black and White Style, Athens and Aigina in the Orientalizing Period*. New Haven.

Motte, A. 1973. *Praires et jardins dans la Grèce antique*. Brussels.

Musée du Louvre, 1990. *Euphronios, peintre à Athènes au VIe siècle avant J.-C.* Paris.

Neeft, C.W. 1987. *Protocorinthian Subgeometric Aryballoi*. Allard Pierson Series, vol. 7. Amsterdam.

Neer, R.T. 2002. *Style and Politics in Athenian Vase-Painting, the Craft of Democracy, ca. 530–460 B.C.E.* Cambridge.

Neils, J. 1981. "The Loves of Theseus: An Early Cup by Oltos." *American Journal of Archaeology* 85: 40–41.

Neils, J. 2000. "Others Within the Other: An Intimate Look at Hetairai and Maenads." In *Not the Classical Ideal: Athens and the Construction of the Other in Greek Art*, edited by B. Cohen, 203–226. Leiden.

Noble, J.V. 1988. *The Techniques of Painted Attic Pottery*. Rev. ed. London.

"Noticias: Objetos del Museo del Prado que deben trasladarse al Arqueológico." 1871. *Revista de Archivos, Bibliotecas y Museos* 1: 26

Novick, P. 1988. *That Noble Dream. The "Objectivity Question" and the American Historical Profession*. Cambridge.

Oakley, J.H. 1995. "Nuptial nuances: Wedding Images in Non-Wedding Scenes of Myth." In *Pandora. Women in Classical Greece*, edited by E.D. Reeder, 63–73. Princeton.

Oakley, J.H. 2000. "Some 'Other' Members of the Athenian Household: Maids and Their Mistresses in Fifth-Century Athenian Art." In *Not the Classical Ideal: Athens and the Construction of the Other in Greek Art*, edited by B. Cohen, 227–247. Leiden.

Oakley, J.H. 2003. *Picturing Death in Classical Athens: The Evidence of the White Lekythoi*. Cambridge.

Oakley, J.H. and W. Coulson, O. Palagia. 1997. *Athenian Potters and Painters: The Conference Proceedings*. Oxford.

Oakley, J.H. and R.H. Sinos. 1993. *The Wedding in Ancient Athens*. Madison.

Oenbrink, W. 1996. "Ein 'Bild im Bild'-Phänomen. Zur Darstellung figürlich dekorierter Vasen auf bemalten attischen Tongefässen." *Hephaistos* 14: 81–134.

Ogden, C.K and I.A. Richards. 1953. *The Meaning of Meaning*. London.

Olmos, R. 1973. *Cerámica griega*. Guías del Museo Arqueológico Nacional 1. Madrid

Olmos, R. 1976. "Contribución al estudio del Pintor de Aquiles en Madrid." *Archivo Español de Arqueología* 49: 9–38.

Olmos, R. 1980. *Catálogo de los vasos griegos en el Museo Arqueológico Nacional I: Las lécitos áticas de fondo blanco*. Madrid.

Olmos, R. 1992. "Introducción a la copa de Aison." In R. Olmos (coord.): *Coloquio sobre Teseo y la copa de Aison*. Anejos de Archivo Español de Arqueología XII, CSIC, 9–35. Madrid.

Olmos, R. 1993. *Catálogo de los Vasos Griegos del Museo Nacional de Bellas Artes de La Habana*. Instituto de Conservación y Restauración de Bienes Culturales, Madrid.

Olmos, R. 1998. "El casco griego de huelva." *Clásicos de la Arqueología de Huelva* 1: 37–78. Huelva.

Olmos, R. and L.J. Balmaseda. 1977–78. "El tema de las muchachas en la fuente." In *Archivo Español de Arqueología* 50–51, 15 ss. Madrid.

Olmos, R. and C. Sánchez. 1988. *Imágenes de la antigua Atenas*. Ministerio de cultura. Dirección General de Bellas Artes y Archivos. Dirección de los Museos Estatales. Madrid.

Otto, W.F. 1960. *Dionysos, Mythos und Kultus*. Frankfurt am Main.

Palagia, O. 1984. "Apollon." In *Lexicon Iconographicum Mythologiae Classicae* vol. II, 183–327. Zurich.

Paradiso, A. 1993. "Erodoto, VI, 137 e la schiavitu minorale." *Metis* 8: 21–26.

Paratore, E. 1957. *Storia del teatro Latino*. Milan.

Payne, H.G. 1931. *Necrocorinthia: A Study of Corinthian Art in the Archaic Period*. Oxford.

Payne, H.G. 1971. *Necrocorinthia. A Study of Corinthian Art in the Archaic Period*. Maryland.

Peschel, I. 1987. *Die Hetäre bei Symposium und Komos in der attisch-rotfigurigen Vasenmalerei 6.–4. Jahrh. V. Chr.* Frankfurt.

Philipp, H. 1990. "Handwerker und bildende Künstler in der griechischen Gesellschaft." In *Polyklet*, edited by H. Beck, 79–110. Frankfurt.

Phillips, J., K.M. 1993. *In the Hills of Tuscany*. Philadelphia.

Pipili, M. 1987. *Laconian Iconography of the Sixth Century B.C.* Oxford

Pipili, M. 1998. "Archaic Laconian Vase-Painting: Some Iconographic Considerations." In *Sparta in Laconia*, edited by W.G. Cavanagh and S.E.C. Walker, 75–81. Proceedings of the 19th British Museum Classical Colloquium held with the British School of Athens and King's and University Colleges (London, 6–8 Dec. 1995), British School at Athens, Studies 4. London.

Pollitt, J.J. 1972. *Art and Experience in Classical Greece*. Cambridge.

Prince, G. 1982. *Narratology: The Form and Functioning of Narrative*. Berlin.

Prince, G. 1987. *Dictionary of Narratology*. Lincoln, Nebraska.

Prince, G. 1990. "On Narratology (Past, Present, Future)." In *Narratology and Narrative*, edited by A. Hardee and F. Henry, 1–14. Columbia, South Carolina.

Rada y Delgado, J. de. 1876. *Viaje a Oriente de la Fragata de Guerra Arapiles y de la comisión científica que llevó a su bordo*. Vol. 1. Barcelona.

Rada y Delgado, J. de. 1878. *Viaje a Oriente de la Fragata de Guerra Arapiles y de la comisión científica que llevó a su bordo*. Vol. 2. Barcelona.

Rada y Delgado, J. de. 1882. *Viaje a Oriente de la Fragata de Guerra Arapiles y de la comisión científica que llevó a su bordo*. Vol. 3. Barcelona.

Ramage, N. 1970. "Studies in Early Etruscan Bucchero." *Papers of the British School at Rome* 38: 1–61.

Rasmussen, T. 1985. "Etruscan Shapes in Attic Pottery." *Antike Kunst* 28: 33–39.

Rasmussen, T. 1991. "Corinth and the Orientalising Phenomenon." In *Looking at Greek Vases*, edited by T. Rasmussen and N. Spivey, 57–78. Cambridge.

Rasmussen, T. and N. Spivey, eds. 1991. *Looking at Greek Vases*. Cambridge.

Rathje, A. 1990. "The Homeric Banquet in Central Italy." In *Sympotica: a Symposium on the Symposion*, edited by O. Murray, 279–288. Oxford.

Reeder, E.D. 1995a. "The Wedding." In *Pandora: Women in Classical Greece*, edited by E.D. Reeder, 126–169. Princeton.

Reeder, E.D. 1995b. "Women and Men in Classical Greece." In *Pandora: Women in Classical Greece*, edited by E.D. Reeder, 20–31. Princeton.

Reeder, E.R. 1984. *The Archaeological Collection of the Johns Hopkins University*. Baltimore.

Rehm, R. 1994. *Greek Tragic Theatre*. London.

Reinsberg, C. 1989. *Ehe, Hetärentum und Knabenliebe im antiken Griechenland*. Munich.

Richardson, N.J. 1974. *The Homeric Hymn to Demeter.* Oxford.

Richter, G.M.A. 1946. *Attic Red Figure Vase. A survey*. New Haven.

Richter, G.M.A. 1969. *A Handbook of Greek Art*. New York.

Richter, G.M.A. and M.J. Milne. 1935. *Shapes and Names of Athenian Vases*. New York.

Rizzo, M.A. 1988. *Un Artista etrusco e il suo mondo. Il Pittore di Micali*. Rome.

Robertson, M. 1972. "'Epoiesen' on Greek Vases: Other Considerations." *Journal of Hellenic Studies* 92: 180–183.

Robertson, M. 1992. *The Art of Vase-Painting in Classical Athens*. Cambridge.

Robinson, D.M. and E.J. Fluck. 1937. *A Study of the Greek Love-Names*. Baltimore.

Rodríguez Adrados, F. 1983. *Fiesta, comedia y tragedia*. Madrid.

Rohde, E. 1894. *Psyche. Seelencult und Unsterblichkeits-glaube der Griechen*. Leipzig.

Rombos, T. 1988. *The Iconography of Attic Late Geometric II Pottery*. Jonsered.

Ruckert, A. 1976. *Frühe Keramik Böotiens, Form und Dekoration der Vasern des späten 8. und frühen 7. Jahrhunderts v. Chr.* Bern.

Rumpf, A. 1927. *Chalkidische Vasen*. Berlin.

Säflund, M.L. 1970. *The East Pediment of Zeus at Olympia*. Gothenburg.

Sebeok, T. 1960. *Style in Language*. Cambridge.

Schauenburg, K. 1957. "Zur Symbolik Unteritalischen Rankenmotive." *Mitteilungen des Deutschen Archäologischen Instituts. Römische Abteilung* 64: 198–221.

Schauenburg, K. 1974. "Zu attischen Kleinmeister-schalen." *Archäologischer Anzeiger* 89: 198–219.

Schauenburg, K. 1981. "Zu Unteritalischen Situlen." *Archäologischer Anzeiger* 96: 462–483.

Schauenburg, K. 1984. "Zu einer Hydria des Balti-moresmaler in Kiel." *Jahrbuch des Deutschen Archaologisches Institut* 99: 127–160.

Schauenburg, K. 1989. "Zur Grabsymbolik apulischer Vasen." *Jahrbuch des Deutschen Archäologisches Institut* 104: 19–60.

Schauenburg, K. 1994a. "Baltimoremaler oder Maler der Weissen Hauben." *Archäologischer Anzeiger*: 543–569.

Schauenburg, K. 1994b. "Zur Mythenwelt der Balti-moremaler." *Mitteilungen des Deutschen Archäolosgis-chen Instituts. Römische Aibteilung* 101, 51–68.

Schaus, G.P. 1986. "Two Fikellura Vase Painters." *Annual of the British School at Athens* 81: 251–295.

Scheibler, I. 1995. *Griechische Töpferkunst: Herstellung, Handel und Gebrauch der antiken Tongefässe*. 2nd ed. Munich.

Schiffler, B. 1976. *Die Typologie des Kentauren in der antiken Kunst*. Frankfurt.

Schnabel, H. 1910. *Kordax. Archäologische Studien zur Geschichte einer antiken Tanzes und zum Ursprung der Griechischen Komodie*. Munich.

Schnapp, A. 1984. "Eros en chasse." In *La Cité des images. Religion et société en Grèce antique*, 67–84. Institut d'Archéologie et d'Histoire Ancienne, Lausanne, Centre de Recherches Comparées sur les Sociétés Anciennes, Paris.

Schnapp, A. 1997. *Le chasseur et la cité. Chasse et érotique dans la Grèce ancienne*. Paris.

Schnapp-Gourbeillon, A. 1981. *Lions, héros, masques. Les représentations de l'animal chez Homère*. Paris.

Schnapp-Gourbeillon, A. 1982. "Les funerailles de Patrocle." In *La mort, les morts dans les sociétés anci-ennes*, edited by G. Gonoli and J.P. Vernant, 77–88. Cambridge.

Schneider-Herrmann, G. 1976. "Eine pästaner Weih-gabe." *Bulletin antike beschaving. Annual Papers on Classical Archaeology* 51: 65–71.

Schöne, A. 1987. *Der Thiasos. Eine ikonographische Unter-suchung über das Gefolge des Dionysos in der attischen Vasenmalerei des 6. und 5. Jhs.v.Chr.* Göteborg.

Schreiber, T. 1999. *Athenian Vase Construction: A Potter's Analysis*. Malibu.

Schweitzer, B. 1971. *Greek Geometric Art*. London.

Séchan, L. 1967. *Études sur la tragédie grecque dans ses rapports avec la céramique*. Paris.

Seeberg, A. 1971. *Corinthian Komos Vases*. Bulletin of the Institute of Classical Studies 27. London.

Sergent, B. 1984. *Homosexuality in Greek Myth*. Boston.

Shapiro, H.A. 1981. "Courtship Scenes in Attic Vase-Painting." *American Journal of Archaeology* 85: 133–143.

Shapiro, H.A. 1983. "Amazons, Thracians and Scythians." *Greek, Roman, and Byzantine Studies* 24: 105–114.

Shapiro, H.A. 1992. "Eros in Love: Pederasty and Pornography in Greece." In *Pornography and Representation in Greece and Rome*, edited by A. Richlin, 53–72. Oxford.

Shapiro, H.A. 1993. *Personifications in Greek Art, the Representation of Abstract Concepts 600–400 B.C.* Zurich.

Shapiro, H.A. 1994. *Myth into Art: Poet and Painter in Classical Greece*. London and New York.

Shapiro, H.A. 1997. "Correlating Shape and Subject: The Case of the Archaic Pelike." In *Athenian Potters and Painters*, edited by J. Oakley, W.D.E. Coulson, and O. Palagia, 63–70. Oxford.

Shapiro, H.A. 2000. "Modest Athletes and Liberated Women: Etruscans on Attic Black-Figure Vases." In *Not the Classical Ideal: Athens and the Construction of the Other in Greek Art*, edited by B. Cohen, 315–337. Leiden.

Shapiro, H.A. 2003. "Brief Encounters: Women and Men at the Fountain House." In *Griechische Keramik im kulturellen Kontext*, edited by B. Schmaltz and M. Söldner, 96–98. Münster.

Shefton, B.B. 1954. "Three Laconian Vase-Painters." *Annual of the British School at Athens* 44: 299–310.

Simon, E. 1972. *Das Antike Theater*. Heildelberg.

Simon, E. 1976. *Die Griechischen Vasen*. Munich.

Simon, E. 1980. *Die Götter der Griechen*. Munich.

Simon, E. 1981a. *Das antike Theater*. Würzburg.

Simon, E. 1981b. *Die griechischen Vasen*. Munich.

Simon, E. 1982. *The Kurashiki Ninagawa Museum: Greek, Etruscan and Roman Antiquities*. Mainz.

Simon, E. 1983. *Festivals of Attica*. Madison.

Small, J.P. 1991. "The Tarquins and Servius Tullius at Banquet." *Melanges de l'École Française de Rome* 103: 247–264.

Small, J.P. 1994a. "Scholars, Etruscans, and Attic Painted Vases." *Journal of Roman Archaeology* 7: 34–58.

Small, J.P. 1994b. "Eat, Drink, and Be Merry: Etruscan Banquets." In *Murlo and the Etruscans. Art and Society in Ancient Etruria*, edited by R.D. De Puma and J.P. Small, 85–94. Madison.

Small, J.P. 1999. "Time *in* Space: Narrative in Classical Art." *Art Bulletin* 81: 562–575.

Small, J.P. 2001. "Hats Off: The Entry of Tarquinius Priscus into Rome." *Etruscan Studies* 8: in press.

Smith, T.J. 1998. "Dances, drinks and dedications: the Archaic Komos in Laconia." In *Sparta in Laconia*, edited by W.G. Cavanagh and S.E.C. Walker, 75–81. Proceedings of the 19th British Museum Classical Colloquium held with the British School of Athens and King's and University Colleges (London, 6–8 Dec. 1995), British School at Athens, Studies 4. London.

Smith, T.J. 2000. "Dancing Spaces and Dining Places: Archaic Komasts at the Symposium." In *Periplous: Papers on Classical Art and Archaeology presented to Sir John Boardman*, edited by G.R. Tsetskhladze, A.J.N.W. Prag, and A.M. Snodgrass, 309–319. London.

Snodgrass, A.M. 1982. *Narration and Illusion in Archaic Greek Art*. Oxford.

Sontag, S., ed. 1982. *A Barthes Reader*. New York.

Souvinou-Inwood, C. 1985. "Altars with Palm-trees and Parthenoi." *Bulletin of the Institute of Classical Studies of the University of London* 32: 125–146.

Souvinou-Inwood, C. 1987. "A Series of Erotic Pursuits: Images and Meanings." *Journal of Hellenic Studies* 107: 131–153.

Souvinou-Inwood, C. 1991 *'Reading' Greek Culture*. Oxford.

Sparkes, B.A. 1960. "Kóttabos: An Athenian After-dinner Game." *Archaeology* 13: 202–207.

Sparkes, B.A. 1996. *The Red and the Black: Studies in Greek Pottery*. London and New York.

Sparkes, B.A. and L. Talcott. 1958. *Pots and Pans of Classical Athens*. Princeton.

Sparkes, B.A. and L. Talcott. 1970. *Black and Plain Pottery of the 6th, 5th and 4th centuries B.C.*, The Athenian Agora, vol. 12. Princeton.

Spivey, N. 1987. *The Micali Painter and his Followers*. Cambridge.

Splitter, R. 2000. *Die 'Kypseloslade' in Olympia. Form, Funktion und Bildschmuck, eine archäologische Rekonstruktion*. Mainz.

Sprenger, M. and G. Bartoloni. 1979. *The Etruscans*. New York.

Stansbury-O'Donnell, M. 1999. *Pictorial Narrative in Ancient Greek Art*. Cambridge.

Steiner, A. 1993. "The Meaning of Repetition: Visual Redundancy on Athenian Vases." *Jahrbuch des Deutschen Archäologischen Instituts* 108: 197–219.

Steiner, A. 1997. "Illustrious Repetitions: Visual Redundancy in Exekias and His Followers." In *Athenian Potters and Painters: The Conference Proceedings*, edited by J.J. Oakley, W. Coulson and O. Palagia. 157–169. Oxford.

Steiner, W. 1982. *The Colors of Rhetoric*. Chicago.

Steiner, W. 1988. *Pictures of Romance*. Chicago.

Steingräber, S. 1984. *Catalogo ragionato della pittura etrusca*. Milan.

Stewart, A. 1983. "Stesichoros and the François Vase." In *Ancient Greek Art and Iconography*, edited by W.G. Moon, 53–74. Madison.

Stewart, A. 1997. *Art, Desire, and the Body in Ancient Greece*. Cambridge.

Stibbe, C.M. 1972. *Lakonische Vasenmaler des sechsten Jahrhunderts v.Chr.* Amsterdam.

Stibbe, C.M. 1994. *Laconian Drinking Vessels and other Open Shapes*. Amsterdam.

Strøm, I. 1981. "Review of T.B. Rasmussen, *Bucchero Pottery from Southern Etruria* (1979)." *Gnomon* 53: 789–792.

Sutton, R.F. 1992. "Pornography and Persuasion on Attic Pottery." In *Pornography and Representation in Greece and Rome*, edited by A. Richlin, 3–35. Oxford.

Szilágyi, J.G. and E. Szász Graziani. 1992. *Ceramica Etrusco-Corinzia Figurata: Parte I, 650–580 a.C.* Florence.

Thompson, J.A.K. 1915. *The Greek Tradition*. New York.

Threatle, L. 1980. *The Grammar of Attic Inscriptions* I. Berlin and New York.

Tiverios, M.A. 1976. *Ho Ludos kai to ergo tou*. Athens.

Todisco, L. 1983. "Un nuovo cratere con scena d'Oltretomba del Pittore de Baltimore." *Archeologia Classic* 35: 45–47.

Todisco, L. 1990. "Teatro e *theatra* nelle immagini e nell'edilizia monumentale della Magna Grecia." In *Magna Grecia. Arte e artigianato*, edited by G. Pugliese Carratelli, 103ff. Milan.

Todisco, L. and M.A. Sisto. 1998. "Un gruppo di vasi attici e il problema delle "Special Commissions" in Italia meridionale." *Mélanges de l'École française de Rome, Antiquité* 110: 571–608.

Torrente Fortuño, J.A. 1960. *Salamanca, bolsista romántico.* Madrid.

Trendall, A. D. 1936. *Paestan Pottery: A Study of the Red-Figure Vases at Paestum.* London.

Trendall, A.D. 1953. "Paestan Post-script." *Papers of the British School at Rome* 21: 161–167.

Trendall A.D. 1970. *The Red-Figured Vases of Lucania, Campania and Sicily: first supplement.* London.

Trendall, A.D. 1987. *The Red-figured Vase from Paestum.* Rome.

Trendall, A.D. 1989. *Red Figure Vases of South Italy and Sicily.* London.

Trendall, A.D. 1991. "Farce and Tragedy in South Italian Vase-Painting." In *Looking at Greek Vases*, edited by T. Rasmussen and N. Spivey, 161–169. Cambridge.

Trendall, A.D. and A. Cambitoglou. 1982. *The Red-Figured Vases of Apulia*, vol. 2. Oxford Monographs on Classical Archaeology. Oxford.

Trendall, A.D. and A. Cambitoglou. 1983. *First Supplement to the Red-Figured Vases of Apulia*, Bulletin of the Institute of Classical Studies of the University of London Supplement no. 42. London.

Trendall, A.D. and A. Cambitoglou. 1991–1992. *Second Supplement to the Red-Figured Vases of Apuli*, Bulletin of the Institute of Classical Studies of the University of London Supplement no. 60. London.

Trendall, A.D. and T.B.L. Webster. 1971. *Illustrations of Greek Drama.* London.

Triantis, I. 1994a. "Oinomaos." In *Lexicon Iconographicum Mythologiae Classicae*, vol. VII, 19–23. Zurich.

Triantis, I. 1994b: "Pelops." In *Lexicon Iconographicum Mythologiae Classicae*, vol. VII, 282–287. Zurich.

Tyrrell, W.B. 1984. *Amazons: A Study in Athenian Myth-making.* Baltimore.

Valavanis, P. and D. Lourkoumelis. 1996. *Drinking Vessels.* Athens.

Vermeule, E. 1979. *Aspects of Death in Early Greek Art and Poetry.* Berkeley.

Vermeule, E. 1984. *La muerte en la poesía y en el arte de Grecia.* Traducción en castellano: Fondo de Cultura Económica. México.

Vernant, J.P. 1985. *La mort dans les yeux. Figures de l'Autre en Grèce Ancienne.* Hachette, Paris. (Translated into Castilian: *La muerte en los ojos*, Barcelona 1986).

Vernant, J.P. 1986. "Conclusion." In *L'Association Dionysiaque dans les sociétés anciennes. Actes de la table ronde organisée par l'École française de Rome.* Collection de l'École Française de Rome 89: 291–303.

Vernant, J.P. 1989a. "Au miroir de Méduse." In *L'individu, la mort, l'amour. Soi-même et l'autre en Grèce ancienne*, edited by J.P. Vernant, 117–130. Paris.

Vernant, J.P. 1989b. "Figures féminines de la mort en Grèce." In *L'individu, la mort, l'amour. Soi-même et l'autre en Grèce ancienne*, edited by J.P. Vernant, 131–152. Paris.

Versnel, H.S. 1990 *Ter Unus. Isis, Dionysos, Hermes. Three Studies in Henotheism.* Leiden.

Vickers, M. and D. Gill. 1994. *Artful Crafts, Ancient Greek Silverware and Pottery.* Oxford.

Vidal-Naquet, P. 1992. "Le chasseur noir et l'origine de l'éphébie athénienne." In *La Grèce ancienne, 3. Rites de passage et transgressions*, edited by J.P. Vernat and P. Vidal-Naquet, 119–148. Paris.

Vierneisel, K. and B. Kaeser, eds. 1990. *Kunst der Schale, Kunst des Trinkens.* Munich.

Villard, F. 1946. "L'evolution des coupes attiques à figures noires." *Révue des Études Anciennes* 48: 173–180.

Vollkommer, R. 1988. *Herakles in the Art of Classical Greece.* Oxford.

von Bothmer, D. 1969. "Euboean Black-figure in New York." *Metropolitan Museum of Art Journal* 2: 27–44.

von Bothmer, D. 1972. "A Neck-amphora in the Collection of Walter Bareiss, II. The Ancient Repairs." *American Journal of Archaeology* 76: 9–11.

von Bothmer, D. 1985. *The Amasis Painter and His World: Vase-painting in Sixth-century B.C., Athens.* Los Angeles.

Wachter, R. 1989. "The Death of the Handsome Panchytos." *Zeitschrift für Papyrology und Epigraphik* 77: 21–24.

Wagner, C. 2000. "The Potters and Athena: Dedications on the Athenian Acropolis." In *Periplous: Papers on Classical Art and Archaeology presented to Sir John Boardman*, edited by G.R. Tsetskhladze, A.J.N.W. Prag, and A.M. Snodgrass, 383–387. London.

Warden, P.G. 2000. "Funerary Ritual." In *Archaic Etruscan Tomb Painting: Five Tarquinian Tombs*, edited by P.G. Warden. CD-ROM. Dallas.

Warden, P.G. 2003. "The Anatomy of an Etruscan Tomb Forgery: Case Unresolved." *International Fine Arts Research Journal* 5 4: 36–42.

Warden, P.G., M.L. Thomas and J. Galloway. 1999. "The Etruscan Settlement of Poggio Colla (1995–1998 excavations)." *Journal of Roman Archaeology* 12: 231–246

Webster, T.B.L. 1955. "Homer and Attic Geometric Vases." *Annual of the British School at Athens* 50: 38–50.

Webster, T.B.L. 1965. "Greek vases in the Stanford Museum." *American Journal of Archaeology*: 69, 63–65.

Webster, T.B.L. 1970. *The Greek Chorus.* London.

Webster, T.B.L. 1972. *Potter and Patron in Classical Athens.* London.

Wehgartner, I. 1992. "Der Vasenmaler Aison und seine Beziehung zu einigen zeitgenössischen Vasenmaler." In *Coloquio sobre Teseo y la copa de Aison*, edited by R. Olmos. Anejos de Archivo Español de Arqueología XII, CSIC, Madrid, 75–96.

West, M.L. 1992. *Ancient Greek Music.* Oxford.

Whitley, J. 1991. *Style and Society in Dark Age Greece. The changing face of a preliterate society, 1100–700 BC. New Studies in Archaeology.* Cambridge.

Williams, D. 1983. "Women on Athenian Vases: Problems of Interpretation." In *Images of Women in Antiquity*, edited by A. Cameron and A. Kuhrt, 92–106. Detroit.

Williams, D. 1986. "A cup by the Antiphon Painter and the battle of Marathon." In *Studien zur Mythologie und Vasenmalerei. Konrad Schauenburg zum 65. Geburtstag am 16 April 1986*, 75–81. Mainz.

Williams, D. 1995. "Potter, Painter and Purchaser." In *Culture et Cité. L'avènement d'Athènes à l'époque archaïque*, edited by A. Verbanck-Piérard and D. Viviers, 139–160. Brussels.

Winkler, J. 1990. "Laying Down the Law: The Oversight of Men's Sexual Behavior in Classical Athens." In *Before Sexuality: The Construction of Erotic Experience in the Ancient Greek World*, edited by D.M. Halperin, J.J. Winkler, and F.I. Zeitlin, 171–209. Princeton.

Woodford, S. 2003. *Images of Myth in Classical Antiquity.* Cambridge.

Zamarchi Grassi, P. 1992. *La Cortona dei Principes.* Cortona.

Ziomecki, J. 1975. *Les représentations d'artisans sur les vases antiques.* Breslaw.

Zunt, G. 1971. *Persephone. Three Essays on Religion and Thought in Magna Grecia.* Oxford.